To Join Together:
The Rite of Marriage

*Studies in the Reformed Rites
of the Catholic Church,
Volume V*

Kenneth W. Stevenson

To Join Together
The Rite of Marriage

Pueblo Publishing Company

New York

Design: Frank Kacmarcik

Scripture quotations contained herein are from the Revised Standard
Version Bible, copyright 1946, 1952, 1971 by the Division of Christian
Education of the National Council of the Churches of Christ in the
USA, and are used by permission.

Excerpts from the English translation of the Rite of Marriage © 1969,
International Committee on English in the Liturgy, Inc. All rights
reserved.

ISBN: 0-916134-84-9

Contents

20   3222

Introduction

The *Ordo Celebrandi Matrimonium* of 1969 is among the
shortest and simplest of all the reformed rites of the
Roman Catholic Church. Like its predecessor in the
Rituale Romanum of 1614, the text is not intended as a
legal norm that is imposed on the Church, but rather
as a sample for local adaptation and development.
But, unlike the previous rite, the new one identifies
two essential ingredients: the consent of the couple
and the nuptial blessing. It also makes proper provision for occasions when the marriage liturgy is not
celebrated within the eucharist.

In a previous book,[1] I attempted to convey within lim-
ited space the main features of the development of the
marriage rites in the East and West, including the rites
of the Reformation, central to which is that of the *Book
of Common Prayer*. Now, a few years later, my friend
and fellow liturgist, Aidan Kavanagh, has rashly en-
trusted to a married Anglican presbyter the task of telling a somewhat different story, which looks at the
new Roman rite in its background and evolution, as
well as in the future paths that it might take. Readers
wanting wider historical scope and fuller documentation must, therefore, refer to the earlier book. But I
have taken this welcome opportunity of correcting mis-
takes and shifting perspectives, which the passage of
time permits.

Among the many people who deserve my thanks, I must mention Father Pierre-Marie Gy, O.P., who was chairman of the Study Group that drew up the new rite, and who generously allowed me access to his many papers on the subject. One significant event since the appearance of the other book was spending the 1983 spring semester at the University of Notre Dame, where I held a Visiting Professorship. Part of my duties entailed delivering a course of lectures entitled "Celebrating Christian Marriage," and I am deeply grateful to the graduate students who attended the class for their friendship as well as for the way in which they helped to bring me out of my historical shell into the light of the present. Many of my comments on contemporary marriage liturgies result, in whole or in part, from this vigorous and warm encounter. Among my colleagues at Notre Dame, Mark Searle deserves special thanks; he steered me gently towards a better appreciation of the intrinsic connection between the marriage liturgy and the human sciences, and he also allowed me to use some of his translations of certain liturgical texts in this book. We hope one day to produce a companion volume, containing various historic and current marriage rites in English translation, together with explanatory notes.

From someone formed in that part of the Anglican tradition that has tended to look to the Fathers for primal inspiration, the Eastern bias in liturgy and spirituality that permeates this book will come as no surprise to the reader. Perhaps this message will find a welcome in North America, at present so fertile a terrain for new ideas in matters of liturgy.

The procreation of children has always numbered among the principal reasons for marriage, and it is therefore appropriate for me to dedicate this book, with Sarah my wife, to our four children, Elisabeth, Katharine, James, and Alexandra.

Kenneth W. Stevenson	26th July, 1985
University of Manchester	Memorial of Joachim and
England	Anne
	parents of Mary.

NOTES

1. Kenneth W. Stevenson, *Nuptial Blessing: A Study of Christian Marriage Rites* (Alcuin Club Collections 64) (London: SPCK, 1982, and New York: Oxford University Press, 1983).

The Tradition

Chapter One

The Context: Mise en scène

INTRODUCTION

Marriage is both a social and a religious institution.
People are married who have religious beliefs as well
as those who do not, and for that reason there is a tension that runs through the marriage liturgy in the
Christian Church, a tension that is felt strongly at present among the Churches of the West, where divergent
views come to the fore. On the one hand there are
those who make a sharp distinction between marriage
as celebrated in a Christian community, by Christian
couples, with a Christian liturgy. On the other hand
there are those who are less ready to demarcate between *Christian* marriage and any other marriage. John
Selden, the seventeenth-century Englishman of affairs,
once wrote, "Marriage is nothing but a civil contract."
He was reflecting the view of many Christians at the
time of the Reformation when it was thought necessary to demote marriage from the league of seven
sacraments.

Christians themselves, therefore, are divided in their
attitude to marriage vis-à-vis other faiths (and none),
and they are also divided, though less so than they
were, about the sacramental status of marriage. The
Catholic tradition, followed by many parts of Protestantism too, has long placed marriage among those
areas of human life deserving to be hallowed by the
Church, and it was for this reason that the medieval

Western Church eventually numbered marriage among the sacraments.

If marriage is an institution, then it also needs a rite by which the two are made one flesh in the Christian community. In the early stages of the development of the marriage liturgy, it is at times not entirely clear how "social" and how "religious" is the rite in question, because much of what was happening took place at home, in a domestic context. Yet the same observation could be made today; the marriage as actually experienced by the couple and their immediate circle is a complex interaction of relationships and attitudes that only the most insensitive liturgist would confine to the words and the prayers recited during the service, whether that is held in church or at home.

Walter Kasper has recently written of marriage:

"There is no area of human life on which most people today are so dependent for personal happiness and fulfillment as that of love between man and woman, a love that is made lasting in marriage and family life. There is also no other sphere in which faith and life are so intimately in contact with each other as in marriage."[1]

But he goes on to say:

"Marriage belongs to the order of creation and to the order of redemption."

Such bold assertions come at a time when theologians are stressing the love aspect rather than the contractual aspect of marriage. Moreover, the Church no longer has the prospect of male, celibate theologians prescribing magnanimously for the faithful just exactly what marriage is all about. We are well into an age when theology and human experience are responding in a fruitful dialogue, so that when the Church formulates a theology or a liturgy it does so on the basis of reflection upon the human condition. What is said or celebrated is, in some sense, a critique of what ordinary people live by.

If marriage does belong to the order of creation and redemption, then it follows that the celebration of marriage is for Christians one of the most vital areas of their liturgical life. Yet this is precisely the reverse of what most Christians "hear" when they go to church. Marriage, like baptism (until recently) has become marginalized, something done by the pastor on a Saturday afternoon, an activity in which the local Christian community has no real interest until the divorce lawyers' voices are audible in the distance. While Roman Catholics today have a rich and vibrant scheme for making new Christians (and eloquent voices to support its ready use in ordinary parishes), they have little comparable to offer for celebrating Christian marriage. It is true, however, that the new marriage liturgies of the Roman Catholic Church, and of the other Western churches, are rich and vibrant in comparison with their predecessors. The liturgical movement has not missed out on marriage. Yet one senses that much more could be done to bring marriage into the mainstream of the Church's life. We do not want another piece of legalistic rigorism, putting fanatical Christian couples through a welter of hurdles before they can consummate their union. Christian marriage should not become a rerun of *The Magic Flute*, in which we all wait until we are worthy. But more could be done by context as well as text to offer to an age that relates uneasily to marriage as an institution something of the wholesomeness, the powerfulness, and the dynamics of what it is to marry "in Christ."

One of the fascinating features of history is that marriage liturgies have varied so much. On the one hand,

Eastern Christians crown the partners as a symbol of the Kingdom of God; on the other hand, medieval Christians in the West veiled the bride as a sign of modesty and beauty. At the Reformation, English Christians heard the sonorous words of Thomas Cranmer:

"Dearly beloved, we are gathered together in the sight of God and in the face of this congregation to join together this man and this woman in holy matrimony. . . ."[2]

History is full of resonances like these, and it is also full of paradoxes. For example, Christians have not always been clear how to describe the marriage liturgy. Thus, in the early Roman Sacramentaries, the nuptial mass is often called "veiling brides," even though the prayers themselves do not mention that veiling. (This suggests that the veiling is earlier than the nuptial blessing, which is the salient feature of these pristine nuptial eucharists.) Eastern Christians usually refer to marriage as the "crowning," for obvious reasons. A later medieval word *sollemnizatio* provided Cranmer in the sixteenth century with the prayer book title "The Solemnization of Matrimony." The 1969 rite of the Roman Catholic Church simply calls it *Ordo Celebrandi Matrimonium*, the order for celebrating marriage. A title is significant because it shows how at least some people perceive what is happening. No doubt new titles will be invented in the future, or old ones revived. But the positive stress on mutual love and joy and witness, which is the hallmark of so much of what the Second Vatican Council had to say about marriage, is boldly reflected in that keyword *celebrandi*,[3] celebrating. Such a word speaks volumes in antithesis to the cold, contractual utterances of past Latin theologians about what does and what does not make up a Christian marriage.

But what of religion and ritual? Once it is admitted that marriage is a salient institution in the life of the community, Christian or otherwise, it is necessary to look, somewhat dispassionately, at the way in which groups and societies have dealt with marriage in a ritual way. In his masterpiece, *Les Rites de Passage*, Arnold Van Gennep examines the various ways in which primitive societies coped with birth, puberty, marriage, and death. He observed that rites of initiation usually are made up of three stages:

rites *préliminaires* (séparation)

    liminaires (marge)

  et *postliminaires* (agrégation)[4]

These are normally translated as rites of separation, liminality, and incorporation, and we are already familiar with the way in which this scheme fits into Christian initiation. The rites of separation correspond with enrollment in the catechumenate. The period of liminality is the catechumenate itself. The rites of incorporation are the final initiation through baptism and eucharist. Moreover, these three stages do not exist in their own right. They exist to help the group or society cope with the essential aspect of initiation: disturbance.

Marriage also fits into such a scheme, both in primitive societies as well as in the rites of the Eastern churches and the old Visigothic churches of Spain. We shall see these in more detail later on. For the moment, it is important to grasp their inner meaning. The first stage, the separation, corresponds with *bethrothal*. Here, the couple (and the community) accept the interim commitment to marry in the future. The way in which this has been described expresses the atmosphere of this separation, which must lead somewhere else, even if it leads to the breaking off of that commitment. Separation is expressed in different forms of ritual. In the West, it eventually came to be dominated by the notion of intentionality, so that when the Catholic Church insisted on consent as an integral part of marriage, "separation" at betrothal became redundant and was a mere prelude to the nuptial mass. The Western practice, therefore, is one that draws betrothal into marriage, so that all the Church has to offer is a liturgy for the third (and final) stage, incorporation. This is what the reformers at Wittenberg, Lambeth, and Trent took over. This is also where we are left today. For the majority of Christians today, what their Church has to offer them is no more than a rite of incorporation.[5]

The question, of course, has to be posed: Was Van Gennep right? There can be little doubt that he was correct when he wrote of primitive societies. There can be little doubt also that his scheme fits in perfectly with what we shall later see to be the inner meaning of the rites of the various Eastern churches, even though most of them now in fact celebrate betrothal and marriage in close sequence. Yet the real question is: Are these three stages a reality that the Church is failing to identify today? To put the question in a technical liturgical way: Are these three stages the "deep structures" of marriage?[6] Are they so deep in the human spirit that they come to the surface willy-nilly, regardless of what the Church may or may not do in its corporate liturgies? And do they imply that recent liturgical renewal, however significant, amounts to no more than playing around with the "surface structures," which liturgists keep telling us are not as important to the real human need as the "deep structures"?

It is our conviction that the answer to these questions must be affirmative. Victor Turner has recently identified the sense of "communitas" as that which is established during liminality and it can be indicated in three ways, which correspond to what many couples actually experience. First, they feel powerless because much is expected of them, but they have no rights. Second, they experience cultural inversion, so that they feel humiliated before being honored (witness many engagement "crush" parties). Third, they know (at times) a suspension of cultural mores; for even in the case of a year's cohabitation, there is still the stage of uncertain yet possible commitment, followed by the liminal stage of "betwixt and between," followed by the stage of actual and total sharing of life together.

For many churchgoing couples, it is true that betrothal is a semipublic reality, even if it is only ritualized by a declaration to the respective families and friends and the solemn exposition of the engagement ring. Moreover, the period of "liminality" may well become one of those popular North American "Pre-Cana" weekends, in which pastors and others involved in the scheme give couples some careful instruction in the teaching of the Church, with some reflection on the relationship as it is progressing. (Some engagements are known to be terminated by marriage-preparation sessions because the couple realize that their relationship is more heat than light.) Then, and only then, the celebration of the marriage takes place after due thought and care, as a real rite of incorporation into a new status and relationship.

It seems, therefore, that the three stages are alive and kicking in ordinary life. It seems also that the Church responds to these stages at the pastoral and educational levels. But, once again, these fine motives have not really touched the liturgy. In the Church of England, there persists the archaic practice of reading the "banns of marriage" at public worship on Sundays. When couples do attend church to hear their banns being read, this is sometimes the only way in which their commitment to marry meets the liturgy, albeit in an oblique and legalistic guise. Similarly, some churches mention couples regularly in the intercessions at Sunday eucharist, so that the community prays for those who are preparing to marry. Yet what a contrast this still is with the great ritual patterns of the Eastern churches, where the ring giving still lies at the heart of the betrothal rites (not the rite of marriage, where it came to be in the West) and where these betrothal rites are no mere statements of commitment to marry in the future but are varied patterns of intercessory prayer and prayer of thanksgiving replete with rich symbolic action. Christians of the West can learn as much from the East about how to get ready to marry as they can about the unity of the eucharistic prayer at Mass in general, and about the theological richness of the epiclesis of the Holy Spirit in particular.

In the ensuing pages, we shall return again and again to this threefold pattern to see how the deep structures of marriage as a ritual process emerge, develop, then fade (in the West) and conjoin (in the East). We shall also take regular stock of the theological themes of prayers as they are added to the respective liturgies. Surface structures are still significant, particularly for Christians who live in the shadow of recent liturgical revision, and as we try to appropriate the vast amount of liturgical activity. The underlying message is that, because marriage is about the way couples share in the love of God, every marriage is the same and yet every marriage is different. Liturgies that evoke rather than define are therefore more likely to reach people who come for God's blessing if they can enjoy rich agglomerations of meaning.

The mythology of the ancient Near East has three important myths that relate to marriage and that form a vital backdrop against which to examine the Old Testament. The first is about the Ugaritic god El, the creator who made both the earth and sky. He is portrayed in one story as producing two sons by two spouses and is a god of fertility. The second myth tells of a divine marriage in which Nikkal marries the moon god. The third is the Epic of Gilgamesh in which Ishtar (corresponding to Venus) is driven by sexual passion toward Tammouz, the god of vegetation.[7]

Thus, we have fertility, marriage, and passion. They are adapted in the Old Testament, whose underlying message eventually emerges as God marrying Israel. If God made Israel and loves her, then this must make demands on how Israel lives in daily life. The two creation myths in Genesis show this clearly. The J-narrative (Gn 2:18–25) makes man and woman equal, even though man is created first, and the notion of man and woman being one flesh makes its first appearance: "Now this, at last—bone from my bones, flesh from my flesh." The other creation myth (Gn 1:26–9, the P-narrative) reflects similar ideas, but God not only *makes* them, he *blesses* them. This theme will recur in later writers and euchology. Perhaps this echoes some kind of liturgical practice of the time; it certainly has later Christian parallels in liturgical prayer.

In the patriarchal tradition, Isaac, though he must marry from the wider family, has to negotiate the marriage with Rebecca's family, and they are betrothed some time before they are actually married. Moreover, when Rebecca leaves home, she receives a blessing from her family, which is about bearing children. But when she sees Isaac before the marriage, she has to veil herself. The marriage is subsequently consummated (Gn 24). Thus, we have negotiation of contract, betrothal, time of engagement, prayer, and consummation, all in a domestic setting. Elsewhere in the Old Testament, there is evidence of the bride wearing elaborate robes and a girdle in her procession (Is 49:18, Jer 2:12) as well as the couple wearing crowns (Is 61:10). The liturgies of the East make much of this later on. Finally, it is worth noting the marriage allusions in two psalms that become popular in later liturgies, Psalms 44 (45) and 127 (128).

Later Judaism provides two important witnesses to marriage. The first is in the book of Tobit, in the marriage of Tobias and Sarah (Tb 7 and 8).[8] The sequence of events is as follows. Tobias asks Raguel for Sarah's hand in marriage, and he consents with the words:

"From now on, you belong to her and she to you;
she is yours for ever from this day.
The Lord of heaven prosper you both this night, my
    son,
and grant you mercy and peace."

The Vulgate text puts this declaration into a proper liturgical form, which reappears in later Visigothic liturgies, so that it needs to be quoted in full:

"May the God of Abraham, the God of Isaac, and the
    God of Jacob
be with you, and may he himself join you together,
and fill you with his blessing."

Here are rich words indeed. The presence of God is identified with being joined together in marriage (no doubt also in sexual union) and with the blessing of God.

Next, the marriage contract is written down by Raguel. The marriage feast begins. After the feast, the couple spend the night together in a special room, but before they sleep, Tobias recites a special prayer, which has a markedly Jewish structure, moving from praise for creation to supplication for the ensuing marriage. In the following chapter, Gabelus blesses Sarah "through" Tobias in a prayer that reappears in the medieval West:

"May blessing be said over your wife and over your
     parents;
and may you see your children and your children's
     children
to the third and fourth generation;
and may your seed be blessed by the God of Israel,
who reigns for ever and ever."

The Vulgate text in general adds liturgical material, but even so, the other texts lay down a clear procedure, almost as if what goes on between Tobias, Raguel, and Sarah is a recognized convention. It is also worth noting, for the purposes of later Latin euchology, that throughout this little book, Raphael and other angels are mentioned and invoked for their protecting power.

The other area of evidence is from Talmudic Judaism, notoriously difficult to date. While Tobit probably comes from the second century B.C., the Talmud is supposed to come from the third century A.D., but it is generally supposed to reflect earlier practice. For Jews, this is not as significant as it is for Christians, because the possible relationship between Talmudic practice (which we know) and early Christian practice (which we do not know during the first two centuries) is at stake. In the Talmud, there are two stages: betrothal and marriage. Betrothal can be enacted by money, by contract, or (improperly) by cohabitation. A short *berakah*, or prayer of blessing God, is recited to ratify the betrothal over each of the partners. The betrothal normally lasted twelve months, and the marriage took place after this lengthy interval. The couple fast all day and confess their sins, as on the Day of

Atonement; they wear crowns of myrtle, and the bride, if a virgin, also wears a long veil as she proceeds with her retinue to the bridegroom's house for the evening feast. At the threshold, the contract is written down. After the feast, the bridegroom himself recites the Seven Blessings, which later tradition passed to the rabbis to be said. According to tradition, these blessings are known to have been established by the time of Rabbi Judah, which means that Jews at the time of Jesus may have known them. They have changed little down the ages, and it is worth quoting them in full because of their structure and themes:

"Blessed are thou, O Lord our God, King of the universe, who createst the fruit of the vine.

"Blessed art thou, O Lord our God, King of the universe, who hast created all things to thy glory.

"Blessed art thou, O Lord our God, King of the universe, Creator of man.

"Blessed art thou, O Lord our God, King of the universe, who has made man in thine image, after thy likeness, and hast prepared unto him, out of his very self, a perpetual fabric. Blessed art thou, O Lord, Creator of man.

"May she who was barren (Zion) be exceeding glad and exult, when her children are gathered within her in joy. Blessed art thou, O Lord, who makes Zion joyful through her children.

"O make these loved companions greatly to rejoice, even as of old thou didst gladden thy creatures in the garden of Eden. Blessed art thou, O Lord, who makest bridegroom and bride to rejoice.

"Blessed art thou, O Lord our God, King of the universe, who hast created joy and gladness, bridegroom and bride, mirth and exultation, pleasure and delight, love, brotherhood, peace and fellowship. Soon may there be heard in the cities of

Judah, and in the streets of Jerusalem, the voice of joy and gladness, the voice of the bridegroom and the voice of the bride, the jubilant voice of bridegrooms from their canopies, and of youths from their feasts of song.

"Blessed art thou, O Lord, who makest the bridegroom to rejoice with the bride."[9]

Much can be said about these blessings, but we shall limit ourselves to a few remarks, to pave the way for later discussions. The *structure* moves smoothly from the opening vine blessing, and blessing for creation in general, to the creation of humanity and the declaration of God's purpose in so doing. Then comes supplication for Zion and for the couple, with reference to the Garden of Eden; blessing for the joy of the couple; and a long blessing and supplication for the joys of married life. In fact, the sequence of ideas is little different from Tobit, except that the opening vine blessing (over a cup) is absent in Tobit, as is the reference to Zion inserted after the fall of Jerusalem.

Later Jewish development moved this part of the rite out of the groom's house so that it took place outside, under a canopy (*huppah*) to represent the groom's home (or divine presence?). A rabbi recited the blessings. Then two features gradually took over: (1) betrothal and marriage were brought together during the Middle Ages and (2) a ring or coin was usually given as a sign of marriage. Both these features may have resulted from Christian influence. Still, the roots of the scheme are social and religious, centered around the family and the local community, with a solemn blessing that reflects the Old Testament's positive teaching on marriage as being about the relationship between God and his people, as well as about covenant, creation, procreation, and redemption, all celebrated in joy and gladness.

The New Testament gives us even fewer allusions to marriage than the Old Testament. But we can assume that early Christians regarded marriage as part of their life of faith, whether they were Jewish Christians of the first generation, who grew up with Jewish customs and thought, or later Greek Christians, who sought deliberately to incorporate the Old Testament into their religious views of the world.

Jesus is identified in the Synoptics as the bridegroom, thus extending the imagery of Yahweh as the husband of Israel. Moreover, in the parable of the virgins (Mt 25:1–13), the wedding feast takes place in the evening at the bridegroom's house. This reflects what we have seen in the Talmud. It is the marriage at Cana that is at once the most tantalizing and the most symbolic of all (Jn 2:1–11). Jesus attends the feast as a guest, and when the wine runs out, he turns convention to the wind by using the water reserved for purification to be the "sign" of his Kingdom. At one level, this "sign" suggests the new religion replacing the old. But it is also about Jesus being present at the marriage of an anonymous couple. The first Johannine "sign" takes place at the celebration of marriage in a rural setting. Jesus thus valued marriage as a relationship of primal importance. Moreover, the end of the meal, when the wine ran out, was the time when the bridegroom would have pronounced the Seven Blessings, if the Talmudic practice were observed. It is not impossible to see in Jesus' "sign" a replacement of the conventional Seven Blessings. Acceptance of the Kingdom of Christ and its accompanying blessings are of greater ultimate significance than even the liturgical conventions of a Jewish wedding.

Jesus' words about divorce (Mt 19:1–6) have been much discussed. Often the preconceptions of scholars have been allowed to intrude. The passage becomes the standard lection at the nuptial eucharist in the later West, and it is also the standard reading at marriage throughout the East, with the exception of the Byzantine rite, which prefers John 2:1–11. Moreover, the pronouncement that those married are not to be parted (Mt 19:6) finds a new role for itself at the end of the Middle Ages (in the Lyon rite, 1498) and at the Reformation (Luther and Cranmer) as a formula to be used immediately after the couple have given their public consent to each other.

One rich and at times problematical pericope is the analogy of Christ marrying the Church in Ephesians 5:22–33. It becomes a favorite lection in the East, and in the East-Syrian liturgy forms the basis, along with the Song of Songs, for some of the richest marriage hymnody in the entire Christian liturgical repertoire. For some modern Christians, the stumbling block is the theme of male domination. The stress on obedience is, it must be allowed, stronger than in the Old Testament, but conversely husbands must *love* their wives and not use them merely for sexual gratification. In the passage there is probably reference to the twofold stages of betrothal and marriage, and Christ's sacrificial death is understood to be a "washing" that corresponds with the ritual washing of the bride before the marriage. The theme of "one flesh" (Gn 2:24) reflects the need for unity among Christians under Jesus himself. Modern prayer writers, captivated as they are by the covenant theme, tend to avoid using this passage for inspiration, though it must be admitted that it forms the basis of a central portion of the Gregorian Sacramentary nuptial blessing and, by derivation, a central composition in Cranmer's Prayer Book rite.[10]

The question needs to be asked: How did early Christians marry? Some scholars have been honest enough to reply, "We just do not know." Others have taken the casuistic approach and have argued *ex silentio*, always a risky exercise, that there was no Christian marriage rite as such. My own conclusion is that there *was* a marriage rite, that it consisted of an adapted version of Jewish practice, and that it persisted at least in those parts of the early Christian world where Jews had gone before and were still influential on the new religion. Further, we shall see in Chapter 3 how Jewish inspired was much of the ambience of the Eastern rites, particularly those of the Syrian-Armenian family. My suggestion is that early Christians knew a sequence of betrothal and marriage, together with negotiation and contract, and that the marriage rite took place at home with a lengthy blessing over the couple, in a Christian form of the Talmud-type of prayer quoted earlier. Jewish origins continue to be a marked feature of liturgical study, and there seem to be good reasons for this hypothesis to be given serious consideration.

Such a theory is supported by subsequent early Christian evidence. For example, the legendary marriage of *Joseph and Asenath*, which may be late Jewish or early Christian, produces a scheme similar to what we have seen already. Although no less a person than Pharaoh is the celebrant, convention takes over in the fact that the couple are first of all betrothed; they later come before him for crowning and blessing, and the marriage feast follows immediately. At the blessing, Pharaoh's hands are placed upon the couple's heads. Journeying further into the apocryphal, the Christian *Acts of Thomas*, probably second or third century Syrian, tells of a marriage that the apostle happens to attend. A blessing is coaxed from him, which consists of a lengthy series of thanksgivings, which ends thus:

". . . Yea, Lord, I ask of Thee on behalf of these young people, that whatever Thou knowest to be beneficial for them, Thou wilt do for them.

"And he laid his hands upon them, and said to them:
'Our Lord be with you.'

"And he left them, and went away."[11]

So much for liturgical evidence. Literary evidence is not lacking. Ignatius, Athenagoras, and Dionysius of Corinth all refer to marriage, and one gets a picture of marriage as something of importance to the community, with a procedure of its own. Roman imperial law allowed local religions to keep their own customs so long as the consent of the partners was explicit, a ruling which the later Roman Catholic Church was to make so central to the marriage rites as to dominate the liturgy in a curious manner. Clement of Alexandria (ca. 150–215) repeats Athenagoras' definition that marriage is for the procreation of children, but he also stresses that marriage is not a way of giving in to passion but is a dignified relationship, blessed by God (citing Gn 1:28 and Eph 5:22–33). Clement also expresses his dislike of bridal wigs because it is the real hair that gets blessed, not the false. It is hard not to see some kind of presbyteral ritual behind that theological statement.

Tertullian's views on marriage (ca. 160–225) have been much discussed.[12] Elsewhere he states that virgins are betrothed to be married by a kiss and the giving of the right hand, after which they must be veiled. Like Clement, he also refers to the use of the ring at betrothal. But the two main passages show a positive view of marriage and hint at its liturgical context. In language that seems to tilt at pagan Roman practice by showing how Christian ritual is so much more satisfactory and true, he waxes lyrical:

"How shall we ever be able adequately to describe the happiness of that marriage which the Church arranges, the Sacrifice strengthens, upon which the blessings set a seal, at which angels are present as witnesses, and to which the Father gives his consent?"

Whether or not Tertullian is alluding to a nuptial eucharist is not clear. Moreover, his own prescriptions for a tight-knit community may not reflect any ordinary Christian rite of the time. But the passage must surely refer to a Christian liturgy, presided over by ministers, with a solemn blessing.

THE FOURTH CENTURY

The fourth century is generally regarded as the formative era of Christian liturgy, when Christians moved from informality to formality, from small *ad hoc* buildings to vast basilicas, from teacher's chair to grandiose ambo. To describe the move in those terms is to miss an important element, that of continuity. Nevertheless, what is true of the development of baptism, the eucharist, and the liturgy of the hours between the third and fifth centuries, may also be true of the liturgies of marriage. What we have so far seen is, first, a sequence of betrothal and marriage; second, a formal liturgy for the latter; and third, a domestic context for all, but with the intervention of local ministers. Finally, it may be that the liturgy reached a climax in a solemn nuptial blessing. As we shall see, this was accompanied by crowns in the East and a veiling of the bride in the West.

The East

Basil of Caesarea (ca. 330–379) gives useful evidence. In his Canonical writings to Amphilochius of Iconium,[13] we read of betrothal and marriage as two separate stages; he condemns private marriages conducted by presbyters on the grounds that it cheapens the blessing, while to have the marriage in church is a way of making Christ present to the marriage, as at Cana. Moreover, he uses the word *eulogia* of the blessing and juxtaposes it with *hagiazo;* this recalls the anaphora that bears his name, where in the early Coptic version these two words occur side by side at the institution narrative. (They also appear together at the epiclesis in the later Byzantine version that bears his name.) Marriage and Cana are closely associated. Marriage must move out of domestic surroundings into the public view of the Church, implying that it had not yet done so, hence the need to lay down the law with Amphilochius. Betrothal and marriage are separate and, one assumes, both ideally under Church auspices. Finally, the marriage liturgy has a blessing of the couple that is priestly in its character, theological in content, and probably set in form, at least as far as Basil was concerned.

Gregory Nazianzus (329–389) supplies evidence for a crowning as well as the use of Psalm 127 (128) at the liturgy, and the blessing is obviously a strong prayer for the future of the couple. Crowning appears to be the norm in Cappadocia, as elsewhere in the East.

John Chrysostom (ca. 347–407)[14] stresses that in marriage the two become one flesh and that it is consent, not cohabitation, that makes marriage. Yet there is no evidence for *liturgical* consent until much later; presumably he means consent implicit by the sequence of betrothal and marriage, with contract. Marriage feasting apparently went on for seven days, as in Judaism. He also defends the use of crowns because they are symbols of the couple's victory over passion. The use of *Arrhas* (pledges) is encountered in Chrysostom's writings. This is symbolized by a ring given at betrothal, where it appears in the Byzantine liturgy today. Marriages are to be conducted by priests, who pray over the couple, invoking God's strength and power on their future life together.

The *Lausiac History* (ca. 419–420)[15] tells the tale, at one point, of an Egyptian marriage, of Amoun of Nitria, who is bullied into matrimony by his uncle. He gives in, and is "crowned" and goes through the whole marriage. But he refuses to consummate the marriage. It is interesting that "crowning" refers to the whole rite, as today in the Byzantine rite.

The West

Crowning in the East was the norm. Veiling, by contrast, takes over in the West, for which we have abundant evidence. Pope Siricius I (384–399)[16] wrote to Himerius of Tarragona that brides must be veiled and that the veiling is to be associated with the blessing given by the priest. Why Himerius asked for advice is unclear. It may have been because the Visigothic Church in Spain did not bless the bride alone, a fact that is observable from later texts. Yet bridal veiling and blessing of the bride alone emerge as the Roman practice, which may not be unrelated to the pagan Roman emphasis on marriage as being a change of state for the bride.

Ambrose of Milan (339–397)[17] seldom mentions the marriage liturgy, but he frequently speaks of marriage as a *vinculum* (link) or *jugum* (yoke). He also refers to betrothal, which is symbolized by a kiss and is binding. It was the legally binding nature of betrothal that eventually caused it to be absorbed into the marriage liturgy. Ambrose also mentions the bridal veil frequently and sometimes describes it as the "priestly veil." Pope Innocent I (d. 417) lays down the need for marriages to be celebrated in church and before a priest, with the priestly blessing given and the bride veiled. But it is Paulinus of Nola (353/4–431)[18] who gives us the most charming of all accounts in a poem about the marriage of the son of one bishop to the daughter of another bishop. In the part of the poem that alludes to the liturgy, we have evidence of the nuptial blessing being given, which bestows the grace of Christ with angelic help, giving justice and peace, and in a recognized manner the presiding bishop places a veil over the shoulders of *both* the bride and the groom.

Augustine has much to say about marriage.[19] First, it is not merely a "joining" but a *sacramentum* (mystery, solemn obligation). He also frequently gives three reasons for marriage: *fides* (fidelity), *proles* (offspring), and *sacramentum*. Such a triad may have occurred in the liturgy, being mentioned in one of two homilies. Second, Augustine mentions the *tabulae matrimoniales* (marriage tablets) that the bishop writes down and reads out, presumably at the liturgy. (Compare the Jewish custom of writing the contract, noted earlier.) Each time Augustine mentions these tablets, he uses the same expression: "for the procreation of children." We may be sure these words appeared on the normal marriage tablet. Third, Augustine repeatedly alludes to Genesis 1:28 and to the connection between the blessing of Adam and Eve and the procreation of children. It is hard to avoid the conclusion that the blessing was priestly and liturgical, and that the divine blessing of marriage was understood to be the fruitful procreation of children. But the blessing does seem to focus on the *bride*, a feature of the Roman Sacramentaries, as we shall see in Chapter 2. Finally, he refers on one occasion to the bridal veil.

The Western evidence is sufficient to show that while the East crowned the couple, the West veiled the bride, with a blessing that probably focused on her change of state. Moreover, the matrimonial tablets were intrinsic to the North African liturgy, corresponding to the contract alluded to elsewhere. Both East and West asserted the need to be married by the Church, and one senses the need felt by the Church to enter into the lives of people when betrothal and marriage took place. The atmosphere of these fourth-century writers is (with the exception of Gregory Nazianzus) less intimate. Systems are being invented to ritualize important phases in the human life cycle. And the seeds of later differences are sown. Why the bridal veiling in the West? Probably it was a popular folk descendant of the pagan Roman *flammeum,* which all but enveloped the pious virgin as she married her man.

In terms of ritual wholeness, the three stages persist, although the liturgical emphasis falls on the marriage, whose liturgy is becoming more complex and formal. Biblical themes abound in these writers, whether in invoking the examples of holy couples from the patriarchal age, in the marriage of God to his people, or in contemplating the presence of Jesus at Cana.

NOTES

1. Walter Kasper, *Theology of Christian Marriage* (New York: Seabury Press, 1980), p. 1.

2. *Book of Common Prayer,* 1662, preface to the marriage rite.

3. *Ordo Celebrandi Matrimonium* (Vatican City: Typis Polyglottis, 1969). The 1614 rite terms the service "ritus celebrandi Matrimonii Sacramentum" (*Rituale Romanum* (Antwerp: Balthasar Moret, 1826), p. 232), but the word "celebrandi" is a rarity in the later Middle Ages when speaking of marriage.

4. Arnold Van Gennep, *Les Rites de Passage* (Paris: Librairie Critique, Émile Mourry, 1909), p. 14 (see also pp. 165–207). On this discussion, see Kenneth W. Stevenson, "Van Gennep and Marriage—Strange Bedfellows?—A Fresh Look at the Rites of Marriage," *Ephemerides Liturgicae* 100 (1986): 138–151.

5. Victor Turner, *The Ritual Process* (London: Routledge and Kegan Paul, 1969), pp. 94–165. For contemporary outworking, see L. Mpongo, "La célébration du mariage dans les reli-

gions africaines," in G. Farnedi (Ed.), *La Celebrazione Cristiana Del Matrimonio* (Studia Anselmia 93; Analecta Liturgica 11) (Rome: Pontificio Ateneo S. Anselmo, 1986), pp. 343–360.

6. Aidan Kavanagh, *On Liturgical Theology* (New York: Pueblo, 1984), pp. 79ff. See also Robert F. Taft, "The Structural Analysis of Liturgical Units: An Essay in Methodolgy," *Worship* 52 (1978):314–329 (or Robert F. Taft, *Beyond East and West: Problems in Liturgical Understanding* (Washington: Pastoral Press, 1984), pp. 151–164).

7. See Kenneth W. Stevenson, *Nuptial Blessing: A Study of Christian Marriage Rites* (Alcuin Club Collections 64) (London: SPCK, 1982, and New York: Oxford University Press, 1983), pp. 3ff. We shall only refer to this book again when a particularly important matter is under discussion. The reader who requires more detailed discussion in this historical section must have recourse to this earlier book as a matter of course.

8. See Kenneth W. Stevenson, "The Origins of Nuptial Blessing," *Heythrop Journal* (1980):413 (whole article, pp. 412–416). See also R. H. Charles, *The Apocrypha and Pseudepigrapha of the Old Testament* (Oxford: Oxford University Press, 1913), I, pp. 174ff.

9. Joseph Hertz (Ed.), *The Authorized Daily Prayer Book* (New York: Bloch, 1946), p. 1013. See also K. Hruby, "Symboles et textes de la célébration du mariage judaïque," in *La Celebrazione Cristiana Del Matrimonio*, pp. 15–28.

10. See (Barnabas Lindars) "The New Testament Evidence," in *Marriage and the Church's Task*, Appendix 4 (London: Church Information Office, 1978), pp. 136–161. For a discussion of John 2:1–11, see Barnabas Lindars, *The Gospel of John* (New Century Bible Commentary), 2d ed. (London: Oliphants, Marshall, Morgan and Scott, 1977), p. 130.

11. On Joseph and Asenath, see E. W. Brooks, *Joseph and Asenath* (London: SPCK, 1918), pp. 61f. On the Acts of Thomas, see Korbinian Ritzer, *Formen, Riten, und religiöses Brachtum der Eheschliessung in den christlichen Kirchen des ersten Jahrtausends* (Liturgiewissenschaftliche Quellen und For-

schungen 38) (Munster: Aschendorff, 1962), pp. 54–57. Hereafter referred to as *Ritzer*.

12. See *Ritzer*, pp. 58–67, but see also H. Crouzel, "Deux textes de Tertullien concernant la procédure et les rites du mariage chrétien," *Bulletin det Littérature Ecclésiastique* 4 (1973):3–13.

13. *Ep. ad Amphilochium* 199, P. G. 32:721–723.

14. *Hom. 9 in 1 Tm*, P. G. 62:546.

15. R. Meyer (Trans.), *Palladius: The Lausiac History* (Ancient Christian Writers 34) (Westminster: Newman, 1965), pp. 41–42.

16. *Ep. 1. 4, Ad Himerium*, P. L. 64:632.

17. See Stevenson, *Nuptial Blessing*, pp. 26–27, and nn. 29–39 (pp. 218–219).

18. Text in *Ritzer*, p. 343. For a discussion, see Stevenson, "The Origins of Nuptial Blessing," pp. 414–415.

19. See Stevenson, *Nuptial Blessing*, pp. 29–30, and nn. 48–60 (p. 219). On early Christian marriage procedure, see John K. Coyle, "Marriage Among Early Christians: A Consideration for the Future," *Église et Théologie* 8 (1977):73–89. See also E Mélia, "Symboles et textes de la célébration du mariage dans la tradition patristique et liturgique en Orient," in *La Celebrazione Cristiana Del Matrimonio*, pp. 29–50; and B. Studer, "Zur Hochzeitsfeier der Christen in den westlichen Kirchen der ersten Jahrhunderte," ibid., pp. 51–86.

Chapter Two

Join Together? The Western Evidence

INTRODUCTION

In Chapter 1, the early evidence pointed to a Christian version of the two-stage procedure of betrothal and marriage that was known in antiquity in general and Judaism in particular. From the fourth century, there was a growing emphasis on the need for Christian couples to come to church for their marriage celebration, which had its own particular symbolism as a formal liturgy.

In this chapter, the variegated rites of the medieval West will be looked at and described according to the evidence. It needs to be pointed out that a service book, especially one written for an important ecclesiastical center, may not reflect what every local church was able to do, particularly with a rite like marriage. Thus, the nuptial masses that are contained in the Roman Sacramentaries are one thing; the domestic rites contained in a few local books are another. The former witness to an established liturgical form in which couples come to church for the church's blessing. The latter witness to a more informal missionary church, still part of the home, providing a simpler liturgical rite.

These two patterns could be called "stratum 1" and "stratum 2." Although they may have roots that go back to the fourth century, they are eventually put together so that, in the ninth century, the domestic rite follows the nuptial mass. This could mean that we have another "ideal" form, or that many couples only bothered with the domestic rite itself if they wanted a marriage rite at all. It must be borne in mind that the Middle Ages in the West is one continuous story of legislation and pressure against clandestine marriages—which means that many folk simply lived together and did not think it necessary to come to church.

The next stage in the story comes at the beginning of the twelfth century with the new rite of consent, which in the Anglo-Norman tradition takes place at the church door and incorporates part of the "stratum 2" domestic rite, particularly in the blessing of the ring. This "stratum 3" rite of consent therefore begins an elaborate marriage rite that becomes the standard form throughout the West and consists of the following:

Rite of consent, with the ring blessing, at the church door

Procession into the church

Nuptial mass, with the nuptial blessing

Blessing of the bedchamber (and couple) at home afterwards

The three strata put together in this way lay the foundations for the even more elaborate rites contained in the Northern French and British Manual services of the fourteenth and fifteenth centuries. Indeed, it is significant to note that from the beginning of the twelfth century, very little of substance changes, except that forms of consent and ring giving vary considerably from one tradition to another, although in Britain they are fairly uniform. More significantly still is that the three strata make up a *single* marriage celebration. If betrothal persisted after the twelfth century at all (and evidence suggests that it did, in France), this made little difference to what the Church did at marriage. This development was largely due to the scholastic theologians, led by Yvo of Chartres and Peter Lombard, who not only numbered marriage among the (now seven) sacraments, but made a sharp distinction between consent at betrothal (*verba de futuro*) and consent at marriage (*verba de praesenti*). Such an emphasis should not be interpreted in exclusively "intellectual" terms, for the will is taken to mean movement of the subject towards the end aimed at, in a way that affects the whole personality.[1]

But Van Gennep's three stages do persist in the Visigothic tradition, and we shall be looking at four rites that bear the marks of this pristine pattern, where a rich and complex nuptial mass only comes as the climax to two preparatory rites, the blessing of *Arrhas* (pledges) and the blessing of the bedchamber. All four of these rites date from the tenth or eleventh centuries, although scholars regard them as embodying traditions that are much older. It is therefore significant that, although the Visigothic marriage rite eventually went the way of the remainder of the West, it should, for some time at least, retain a three-stage rather than a one-stage marriage rite.

Then, in the rest of Europe, we encounter even greater variety, but within a single rite of marriage. Thus, in Scandinavia, different influences are to be noted. Although the Anglo-Norman rite of three strata is the norm and provides early Lutheranism with an excuse for a nuptial mass, Germany on the other hand proves to be exceptional, for in many places noneucharistic marriage rites persist, perhaps descendants of older domestic liturgies. These provide German Lutherans with the material with which to formulate their sixteenth-century vernacular rite.

The three Sacramentary traditions all provide forms
for the nuptial mass, and these consist of variable
prayers for the eucharist and the special feature that
distinguishes a nuptial mass from any other, the nuptial blessing before Communion. Whereas the Leonine
and all Gregorian texts call the mass "a veiling of the
bride," the Gelasian uses the title *actio nuptialis*.

There are certain problems surrounding the texts in
the Leonine.[2] The nuptial mass comes in the month of
September. The sequence of the prayers is not entirely
clear. Most noticeable is that the long nuptial blessing
(*pater mundi conditor*, "Father founder of the world")
appears *last*, preceded by a prayer that uses the future
tense in referring to the joining together of the couple.
This may mean that at such an early date the nuptial
blessing was regarded as the performative part of the
rite, the liturgical high point. The nuptial blessing itself is rich although not always clear. The sequence of
ideas bears a remarkable resemblance to what we have
seen elsewhere, including the Seven Blessings of the
Talmudic traditions. The themes covered are creation,
creation of man and woman, procreation, children for
this woman, and prayer for a good marriage. The
prayer then takes on a second wind and starts including various Old Testament characters, that the woman
may imitate them in their various attributes and eventually enjoy heavenly felicities.

The prayer, for all its chauvinism (women being the
weaker sex), provides a firm foundation for a theology
of marriage, which is based on the Bible and the Fathers. God instituted marriage, the primary purpose of
which is the procreation of children. But it is also a
union between man and woman that is blessed in its
own right as a means of knowing the love of God and
growing into it. It is not a purely social relationship; it
is also a religious one. The main point of difference be-

tween our own age and the age in which these fine prayers were written is that the emphasis falls on the bride. Both the *Hanc igitur* and the nuptial blessing pray throughout exclusively for the bride, which implies that for this Roman Christian age, marriage is God-given and primarily about the woman's change in state.

Various reasons can be offered for this emphasis. Pagan Roman society also viewed marriage in these terms, as one can see from the secular poetic tradition represented by writers such as Catullus. But the question must still be asked, why? I think that it is a deliberate way of fixing the spotlight on the "weaker sex," so that marriage is "the bride's day," as it is in popular folk religion today even down to the quaint detail that the bride, already the center of all the fuss, is allowed to be two minutes late. Out of a society that plays down the role of the woman must come a liturgy that plays it up.

The Gelasian and Gregorian Sacramentaries provide a similar scheme, with a nuptial mass that reaches a climax at the special blessing before communion.[3] Whereas the Gelasian book changes the Leonine's nuptial blessing, the Gregorian traditions rewrite it altogether. Since the Gregorian nuptial mass becomes standard throughout the later West and forms the basis for the first nuptial blessing in the 1969 *Ordo Celebrandi Matrimonium*, it is worth quoting in full.

"O God, you have made all things out of nothing by your power. When you had ordered the beginnings of the universe, you established for man, made in the image of God, the inseparable help of woman, bringing the woman's body into being out of man's flesh, and teaching (us) that what it had pleased you to create from a single beginning should never be put asunder.

31

"O God, you have consecrated the bond of marriage
with such an excellent mystery as to prefigure in the
covenant (*foedus*) of marriage the sacrament of Christ
and his Church.

"O God, through you a woman is joined to her husband, and society is chiefly ordered through that
blessing which was neither lost by original sin nor
washed away in the flood.

"Look with kindness upon your maidservant, who is
to be joined in the relationship of marriage, as she
asks to be strengthened with your protection. May
her yoke be one of love and of peace. May she
marry in Christ, faithful and chaste.

"May she continue to imitate the holy women: may
she prove loving to her husband, like Rachel, wise,
like Rebecca, long-lived and faithful, like Sarah.

"May the author of lies never subvert a single one of
her acts;
may she remain steadfast in the bond of faithfulness
and in the commandments joined to one marriage-
bed;
may she flee all unlawful relations;
may she fortify her weakness with the strength of
discipline;
may she be serious and modest,
respected for her honor, learned in heavenly wis-
dom.

"May she be fruitful with children, upright and innocent;
and may she come at last to the rest of the blessed
and to the heavenly kingdom.
May she see her children's children
to the third and fourth generation,
and come to a desired old age."[4]

The language, and sequence of ideas are not unfamiliar. Whereas the Leonine's prayer logically prays for
the bride to attain heavenly promises *after* the produc-

tion of children, the Gregorian text curiously inverts this order; perhaps this is a way of implying that children are not quite so central to a good marriage. Apart from a better coherence, the Gregorian prayer introduces one theme not contained in the Leonine, the analogy from Ephesians 5, which was discussed in Chapter 1. Indeed, this theme seems so important that it provides an opportunity of introducing the sentence following from the prayer. Like the Leonine, the ending of the prayer echoes the "children's children" motif from the Raguel prayer, quoted in Chapter 1. If ever there was a prayer for a bride that combined so succinctly and evocatively the human and legal images of marriage, then the Gregorian nuptial blessing is it.

There are, however, two ancillary questions that are germane to the actual use of the Gregorian nuptial rite as the basis for the future Western marriage rite. The first concerns the question of readings, which of course do not appear in the Sacramentaries. Early lectionaries provide some obvious choices. For the first reading, 1 Corinthians 6: 15–20 and 1 Corinthians 7:32–35 are popular alternatives. Paul wrestling with the pastoral aspects of marriage is a clear winner for the Western mind. On the other hand, Ephesians 5:22–33, so popular in the East, is exceptional in the West, at least for the time being. This is somewhat surprising, in view of the Gregorian Sacramentary's introduction of the Ephesians analogy into the body of the nuptial blessing. For the gospel, Matthew 19:1–6 becomes by far the most popular, although there are signs of the use of John 2:1–11 in some early books. There are exceptions, too. For example, the so-called Pontifical of Poitiers, a tenth-century book, has an unusual pair of readings, the first one being Isaiah 61:10–11 (wedding garlands), and the gospel is John 3:27–29 (Jesus as bridegroom).[5]

The second question concerns the direction of the nuptial prayer and its context in later rites. We have already observed how exclusively bridal is the nuptial blessing. This is hardly surprising in view of the evidence supplied by Ambrose and Augustine, to name but two. An interesting variant can be detected in certain manuscripts of the Gregorian Sacramentary, which may reflect a certain uneasiness with its bridal focus as the prayer traveled North and West in Europe.

What happens to the prayer? Two things. First, there is a tendency to pluralize the final verbs,[6] so that, while the main body of the prayer continues to focus on the bride, the *conclusion* prays that *they* may come to the heavenly kingdom, that *they* may see their children's children, and that *they* may come to a desired old age. The plural-ending version of the nuptial blessing abounds in later service books, and we can only conclude that it was a deliberate rewriting of the ending of the prayer so that both bride and groom are prayed for. The significance of this alteration was not lost on the compilers of the 1969 *Ordo*, since the plural-ending text appears in the 1570 *Missale Romanum* and thus became standard throughout the West after the Council of Trent. Although the ending is important, it could nonetheless be taken to underline more emphatically the theology of the prayer; the *bride* is prayed for, so that *both* may enjoy everlasting happiness and see their offspring "to the third and fourth generations."

Second, the prayer is often supplemented with other blessings. These vary from one tradition to another. Pontificals and Benedictionals contain several texts. The most common is from the Lanalet Benedictional, which is a tenth-century English book. After the nuptial blessing in the mass would be inserted the following prayer, entitled "blessing of bridegroom and bride."

"May almighty God, who by his own power created our first parents, Adam and Eve, sanctified them with his blessing and joined them in a holy union, sanctify and bless your hearts and bodies and conjoin you in a union of true love. Amen.

"May he who sent the archangel Raphael to prepare the marriage of Tobias and Sarah send his holy angel from his heavenly throne to comfort you in his holy service, show you the path of righteousness and protect you for ever from all evil. Amen.

"May he who willed that his only-begotten Son, our Lord Jesus Christ, redeemer of the world, should be born of a virgin, and who consecrated marriage by his presence and his miracle, when he turned water into wine, may he be present also at your nuptials and deign to bless you and make you holy. Amen.

"And may he grant you quiet times, health of mind and body, joy in the birth of holy children and, when the labors of this present life are done, may he grant you to come faithfully into the company of his holy angels. Amen."[7]

The style of this prayer is quite different from the sophisticated *oratio* structure of the Gregorian nuptial blessing. It comes in short paragraphs, each with its own theme, each ending with an "Amen." But the sequence of ideas is still the same: creation of Adam and Eve, angelic protection to Tobias and Sarah, Christ's presence at Cana, and a blessed marriage with children. What differs is the actual themes covered, for nowhere in the Sacramentaries do we encounter angelic protection. The compiler of this prayer, by contrast, uses biblical ideas and characters in preference to legal themes.

The Lanalet prayer appears in many later service books, either in its entirety or else in a shortened form, consisting of the first paragraph only. The prayer is but one part of the complex story of medieval Western euchology, in which the whole marriage liturgy, especially the latter part of the nuptial mass and the premass rite of consent, are given extra blessings and prayers over the couple. Almost without exception, this prayer blesses both bride and groom. There can be no clearer hint that the solemn prayer over the bride, venerable as it was by virtue of being contained in the Sacramentary of Gregory ("stratum 1" in every sense), was regarded as inadequate to express ever-growing ritual needs.

DOMESTIC RITES

The evidence for these rites is not as full as we would like, because a missionary church does not lay down as firm lines for its liturgy as does a metropolitical city. Two texts have come down to us that illustrate in different ways how marriages were blessed apart from the solemn celebration of the eucharist.

The first is the Pontifical of Egbert,[8] a tenth-century manuscript that probably reflects eighth-century use either in York by Egbert or in Normandy. It contains two marriage rites, which are very similar but for the blessing of the ring. This appears in the first of two contained in Egbert, together with a series of short marriage prayers, which include the blessing of the bedchamber. The second set of prayers lacks both the ring prayer and the blessing of the bedchamber. These prayers are different in style both from the long Gregorian nuptial blessing and the Lanalet prayer. They are short and to the point. Moreover, the fact that the Pontifical of Egbert contains two rites may be as much a reflection on the arrangement and date of the manuscript as on the fact that some couples wanted a wedding ring blessed and others did not. Conceivably, part of these rites was tacked on to a nuptial mass in church. The ninth- or tenth-century "Durham Collectar" contains the Gregorian mass and adds a set of Egbert prayers to the end of the service. More likely, they were used in various contexts, at the end of mass as well as at home.

The second text dates from the eleventh century and is probably from the North of Italy.[9] It resembles the Egbert prayers in form and content. To balance the eucharistic focus of so many of the official marriage rites, it, too, is worth quoting in full.

Prayer over men and women for joining together
"Lord, almighty God, deign to send your blessing upon your servant (N) and your maidservant (N), so that they might live in your love and increase and multiply unto length of days."

Another prayer over men and women for joining together
"Lord Jesus Christ, bless your servant (N) and your maidservant (N) through the prayer of Moses whom you delivered in the Red Sea from the face of Pharaoh, that they might find favor before your face on the day of judgment."

Blessing over one man
"May God the Father bless you. May Christ his Son guard you and preserve your body in his service, enlighten your mind, guard your senses, perfect your soul by his grace, and keep you from all evil. May his holy right arm protect you. May he who always helps his saints himself be pleased to help you."

Blessing of the ring when the wife comes to marriage
"Lord, creator and sustainer of the human race, giver of everlasting life, grant your blessing to your maidser-

vant (N), that, equipped with the strength of heavenly protection, she may progress to eternal salvation."

This short series of prayers is a feast of ideas. First, each prayer has a title, which indicates how someone (at least) regarded its function within the whole. Moreover, the first prayer has an alternative, a phenomenon that becomes very common in later medieval service books, especially in marriage rites in England. Then the third and fourth prayers are said over each one of the couple; it is conceivable that the third prayer ("over one man") was added to compensate for the prayer over the ring for the woman. Significantly, the ring blessing is a prayer for the woman and not for the future of the marriage in general. Then there is the style of the prayers. The first and the last are short bursts, concentrating on one idea. The third prayer, by contrast, is a formal blessing, with shorter contrasting petitions for the divine presence. The second prayer is the most unusual of all. It is addressed to Christ, and its theme relates to the passage of Moses through the Red Sea. At first sight this may seem to be a somewhat odd idea to introduce into a marriage prayer. On the other hand, it mixes well with Van Gennep's notions of marriage as a passage from one kind of life to another. Hitherto, prayers have been evocations of divine presence on something new. Here we have the image of the couple *walking through something*, at the end of which they emerge as man and wife. We shall see in Chapter 3 the different ways in which the Eastern rites introduce this kind of idea through imaginative symbolism. The Red Sea theme may well point, in addition, to another notion that Eastern rites carry more effectively than the West: the connection between baptism and marriage.

What can be said of such evidence? Simply that in many cases the priest led a short marriage liturgy at home. Such a rite sometimes included the blessing of the ring; sometimes a blessing of the bridal chamber. Invariably the priest would pray over the couple, taking as implicit their consent to each other, and the whole short liturgy would take place in a domestic context surrounded by the local community, the church in embryo?

THE ANGLO-NORMAN SYNTHESIS

The Gregorian nuptial mass became the standard form for the marriage eucharist throughout the ambit of its authority and influence. Thus we find it embedded in many local rites, such as the Pontifical of Poitiers. Among these rites additional blessings between the nuptial blessing and the kiss of peace before communion are often found. A set of prayers, including a prayer over the ring, is frequently appended to the mass, with or without a blessing of the bedchamber at home. Such a set of prayers is what we find in various books during the tenth and eleventh centuries, such as the Benedictional of Robert and the Red Book of Darley. (The latter has now been identified as a traveling mass book, originating from the New Minister, at Winchester.[10])

A dramatic change occurs in the marriage rite used at Bury St. Edmunds, dated 1125–1135.[11] Its shape—of "stratum 1" (nuptial mass), "stratum 2" (ring prayers and domestic prayers), and "stratum 3" (rite of consent)—results in a considerable shift of emphasis, so that the mass comes as a corollary to the giving of consent, with which the ring is closely associated. This shift changes the balance. Moreover, the domestic prayers at the end are now no longer an integral part of the scheme; they read like an appendage. Another new feature is the blessing of a cup at the end of mass, which is no doubt related to the decline in regular communion.

Here is the shape of the service, with some of the
sources indicated.

1. *Before Mass* (at the
   church door)
   Ring blessing
      benedic hunc anulum   Benedictional of Robert
      creator et conservator   Egbert
   Consent:
      "When this blessing
      has been given, let the
      man be asked by the
      priest if he wants to
      have her for his lawful
      wife. Let the same be
      asked of the woman."
   Giving:
      The dowry and
      other gifts are given.
      The woman is given
      away by "he who
      must give her
      away."
   Ring giving:
      In nomine patris . . .
      "With this ring I
        wed you,
      and this gold and sil-
        ver I give to you,
      and with my body I
        honor you,
      and with this dowry
        I endow you."
   Prayers:
      manda deus (some
        psalmlike verses)   Benedictional of Robert
      deus qui mundi
        exordio   Gelasian

deus Abraham . . .	
ipse vos conjugat	"Raguel" prayer: Robert (and Visigothic)
Psalm 127 (128) (procession into church)	
deus Abraham . . .	
semina	Tobit: Robert (and Visigothic)
omnipotens et	
misericors	Lanalet prayer
respice domine . . .	
Raphael	Egbert, Robert
benedicat et custodiat (alternative prayers for aged couple)	Aaronic Adapted; Egbert

2. *Nuptial Mass*
   Trinity votive mass
   Before Peace:

propitiare, domine	Preparatory prayer from Gregorian Sacramentary
deus qui potestate	Gregorian nuptial blessing
deus Abraham . . . sit in adversis	

3. *After Mass*

benedicti sitis	Found elsewhere
benedic domine hunc potum	

4. *At home*

benedic domine thalamum	Egbert
benedicat vos pater	Egbert

The shape and the sources are complex. Indeed, the whole scheme shows a subtle interweaving of various elements as well as a tapping of the collective memory of earlier marriage euchology.

First, the rite that we have hitherto regarded as either domestic or appended to the mass has now been divided in two, so that the ring blessing comes at the beginning and the domestic prayers are left at the end.

Second, the consent formula is for obvious reasons left as a direction, because it has to be in the vernacular. There seems a slightly conditional aspect to the ring blessing; logic might suggest that the ring should be blessed *after* the consent.

Third, we are given a clue about the type of language used in the vernacular with the giving of the ring and dowry, and gold and silver. This rhymes well and can be picked up easily because of the contrasting nature of the clauses. We come across this kind of formula later in the Sarum Manual vow.

Fourth, like future English texts, the priest has no precise role in the rite except as liturgical president. He thus adds no priestly or paternal remarks once the consent has been given.

Fifth, the Trinity mass replaces those in the Gregorian Sacramentary as the series of mass prayers. Other rites specify more freedom (Trinity or mass of the day) and duplication of prayers (Trinity first, Gregorian second). The Trinity votive mass was festive in style and popular in theme. It was usually only allowed on Sundays. The importance of the marriage service could be given no clearer direction.

Finally, among the various new elements are two that need to be noted. One is the appearance of a supplementary blessing, *deus Abraham*, after the nuptial prayer. This blesses both partners. It could be inserted so that brides who are widows still receive a blessing. The other new feature is the blessing of the cup at the end. This could be a eucharistic substitute, a Cana feature, or even an example of Jewish influence. Such a practice was popular in many later medieval marriage rites, either at the end of Mass (as here), or at home afterwards. It appears to symbolize a sharing of a common life together.

The Anglo-Norman synthesis, which is represented by the Bury rite, becomes standard throughout Northern Europe. Among the many variations and developments, the form of consent and the role of the priest need to be noted. In the fourteenth century, the French rite of Barbeau provides us with the earliest known example of the couple not merely responding affirmatively to the questions put by the priest, but actually stating their consent in a full formula:

"I take you as my wife, and I espouse you;
and I commit to you the fidelity of my body,
  insofar as I bear for you fidelity and loyalty
  of my body and my possessions;
and I will keep you in health and sickness and in any
    condition
  which it pleases our Lord that you should have,
nor for worse or for better will I change towards you
    until the end."[12]

These are similar sentiments that are to be found in other forms of marriage vows, with the underlying themes of commitment, risk, and whatever the future may hold. The French text reads like a minispeech. But the English Sarum Manual text, which is thought to be from the next century (which we regard as earlier) is composed in a different style, resembling more the contrasting phrases from the ring-giving formula of the Latin text in the twelfth-century Bury rite:

"I take thee (N)   cf. Evesham
  to my wedded wife,[13]   (fourteenth century)

to have and to hold,	cf. Bury, and Evesham
from this day forward	cf. Evesham
for better or worse	cf. Magdalen
	(twelfth century)
for richer or poorer	Evesham, Rouen
	(thirteenth century)
in sickness and in health	
till death us depart	cf. Evesham
if holy Church it will ordain	
and thereto I plight thee	
my troth."	Evesham

The fourteenth-century Evesham book referred to has a Latin formula for consent added in a later hand, which resembles the Sarum form closely. This vow may well be the result of vernacular piety, with its contrasting cadences, and may be earlier than the fifteenth century. The Sarum version forms the basis of the texts in the other British Manuals, as well as the liturgical work of Thomas Cranmer in the 1549 and 1552 Prayer Books of the Church of England. It also forms the starting point for the innovation at this point in the 1969 *Ordo*.

The other matter that is the subject of variation in the late Middle Ages concerns the role of the priest. The British texts, followed by some Scandinavian ones, give the priest no special formula to pronounce after the consent. The Visigothic rite, as we shall see, knew of a custom whereby the priest hands the woman over to the man after Communion. French rites influenced by the Visigothic custom reproduce this role in some rites of consent before mass. German rites, on the other hand, opt for an intermediary role. The late medieval Rouen rite, however, provides the priest with a formula that says:

"And I join you together,
in the Name of the Father. . . ."[14]

Theologians of liturgy often make words say what they want them to say. For my part, I can only interpret this formulation as a bold statement about what the priest is there to do. He elicits consent from the couple and then joins them together. Moreover, the word "conjungo" has appeared before in various prayers as a suitable way of expressing marital union. Unsurprisingly, at a time when consent was being emphasized as a needful condition of marriage, the priest also emerges as the representative of the church, which requires marriage to be celebrated publicly and sacramentally.

VISIGOTHIC CREATIVITY

The Anglo-Norman synthesis brings together the mass, with domestic rite and consent. The old Visigothic rite by contrast takes a different line, one that is reflected in no fewer than four texts from two different areas of Visigothic influence.[15]

The first two texts are from the *Liber Ordinum*, a collection of old Spanish services put together in the middle of the eleventh century at a time when the old native liturgical customs were under threat from romanizers. The *Liber Ordinum* texts probably emanate from Old Castile in central Spain. We know that some of the prayers go back to the eighth century, because they appear under a different guise in a short domestic marriage rite contained in the Bobbio Missal. We have already had occasion to note different styles in Latin euchology. In the Visigothic area, Latin almost becomes a new language. Most important of all is that the Visigothic rites were resistant to romanization.

Thus in the other two texts, from Catalonia (the Sacramentary of Vich and the Pontifical of Roda, both from the tenth to eleventh century), many of the features that are noticeable in the *Liber Ordinum* are carried on. The one that is most peculiar, apart from the style of Latin, is that the marriage rites are spread over three (and, in one case, four) phases. The mass is always the last; the first two or three phases differ:

Liber Ordinum "B"	Liber Ordinum "A"	Roda/Vich
Blessing of chamber		Blessing of Arrhas (pledges)
Vespers		
Blessing of Arrhas	Blessing of Arrhas	Blessing of chamber
Nuptial Mass: nuptial blessing *after* Communion	Nuptial Mass:	Nuptial Mass: nuptial blessing *before* Communion

Roda and Vich are identical in shape, but not in content. However, the phasing of marriage over the traditional stages is apparent in all ("A" is probably incomplete). The one item that stands out is the proper for Vespers in "B." Unfortunately, the manuscript breaks off, but what little there is gives abundant evidence for a liturgy of the hours that prays for the couple as they prepare to be married.

The two preparatory rites, of *Arrhas* and of chamber blessing, show great similarity between the service books, which points to considerable stability in a *rite de passage*. One prayer occurs in all four texts; it does not actually bless the *Arrhas*, but rather the *giving* of the *Arrhas*.

"Lord, almighty God, you commanded Abraham to give Isaac to Rebecca through the exchange of rings as an image of holy matrimony, that by the offering of rings the number of children might be increased. We pray you to sanctify with your power this offering of the *arrhae* which your servant (N) makes to his beloved bride (N); so that, protected by your blessing, and joined in the yoke of love, they may know the joy of being happily counted among your faithful ones for ever."[16]

Clearly, this prayer looks forward to a union to be experienced, but it also looks back to and implies a love that is already sown in the hearts of the couple. There is also a hint that the prayer has been composed to ritualize what is a long-standing folk custom. The *Arrhas* persisted in Spain, and it was later found in France, too. But what is interesting in *Liber Ordinum* is that the *Arrhas*, though venerable, is accompanied by the newer symbol, the ring, and that, for the first time in the West, there are *two* of them.

Where the Castilian and Catalonian rites differ is over the shape of the nuptial mass. The Catalonian rites have been romanized more, so that the Gregorian prayers, including the nuptial blessing, appear again, but it is so embedded among Visigothic prayers as to be hardly noticeable. The priest hands the woman over to the man after Communion in the Castilian rites; in the Catalonian rites, she is handed over immediately prior to the nuptial blessing, which comes before Communion, as in the Roman books. Thus, the local custom has been made to fit the Roman order.

Another custom, which became popular in the later Middle Ages in Northern Europe, was to place a large veil over the couple. Elsewhere this became a canopy, like the Jewish *huppah*. It was probably regarded as a symbol of the *shekinah* at a special part of the service in order to give it a special point. The Visigothic rites tied a special cord around the couple to symbolize the binding together of man and wife.[17] With two exceptions, which we think are the result of Roman influence, all the Visigothic blessings are of both bride and groom throughout.

One of the nuptial prayers that appears in all four texts is particularly florid in style and may be compared in basic shape with the Gregorian Sacramentary nuptial blessing quoted earlier.

"O God, when the world was itself newborn, you shaped woman out of the bone of the man, for the purpose of continuing the human race, thereby revealing the unity of genuine love; for in making two out of one you have shown that the two are one. Thus you established the basis for the first marriage, namely that the man should take to wife what was a part of his own body, knowing it to have been made out of part of himself. Look graciously down from your heavenly throne and be pleased to hear the prayers we offer for your servants, (N) and (N), whom we join in marriage by blessing their union. Bless them with your merciful kindness and by the kindness of your mercy sustain them. Grant them, Lord, to be of one mind in the fear of your name and to show their love in the goodness of their mutual behavior. May they love one another and never be estranged from you. May they render to one another the debt of marriage in such a way as never to cause offense to you. May they never turn away after another, but please you by remaining faithful to one another. Grant them, Lord, an abundance of this world's goods and a large family of children. Let them be popular with their fellow human beings and blessed by you, so that their hearts and bodies might be overflowing with the sweetness of your blessing. Grant them to enjoy length of days in this life and to desire the unending life that is to come. Let them so negotiate all temporal business that they will continue faithfully to long for eternal things. May they handle the goods that pass away in such manner as not to lose those that abide. Serving you in fidelity and truth, let them see their children's children that, after a long life in this present world, they may attain to the kingdom of heaven."[18]

Succinctness is clearly not an attribute of Visigothic prayer writers. And yet for those of us who struggle with modern prayers, it comes as a sobering thought that many people like things to be said more than once in the liturgy, and homely allusion is a tender aspect that is often lacking in the somewhat cold and clinical expressions that modern revisions have given us, whether these have been produced from Latin originals or composed afresh. This prayer looks to the nuptial blessing as the performative part of the rite, and it regards strong intercession for the couple as an essential part of the rite.

All in all, the Visigothic ambience, however romanized, takes us into a different world. Similarities of theme in euchology are still recognizable; the sequence of ideas (creation, creation of man and woman, marriage, the couple, marital virtues, and offspring-eternity) is equally noticeable. Still, there is a passion and a humanity that we have not encountered so far. Perhaps this finds ultimate expression in that when the Visigothic rites *do* take over consent at marriage the question asked of the bridegroom and bride is not "do you *want* each other?" but "do you *love* each other?"[19]

GERMAN AUSTERITY

Some German rites reproduce the pattern we have already seen in the Anglo-Norman synthesis. However, there are some that have short, noneucharistic rites, and these deserve brief mention as yet one more variant in the whole story.

For example, the 1485 Cologne rite comes in three parts. First, the ring is blessed with formulas that we

49

have already seen. Next, the bride and bridegroom are blessed in a series of short prayers, including Psalm 127 (128). Finally, the bride is solemnly "led into" church, again with Psalm 127 (128), and the priest recites a prayer over her alone in which marital virtues and fruitfulness are alluded to. This last rite follows the consummation of the marriage.

The Magdeburg Agenda of 1497 has an even barer scheme, but the Gregorian nuptial blessing (without mass) is given, in the plural-ending version. The Meissen rite of 1512 has a similar format, but the formula after consent reflects some of the discussion about priestly roles already mentioned: "May God confirm the marriage which has been contracted between you; and I solemnize it in the face of the church: In the Name of the Father . . ."[20]

The German rites from other sources reflect a similar austerity, which bears testimony to the noneucharistic form of marriage as something that the medieval nuptial mass could not dislodge everywhere.

CONCLUSION

The Western medieval development is both rich and complex. It can be summarized, however, in the following four features.

First, although the nuptial blessing is the first and earliest part of the marriage liturgy, it eventually gives way to the consent of the partners as the part of the rite identified by the scholastic theologians as performative. Their premise was that *consensus facit nuptias* (consent makes marriage). So it is for this reason that the rite of consent was *prefixed* to the marriage rite, from the twelfth century onwards, and clothed with various interpretative symbolism, such as the giving of the ring. As consent in marriage ascends in importance, so betrothal before it wanes.

Second, there appears to have been some inner scepticism about the view that the consent is central, even though it necessarily took place in the vernacular, which was a rarity in medieval Western worship. Such a scepticism is shown by the relationship between the (modern) consent and the (older) nuptial blessing during mass, for this special blessing was frequently given its own special liturgical emphasis. The couple were often veiled, or else a canopy was held over them; the nuptial blessing would be introduced by the eucharistic dialogue (*Sursum corda*), and sung to a preface chant. Aidan Kavanagh has recently written about the interplay between "primary" and "secondary" theology in the worship of the church.[21] Here it seems is a good example, for by the twelfth century the rest of the marriage liturgy has developed its own symbolism and ecclesiological focus, and this has reached such a peak that it cannot suddenly take a back place by the *fiat* of a canon lawyer or a theologian. I would hazard a guess that consent and blessing came across *in actual celebration* as being the two climaxes of the liturgy, but that consent was preliminary and blessing central.

Third, this ambivalence about the relationship of consent with the rest of the liturgy is highlighted by the different ways in which various countries understand the role of the priest. For if consent is to be central, what is the priest there to do? Late-medieval theologians looked for irreducible minimums in their sacramental thinking. While all this was going on in the seminar room, something else was taking place in the liturgies of ordinary people, and different countries produced their own answer to what the priest "does." Thus, in England, he presides, and does no more, for there is no special formula for him to recite after the consent has been made. In Spain, he "hands over" the woman to the man at the end of the mass, as a *pater familias* figure. Germany is more neutral; here, the priest "solemnizes" the union made by consent. Finally, Normandy goes over the top, with the priest reciting the definitive formula, "I join you together." These, surely, are all secondary theological interpretations at a local level of what it means to preside at this sacrament as well as different answers to an issue that the Middle Ages does not properly resolve. Ultimately, however, it is the notion of marriage as *churchly*, rather than *contractual*, that is at stake.

Fourth, marriage becomes as public as possible. The earlier tradition, represented by the nuptial mass in the Sacramentaries, the Visigothic rites, and the domestic-missionary rites, offered couples what was available as local regions had formulated their service books, and, indeed, as the missionary thrust Northwards was slowly making the church part of the life of society. The emphasis on consent went hand in hand with the requirement that such a consent be made *publicly*. Such a notion of marriage liturgy stood in direct contrast with the older model of the mobile priest coming to the home, probably in the context of the marriage feast, and reciting prayers and blessings. Thus, the Fourth Lateran Council of 1215 decreed that banns of marriage must be read on three preceding Sundays,[22] so that everyone knows, impediments can be alleged, and the marriage has as high a public profile as possible. All this gives the church an increasing responsibility in civil society. No wonder, then, that the liturgy celebrated on these occasions should have moved so far from its roots.

NOTES

1. See J. Dauvillier, *Le mariage dans le droit classique de l'église depuis le décret de Gratien (1140) jusqu'à la mort de Clement V* (Paris: Receuil Sirey, 1933), pp. 55–136.

2. See Korbinian Ritzer, Formen, Riten, und religiöses Brachtum der Eheschliessung in den christlichen Kirchen des ersten Jahrtausends (Liturgiewissenschaftliche Quellen und Forschungen 38) (Munster: Aschendorff, 1962), pp. 174–182 (discussion) and pp. 345–347 (text). Hereafter, this book is referred to as *Ritzer*. On the future-tense verb in prayer no. 4, see our review of the 1982 reprint of *Ritzer*, in *Theologische Revue* 80 (1984), col. 157 (whole review, coll. 156–158).

3. Text of Gelasian in L. Eizenhöfer, P. Siffrin, and L. Mohlberg, *Liber Sacramentorum Romanae Ecclesiae* (Rerum ecclesiasticarum documenta; series maior: Fontes; 4) (Rome: Herder, 1960), pp. 208–210. Text of Gregorian in J. Deshusses, *Le Sacramentaire Gregorien* I (Spicilegium Friburgense 16) (Fribourg: University Press, 1971), pp. 308–311.

4. Latin text, Deshusses, op. cit., pp. 310–311 (no. 838) (Mark Searle, Trans.).

5. Kenneth W. Stevenson, *Nuptial Blessing: A Study of Christian Marriage Rites* (Alcuin Club Collections 64) (London: SPCK, 1982, and New York: Oxford University Press, 1983), pp. 33–34. See also Aldo Martini, *Il Cosidetto Pontificale di Poitiers* (Rerum ecclesiasticarum documenta; series maior: Fontes; 14) (Rome: Herder, 1979), p. 336 (lections).

6. Kenneth W. Stevenson, " 'Benedictio Nuptialis': Reflections on the Blessing of Bride and Groom in Some Western Mediaeval Rites," *Ephemerides Liturgicae* 93 (1979):457–462 (whole article, pp. 457–478).

7. Latin text, G. H. Doble, *The Lanalet Pontifical* (Henry Bradshaw Society 74) (London, 1937), p. 65 (Mark Searle, Trans.).

8. Text in W. Greenwell, *The Pontifical of Egbert* (Surtees Society 27) (London, 1853), pp. 125–126 (with blessing of the ring), and p. 132 (without blessing of the ring).

9. Text in *Ritzer*, p. 353 (Mark Searle, Trans.). The second prayer appears, adapted, in some medieval marriage rites elsewhere, e.g., in the twelfth-century "Magdalen" Pontifi-

cal, for which, see H. A. Wilson, *The Pontifical of Magdalen College* (Henry Bradshaw Society 39) (London, 1910), p. 203.

10. See W. G. Henderson, *The York Manual* (Surtees Society 63) (Edinburgh, 1875), p. 159, for the Red Book of Darley. See H. A. Wilson, *The Benedictional of Archbishop Robert* (Henry Bradshaw Society 24) (London, 1903), pp. 149–151.

11. See Jean-Baptiste Molin and Protais Mutembe, *Le rituel du mariage en France du XIIè au XVIè siècle* (Théologie Historique 26) (Paris: Beauchesne, 1973), pp. 289–291. My own translation, with Molin's, and my own appended sources.

12. See Molin and Mutembe, op. cit., p. 306. My own translation.

13. See Stevenson, *Nuptial Blessing*, pp. 79f. The "Evesham" book mentioned in this discussion is an early fourteenth-century monastic liturgical text, for which, see H. A. Wilson, *Liber Evesham* (Henry Bradshaw Society 6) (London, 1983), col. 35, where the "later hand" adds the active vow. Peter Lombard maintained that consent at marriage required only the minimal formula, "I take you for my husband"/"I take you for my wife"; see *Sententiae, P. L.*, 192, 210.

14. See Molin and Mutembe, op. cit., p. 304, where the text reads (incorrectly) "conjugo" instead of "conjungo." See also Kenneth W. Stevenson, "The Marriage Rites of Mediaeval Scandinavia: A Fresh Look, "*Ephemerides Liturgicae* 97 (1983):550–557, where "zones of influence" reflect the way in which the priest's role is understood. See also A. Duval, "La formule 'Ego vos conjungo' au Concile de Trente," *La Maison-Dieu* 99 (1969):144–153, on the history and further development of this formula.

15. See Stevenson, *Nuptial Blessing*, pp. 47ff. Texts arranged in *Ritzer*, pp. 357–364, where the tenth-century "Liber Antiphonarius" of Léon is also provided, which is another witness to the influence of the Liturgy of the Hours on marriage rites. See also Stevenson, "Van Gennep and Marriage—Strange Bedfellows?"—A Fresh Look at the Rites of Marriage," *Ephemerides Liturgicae* 100 (1986):145ff., and J.

Pinell i Pons, "La liturgia nupcial en el antiguo rito hispanico," *La Celebrazione Cristiana Del Matrimonio,* pp. 87–106.

16. Text in M. Férotin, *Le liber Ordinum en usage dans l'église wisigothique et mozarabe d'Espagne du cinquième au onzième siècle* (Monumenta Ecclesiae Liturgica V) (Paris: Firmin-Didot, 1905), coll. 435–436. The prayer also appears in the Vich and Roda books (Mark Searle, Trans.). It should be noted that the Visigothic domestic rites bless the "chamber," whereas the other Western rites bless the "couple."

17. The "jugale" is mentioned by Isidore of Seville, *De Ecclesiasticis Officiis* II 20, 7 (*P. L.* 83, 811 C). (Text in *Ritzer,* p. 356.) The cord used was colored red and white.

18. Text in Férotin, op. cit., coll. 438–439 (Mark Searle, Trans.).

19. Molin and Mutembe, op. cit., p. 65. Subsequent rites synthesize "love" and "will to marry," before the latter takes over altogether.

20. A Schönfelder, *Liturgische Bibliotek,* I (Paderborn: Schöningh, 1906), p. 26. See also Stevenson, *Nuptial Blessing,* pp. 88–91.

21. See pp. 188ff.

22. J. D. Mansi, *Sacrorum conciliorum nova et amplissima Collectio* 22 (Florence: Venedig), col. 1038.

Chapter Three

Crown Them in Love. The Eastern Evidence

INTRODUCTION
If the Western marriage rites are typified by a nuptial blessing of the bride alone and later by a public consent to be married, the Eastern rites are typified by the crowning of the bridal pair in a rich liturgy of the word, with symbolic action, and a strong corporate focus on marriage as a mystery of the church. Thus, the words "crown them in love" appear toward the end of one of the main marriage prayers in the Byzantine rite.

But the Western rites varied greatly from one tradition to another—Visigoths with their lengthier rich euchology; medieval English with their elaborate vernacular vows; Germans with their simple rite, celebrated without the eucharist. Local rites grew and developed their own shapes and forms, and the Sacramentaries insinuated their own sort of uniformity as time went on. The Eastern rites, on the other hand, take us into a different world characterized by a remarkable similarity. If you attended a wedding according to each of the Eastern rites in turn, you would be able to identify common ground between, say, Maronite, Coptic, and Byzantine that you would not find were you to be in a position to move in a similar fashion through the Western rites discussed in Chapter 2.

What is this common ground, apart from the crowning of the partners? The common ground is that each clearly reproduces the deep structures of marriage ritual identified by Van Gennep. Each of the rites has a liturgy of betrothal that is normally separate from the marriage celebration. This rite of betrothal is not a legal-sounding form of consent; it is a liturgy in its own right, which prays for the couple as they offer their resolve to God. When betrothal precedes marriage by some time, there is no pressing need to make the couple express their consent publicly. Moreover, some of the Eastern rites add other intervening shortened rites, such as the Armenian blessing of robes, as ways of ritualizing folk customs.

One of the pieces of baggage that a certain type of Westerner brings to even the most cursory glance at Eastern liturgies is that scholastic minimalism that searches for the corresponding sacramental "magic words." So the old-fashioned pious Latin, who has at last found the consecration formula in a Syrian anaphora, will not cease from mental strife until a form of consent has been uncovered, somewhere. It is significant that the preliminary questions about willingness to marry in the Byzantine rite appeared soon after betrothal and marriage became celebrated to all intents and purposes together. Still it is equally significant that the Maronite rite had the Latin form of consent imposed on it, without any reference to its prior history; and each of the Eastern rites in communion with Rome had to follow suit.

Of course consent matters. It is so easy for Westerners to reflect their own presuppositions in what they find when they look at these vibrant and venerable rites. Thus, in the Syrian betrothal liturgies, the ring is central, because the ring was anciently the sign of betrothal. Similarly, the marriage prayers of all these rites reflect the joy and celebration aspects of marriage in a way that we have only met in the Visigothic service books. Moreover, betrothal was so important that, even though only the Coptic and Armenian rites have a full liturgy with lections, *each one* of the rites from the Armenian-Syrian family employs a special symbolism at betrothal, as if there were a need to make this rite significant in the lives of ordinary men and women.[1] Thus, betrothed Armenian couples exchange crosses; the Syrian orthodox priest goes to the home of each partner to act as a sort of intermediary; the Maronites include an anointing of the couple (which they probably took from the Copts); and the East Syrians make a curious mixture of water, ash, and wine in a chalice (the *henana*) for the couple to drink, to symbolize the dying of the old relationship in order to come to life in the new.

Unfortunately, we do not have the detailed historical texts of these rites with which we can trace their development in the detail that we can in the Western rites. Literary evidence unites in a liturgy of crowning by the fourth century, as well as in some form of betrothal. Thereafter, the scholar can be sure of the course of history in the Byzantine rite, but not so among the others, although the Armenian rite of the ninth century is known to us in outline. At the same time, comparative liturgy comes to our help and reveals both the deep structures and the surface structures. The former consist of the passage into marriage through betrothal, ancillary ceremonies (in some rites), and the marriage celebration itself. The latter are apparent in the idiosyncrasies of each local rite, for example, the offering of incense in the Coptic betrothal rite. Due to the conservatism of the Eastern liturgies, we can with some fairness assume that we are handling ancient and time-honored holy things. A glance at each one of them will make plain their peculiar ambience.

Gabriele Winkler has taught us all to regard the Armenian rite as no mere eccentric appendage to Byzantium, but rather as a serious cousin of the Syrian rites.[2] We know that Armenians not only used crowns at marriage, but actually *blessed* them, from as early as the fourth century. This practice becomes universal in the East, except in the Byzantine rite. The ninth- and tenth-century texts give us evidence of three stages:

Betrothal, with lections (Prv 3:15–18, Gal 5:14–18, Mt 24:30–35), exchange of crosses, and solemn prayers

Marriage, with lections (Gn 1:26–28 and 2:21–23, Is 61:9–62:5, Eph 5:22–33, Mt 19:1–9, and Jn 2:1–11), and solemn prayers

Removal of crowns, with solemn prayer[3]

Later rites fill out this basic shape. The special lections at betrothal remain, as do these fine prayers. Betrothal is an elaborate rite, with the blessing of jewelry; this is followed by the blessing of robes, with more readings preceded by hymns and censing; and the rite of joining of the right hands, which starts at home and moves from there to church and which involves the giving of consent at the church door. The marriage liturgy may or may not include the celebration of the eucharist, but the solemn prayers over the couple, together with the crowning, take place at the end of the liturgy of the word. The rite moves back to the home for the blessing of a common cup and the removal of the crowns; this later took place after an interval of some days.

Although the sequence of rites has been brought together, it nonetheless embodies the same principle that we have met before. It starts at home with preparations, and these even include blessing jewels and robes for the bride. It then moves from the home to church for public consent and joining of hands. It then moves from the church door into the church itself for the celebration of the marriage, leading up to the great climax when the couple are crowned. It then moves back to the home for the Cana cup and, one week later, for the removal of the crowns. A particular feature of this rite is the rich provision of readings.

The prayers of the Armenian rite repay consideration, because they take us away from Western concepts, and seem to build upon Semitic models, both in shape, literary form, and imagery. Here is the full text of a marriage prayer that appears in a ninth-century manuscript and is still in use today:

"Blessed art thou, almighty God, who madest all thy creatures, heavenly and earthly, alive by thy word: and fashionedst man with thy hands in the image of thy divine form. Thou didst appoint and couple with him, as the companion of his speech and the sharer of his life, the bone which thou didst take of his bones, the flesh of his flesh; and they twain became one flesh. Thou alone art merciful, who for our humanity hast prepared things heavenly and earthly: the heavenly crowns of holy virgins, and the earthly for the yoking together of the wedded.

"Bless, O Lord, the wedlock of these persons through thy mercy, as thou blessedst the wedlock of Abraham and Sarah, of Isaac and Rebekah, of Jacob and Rachel. And as thou hast said through the apostle: Honorable is wedlock and holy the bed: So keep holy the marriage bed of these persons and graciously bestow on them seed according to thy will, that they may be blessed according to thy word which thou spakest: Increase and multiply and replenish the earth. And increase them with the increment of holiness, to the end that their seed may become numerous upon the earth, and may become worthy of the adoption of thine inheritance, glorifying Father and Son and holy Spirit, now and ever and to eternity."[4]

This prayer manifests the deep structure of Jewish euchology in the way that it moves from blessing to supplication. It also uses biblical allusions; the opening P-narrative (Gn 2), the patriarchal couples, the marriage bed as honorable (Heb 13:4), and the command to increase and multiply (Gn 1:28). Moreover, beneath the Jewish shape and the use of biblical allusion there is the same sequence of ideas we have met before, which perhaps points to a deep structure for the solemn marriage prayer in both East and West. Such a sequence begins with creation and then creation of man and woman; then it turns to the institution of marriage; thereafter it prays for the couple, both for their future offspring and their life together under God's care.

The Armenian rite for the removal of the crowns consists of a prayer that survives into contemporary usage. Like some of the Western texts we have already seen, it uses the theme of angelic protection:

"Lord God almighty, by thee have been blessed the crowns of thy servants and handmaids. Do thou likewise by thy command, Lord and creator, enjoin the taking of the crowns off the heads of these persons, and instead of the crowns that pass away may the angel of peace guard them holy and spotless, one in spirit and in counsel, until the day cometh of our Lord Jesus Christ, with whom to the Father almighty in fellowship with the holy Spirit are due glory, rule, and honor."[5]

Like other prayers we have seen, this one stresses the eschatological character of marriage.

The thirteenth-century Nomo-Canons of Bar Hebraeus[6] provide us with evidence for the enforcement of the following as needful for a proper marriage:

Presence of a priest and witnesses

Use of a ring

Use of a cross

Priestly blessing

Nowadays, betrothal normally takes place on the eve of marriage, but originally it was distanced in time. There are four main parts of the "passage" to marriage in the Syrian rite. These are betrothal, the joining of the right hands, the blessing of the rings, and the blessing of crowns. Similarity with the Armenian rite is obvious.[7] Here are the main elements:

1. *Betrothal*
The priest goes to the home of the bridegroom, then to that of the bride, and offers the ring to the bride. The ring (if accepted) is blessed and then placed on her finger. The blessing is elaborate in comparison with any Western formula.
2. *Joining of right hands*
The priest asks for the consent of the couple, then joins the right hands.
3. *Marriage—Blessing of rings*
Introductory prayers
Psalm 50 (51)
Preparatory prayer for the couple
Psalm 44 (45)
Sedro (Psalmic prayer), chant, censing
Blessing of rings
Giving of rings

4. Marriage—Blessing of crowns

Opening prayer
Psalm 20 (21)
Sedro (Psalmic prayer)
Ephesians 5:20–33
Matthew 19:1–11
Prayer over crowns (lengthy)
Signing of crowns
Crowning, with brief formula
Long blessing prayer
Prayers
Signing of couple (with threefold sign of the cross)
Concluding prayers over couple
Removal of crowns
Concluding chant

The order of elements is as elaborate as the Armenian. Several issues are raised of which we need to take note.

First, the role of the priest at betrothal presupposes a position of respect in the community. He acts as an intermediary between the couple.

Second, however, there seems to be some duplication between the betrothal and the joining of the right hands, as each rite appears to have a similar function. It could be that betrothal (as a simpler, domestic rite) is considerably older than the joining of hands (which in the Syrian Orthodox rite seems to take place in church, though it could take place at home).

Third, in the marriage rite the rings are blessed, with one for each partner, whereas the earlier rite of betrothal only used one ring. Here at long last is a rite that celebrates betrothal with what we would call an "engagement ring" as well as marriage with what we would call a "wedding ring." The preparatory character of this part of the rite is reflected in the choice of Psalm 50 (51).

Fourth, like the Armenian rite, and the other Eastern services that we shall be looking at, the crowning comes at the end of a liturgy of the word as a symbolic act interpreting the readings, chants, and prayers.

Finally, the removal of the crowns, originally a separate rite, is now an appendage to the marriage service itself. Similarities with the Armenian rite include the fact that the Syrians once blessed robes, but this has now disappeared altogether.

The Syrian rite, then, sees marriage as a "passage," and this is reflected in the coherence of the actions, gestures, and prayers of the liturgy. The opening prayer of the marriage rite expresses not only the aspirations of the couple, but the identification of the whole community with them, the human qualities divinized by God's grace and the element of sacrifice in the life of faith:

"Be present, Lord, so that the beginning of our joy may be in you, and the end of our gladness may also be in you; may our souls and spirits delight in you, and our sadness be turned away through your mercy; may our goods be multiplied through your kindness, may blessings abound in us; and may the minds of our bridegroom and bride be illuminated and perfected, so that with you and with the saints who have pleased you, we may produce good things that do not fail, and in the company of your saints and the ranks of your beloved, we may give glory and thanksgiving, Father, Son and Holy Spirit."[8]

MARONITE RITE

The Maronite rite comes in two parts called "Testament" (betrothal) and "Crowning" (marriage). But, as we shall see, they embody several of the features that we have already seen in the Armenian and Syrian rites.[9] The structure is as follows:

64

1. *Testament* (*betrothal*)
The priest asks for consent
The priest joins the right hands
Prayer for the couple
Anointing of the couple with imagery from the anointing at Bethany, Mark 14:3ff.
Blessing of rings and other accoutrements
2. *Crowning* (*marriage*)
Procession with candles
Bride dressed in special attire
Introductory prayer
Censing of cross, altar, and crowns by deacon
Prayer for forgiveness, reconciliation, and renewal
Sedro (Psalmic prayer) on the theme of Adam and Eve, and Cana-theme chant
Ephesians 5:22–27
Matthew 19:3–6
Consent and stole wrapping (cf. Latin usage)
Ring blessing
Ring giving
Crown blessing and crowning
Long hymn (attributed to Ephrem)
Blessing of each, with hand laying
Removal of crowns
Concluding prayer

There is little in the Maronite rite that does not also appear in the Syrian, apart from the use in the Syrian of the priest as intermediary. We have the same phasing, the ecclesiological dimensions to the whole series of rites, which is heightened by the fact that the "Crowning" liturgy takes the place of one of the liturgies of the hours. The somewhat mannered character of the consent form in this marriage rite is demonstrated by its insertion very near to the liturgical climax. Moreover, in the crown blessing prayers, the "male" and "female" aspects are emphasized, so that "his" prayer mentions Abraham, Isaac, and Jacob, whereas "her" prayer mentions Sarah, Rebecca, and Rachel. This is more explicit than the Syrian rite and it illustrates that once a prayer begins to focus on one partner as distinct from the other, the liturgy starts to define different roles in marriage. The removal of the crowns at the end is doubtless a relic from the days when this would take place some time after the marriage.

Of particular interest is the practice of anointing of the forehead at betrothal. As we shall see, the Copts anoint at the marriage itself, using baptismal and kingship imagery. In the Maronite rite, however, the biblical interpretation is otherwise. In the Bethany lection (Mk 14:36), oil is not a symbol of the kingdom, but rather a preparation for a change of state: marriage is a dying to the old (separate) relationship in order to live to the new (united) one. Perhaps the baptismal character of this anointing is different from the Coptic in that the Maronites are thinking of the prebaptismal unction. It certainly shows how symbolism was natural to live in and enjoy in these Eastern rites.

To conclude, three texts exemplify the spirit of this liturgy.[10] First, the fine Cana chant immediately before the readings:

"Alleluia and glory to you, Lord, Christ, Spouse who was invited to the wedding in Cana of Galilee, who blessed the bridegroom and bride and made their good abound; in your mercy may your right hand, filled with all spiritual goodness, be placed also on the bridegroom and bride, and bless them at the same time, so that they may sing your glory, and that of your blessed Father and Holy and life-giving Spirit, Alleluia, Alleluia!"

Second, a prayer near the end of the rite, which stresses the ecclesiological aspects of marriage as a celebration of the redeemed community:

"May the God who blessed Juda with the race from which was born the Christ, who won the nations by his cross, bless the bridegroom, bride, and paranymphs (attendants) here present, and may he protect this assembly by his victorious cross. May their works begin and end in righteousness; may they produce children agreeable to God in this passing world, and may they reach the other world, that which does not pass away, at the gate of life eternal."

Third, the prayer that follows the previous one, which is once more kingdom centered:

"May God go with you from the height of his temple, guarding your bodies and your souls. May he be for you a wall and protection against the temptations of the enemy. May he protect your life from warfare and famine, from wicked and sinful men; and may he in the end make you worthy to hear the word which surpasses all that is good—come, blessed of my Father, inherit the kingdom of ages of ages, Father, Son, and Holy Spirit."

EAST-SYRIAN RITE

The early history of the East-Syrian marriage rite is less shrouded in mystery.[11] It emerges with the same sort of structure that we have already encountered: betrothal with the consent of the couple, the presence of the priest, and the use of a cross. As early as the time of Patriarch Iso bar Nun (832–838), we know that the *henana* was used at betrothal, the mixing of ash with water, which is placed in a chalice filled with wine. The cross, used for blessing at betrothal, is thus a peculiarity of each of the Syrian-Armenian family of marriage rites. The East-Syrian[12] scheme resembles the others closely:

1. *Consent*
A woman is sent to the bride's house, offering a ring

2. *Joining of right hands*
Lengthy blessing, mentioning the three patriarchal couples
Signing of the hands
3. *Betrothal*
Chant, based on psalter
Two very long blessings
Blessing with chalice
Blessing of the ring, placed in a chalice
Ash placed in a chalice (with water and wine)
Mixture drunk by couple (two-thirds by man, one-third by woman)
4. *Blessing of robes*
Chants and prayers, rich in symbolism
Blessing of crowns
5. *Crowning* (Marriage)
Chants, with crowning
Ephesians 5:21–6:5
Matthew 19:1–11
Blessing (attributed to Ephrem) with hand laying: bridegroom
Blessing (attributed to Ephrem) with hand laying: bride
Blessing for attendants (paranymphs)
Doxology
Signing of the couple
(Wedding feast)
6. *Making of bedchamber*
Prayers and chants

We note the same phasing, but three features stand out.

First, the *henana* is idiosyncratic and corresponds to the anointing at betrothal in the Syrian rite. The use of ash in this way is probably a symbol of passage, as we have suggested. The ash is used in no other rite, but fits well where it is placed here.

Second, the crowning takes place at the beginning of the marriage proper, not after the readings, as in the other rites we have seen so far. In the Byzantine rite, the Italo-Greek tradition similarly places the crowning before the lections (but after introductory prayers), and this is how the later rite develops.

Third, the crowns are not formally removed, probably because the liturgy ends with the making of the bedchamber, and that is seen as sufficient evocation of the consummation of the marriage.

Other smaller aspects stand out too, including the fact that a woman is used as intermediary at the beginning of the scheme, whereas the Syrian rite uses the priest. But there is one overriding phenomenon that makes the East-Syrian liturgy stand apart from all others, namely the very rich tradition of hymnody, in particular addressed to the Spouse-Christ. Here is a small example:[13]

"O Christ, adorned spouse, whose betrothal has given
    us a type,
complete the foundation and the building, and their
    (the couple's) laudable work;
sanctify their marriage and their bed;
and dismiss their sins and offenses;
and make them a temple for you and bestow on their
    marriage chamber your light;
and may their odor be as a roseshoot in paradise,
    and as a garden full of smells,
    and as a myrtle tree may be for your praise.
May they be a bastion for our orthodox band and a
    house of refuge."

Similarly rich are the prayers of the priest. Here is the prayer said over the robes:

"O God, who formed the body and prepared the soul,
and made man in his own image and likeness,
and adorned garments for the upholding of men;

may (God) bless these garments,
and may they be a joy for those who wear them;
as they cleave to the limbs of people as clothing,
and are adorned with beautiful things,
so may also these servants cleave to one another in
    love,
and may live united in the concord and fear of God,
through the grace and mercy of Christ our Lord."

Here are themes of the symbolism of clothing applied
to marriage in a way ritualizes folklore and "sacralizes
the secular," as Westerners would understand it. All
in all, the East Syrians take us into a Semitic-inspired
rite, like the other liturgies of this family, where domestic and ecclesial mix freely, biblical and natural
symbols intertwine in word, song, and action. Above
all, in each of these rites, marriage is phased as a passage from one form of existence to another. Each rite
has different peculiarities. But each builds up to the
crowning as the ultimate adornment of the liturgy,
pointing to marital union as the climax to which the liturgy leads. Perhaps the concluding prayer from this liturgy says it all:

"Lord, you blessed the righteous of old,
Abraham, Isaac and Jacob,
and you increased, multiplied, exalted and pardoned
    them.
Bless these your servants, and bless their pure
    marriage bed
that they may live together in love and concord,
and that their children may be worthy of the
    ornaments of this day,
and to ascribe glory to him who has allowed them
    to share in each other.
May he perfect you and everyone in this assembly,
and may his mercies abound towards us for ever,
    through the prayers of Mary the mother of life and
        light,

70

and through the prayers of all the saints and
    martyrs of the Lord,
now and for ever and ever."

COPTIC AND ETHIOPIC RITES

The need to marry in church is attested in Egypt as
early as the fourth century. The next step in the story
does not come until the tenth and eleventh centuries,
in the form of a series of prayers from the Euchologion of the White Monastery.[14] This monastic estab-
lishment in Upper Egypt (not far from the present city
of Sohag) was the center for classical Coptic culture,
so the fact that there is a marriage rite of relatively
early date is of considerable importance. Its sequence
follows thus:

Blessing of the crowns

Blessing of oil for the anointing of the couple

Blessing of bread

Blessing of wine

A Euchologion, since it contains as a rule only prayer
texts, does not contain everything necessary for a full
liturgy, so the baldness of these prescribed prayers
must not mislead us. What we have here is enough to
tell us a great deal about the roots of the Coptic rite of
marriage.

First, crowns are not only used but blessed. Second,
oil is used at marriage. And third, bread and wine are
blessed. Moreover, the themes of the prayers are rich,
and the prayer over the crowns is similar in structure
and content to later practice. We have already met the
blessing of the cup, from as early a time as the eighth
century, and we shall meet it again in the Byzantine

rite. Here is yet one more point of similarity among the various Eastern liturgies.

In the thirteenth century, under Pope Cyril III (1235–1243), we learn that marriage consists of two stages. Betrothal had the dowry and a giving of gifts, including a cross and a ring. Marriage includes the use of incense, crowning, and the eucharist.

The modern texts expand on this skeleton considerably:[15]

1. *Betrothal* (in the early morning)
Thanksgiving prayer
Censing
1 Corinthians 1:1–10
John 1:1–17
Three intercessory prayers
Creed
Three betrothal prayers
Thanksgiving
Blessing of robes—tunic, cincture, veil; clothing of bride
Bridegroom goes to bride to give her a cross and the ring
Both are veiled
Hymn
2. *Marriage*
Thanksgiving (preceded by consent)
Censing
Ephesians 5:22–6:3
1 Peter 3:5–7
Acts 16:13–15
Matthew 19:1–6
Special litany, with twelve petitions for the couple
Three solemn marriage prayers
Anointing—blessing of oil precedes
Blessing of crowns and crowning
Blessing of couple

Chants
Eucharist (no longer)
3. *Removal of crowns* (after two days, originally seven)

Once more, similarities are obvious. Marriage is
phased. The crowning takes place after the liturgy of
the word. Robes are blessed within the whole liturgical framework, and the ring is still, formally, part of
the betrothal rite. Two special features stand out. The
couple are veiled at the end of the betrothal service.
This is yet one more symbol of the passage character
of the entire scheme. The couple have been standing
in separate parts of the church, at the head of the
men's and women's side, respectively. Only now do
they come together in church. The veil conceals them
and also unites and blinds them. The other special
characteristic to which we have already alluded is the
custom of anointing immediately before the crowning.
The prayer recited over the oil beforehand is an adaptation of the old oil prayer contained in the *Apostolic
Tradition* of Hippolytus, which forms the basis of oil
prayers in both East and West. But it is extended to refer to marital virtues thus:

" . . . a weapon of truth . . . and justice . . . the unction of purity and integrity. . . . Incorruptible light
and beauty . . . for comeliness and true decoration . . . for virtue, salvation, and victory against all
the assaults of the enemy . . . for the renewal and salvation of their souls, bodies, and spirits . . . for the
riches and fruits of good works . . . for the glory and
honor of your name."[16]

Each of these short phrases leads into an intercalated
"Amen." There can be no doubt whatever of the value
placed on this ceremony.

The symbolism of the numbers 3 and 12 appears
throughout both the services, and the lections are almost as full as those in the Armenian liturgies. How-

ever, the connection between solemn thanksgiving and censing is noticeable at the start of betrothal and marriage. Here is the text of the thanksgiving immediately before the blessing of the robes:

"We thank you, Lord God almighty, for you adorned the skies with your word and founded the earth and everything that is in them; and you have gathered together everything into one place of meeting, and you have made two people into one.

"Now, therefore, our Master, we ask you to make your servants worthy through the nature of the sign of your word in the yoke of betrothal, so that an indivisible love may be in them toward one another in each of them being joined firmly to the other.

"Build them on the foundation of your holy Church, that they may walk in the attitude and joining of the yoke of the word that has been agreed between them. For you are the yoke of love and the giver of the law for joining them, making unity in the joining of two through your word, so that they may fulfill the command of your only-begotten Son Jesus Christ our Lord, who completed it, with whom you are blessed in the Holy Spirit. . . ."[17]

Ecclesial and biblical, pastoral and tender, this unique prayer echoes themes that we have already encountered.

The Ethiopic rite is a cousin of the Coptic, and it has more flexibility about it, for example, in the form of giving the gifts at the betrothal and whether or not the eucharist is celebrated during the marriage. At the beginning of the rite, the priest cuts a piece of hair from the bridegroom's head and places it on the bride's, and then cuts some of the bride's hair and places it on the groom's head. This is yet one more curious custom, symbolizing in one more way the union of the

74

couple. If the eucharist is celebrated, the crowning comes at the end, as a climax, and the couple walk around the church three times before departing.

The roots of the Byzantine rite are similar to those of the Syrian family. We have already seen evidence for this in fourth-century writers and earlier. This presupposes betrothal and marriage, the latter celebrated normally in church before a priest with a crowning and blessing. The earliest liturgical texts that have come down to us come from an eighth-century manuscript, *Barberini 336*,[18] which is Italo-Greek in origin. The following scheme appears:

1. *Betrothal* (called *Arrhas*)
A long prayer, invoking the example of the betrothal
    of Isaac and Rebecca
Deacon tells everyone to bow their heads
A short blessing, based on Ephesians 5
2. *Marriage* (called crowning)
Short litany by deacon, with three special biddings for
    the couple
Three priestly blessing prayers:
    First prayer with images from the bible, and "fitting
        together" the couple as well as allusion to the
        crowning, which follows
    Second prayer is more theological and perhaps later
        than the first
    Third prayer over common cup mentioning Cana

No psalmody appears in this manuscript, although Psalm 127 (128) is quoted by Gregory Nazianzus, possibly from the liturgy. Neither are there any readings, though later texts provide Ephesians 5:20–33 and John 2:1–11. We may assume that *Barberini 336*, together with the psalm and readings suggested, forms the first stratum of what was later to become the Byzantine liturgy of marriage. The first of the three priestly prayers is a fine composition and one that repeats themes and shapes that we have already met:

"Holy God, who made mankind out of chaos and from his rib provided woman, and yoked her as a help to him, because it pleased your great goodness that he should not be the only man on the earth; even now, Lord, stretch forth your hand from your holy dwelling place, and fit together this your servant and this handmaid, that the woman may be joined by you to the man. Yoke them together in unity of mind; crown them in love; unite them to be one flesh; graciously bestow on them the fruit of the womb, the enjoyment of children; for yours. . . ."[19]

The *Barberini 336* text thereafter becomes amplified through the introduction of secondary material that does not destroy the essential simplicity and unity of the original. Legal pressure under Justinian made betrothal binding, and this resulted in the gradual narrowing of the gap in time between betrothal and marriage, so that from the eighth century the two grew close together, and from the tenth they tended to follow immediately upon each other. The ring came to be used from the tenth century, though it was never actually blessed; and from the eleventh century *two* rings appear, as in the Visigothic *Liber Ordinum*. Supplementary blessing prayers, longer than the older forms, appear in the twelfth century. Candles are also carried by the couple at this time, though the practice may be considerably older.

The subsequent elaboration of the liturgy included the following features. First, the relationship with the eucharist becomes more tenuous, and in some rites the presanctified liturgy is introduced. Second, special formulas appear at the crowning, using the conventional Byzantine passive voice, "N *is crowned*." Third, the place of the readings varies. The Palestinian tradition keeps the readings in what is probably the older position, before the crowning, whereas the Italo-Greek has them afterward. This is where they eventually appear in the later standard texts. Fourth, the "dance of Isaiah" and the removal of the crowns become significant parts of the rite. Both these customs, though probably older, first appear rubricated in the fifteenth century. Finally, a form of consent is introduced into the Byzantine rites as a last step. The Russian rite inserts consent at the start of the marriage proper, under the Latin influence of Peter Moghila of Kiev in the seventeenth century.

The complete rite as it is normally celebrated today among the various Byzantine churches takes the following form (*Barberini 336* and other earlier elements italicized):[20]

1. *Betrothal* (at the church door)
Short question on willingness to marry
 . . . with candles
Opening blessing
Litany, with special biddings
Prayer: "Eternal God"
Prayer: "Lord our God"
Ring giving, with short formula
Prayer: "Lord our God, who accompanied Abraham"
2. *Marriage*
Psalm 127 (128)—procession into church
Questions and consent (Russian form only)
Opening blessing
Litany, with special biddings
Marriage prayer: "Blessed are you, Lord"
Marriage prayer: "Undefiled God"
First marriage prayer: "Holy God, who made mankind"
Crowning (with formula)
Prokeimenon
Ephesians 5:20–33

Alleluia
John 2:1–11
Litany (short)—no special biddings
Second marriage prayer: "Lord our God, who in the economy"
Litany (short)—no special biddings
Third marriage prayer: "blessing of common cup"
Troparion
Walk in circle (the dance of Isaiah)
Removal of crowns (originally at home, after an interval)
Short blessing
Final blessing

The early core thus stands out from the later overlay. It also becomes apparent that the Byzantine rite is, in fact, the exception among the Eastern liturgies on a number of points. These include its conservatism in restricting the scheme to betrothal and marriage; it avoids going home too much. It does not use any symbols other than the ring and the crown—no blessing of robes, and no special features such as East-Syrian *henana* or Coptic anointing at betrothal. Furthermore, whereas all the other Eastern rites use a lection from Matthew 19 at marriage, the Byzantine service employs John 2:1–11, perhaps reflecting more faithfully the Cana spirituality of all the Eastern hymns, chants, and prayers.

The prayer "Holy God" quoted above may be considerably earlier than the eighth century because of its simple form and structure. Certainly its themes recur in the other rites that we have looked at. The second prayer from the *Barberini 336* text perhaps reflects a more developed climate when it prays over the couple after they have been crowned:

"Lord our God, who in the economy of your salvation at Cana in Galilee deemed to show marriage worthy of your presence: even now protect these your servants (N and N), whom you have pleased to join together, in peace and harmony.

"Show them that marriage is honorable, keep their marriage bed undefiled, be pleased to keep their life together without taint; and with pure hearts to carry out your precepts, and to reach abundant old age."[21]

If the previous prayer expresses the simple themes of creation and redemption that lie deep in the Eastern collective memory of marriage spirituality, then this second prayer expresses the Cana spirituality abundantly, through its confidence of the presence of Christ to redeemed humanity.

CONCLUSION

It is now possible to highlight the principal differences between the Eastern and Western rites of marriage.

First, whereas in the West liturgical symbolism is relatively underdeveloped, the Eastern rites enjoy a rich and lavish use of symbolism.

Second, the Western rites place more emphasis on contract and the legal aspects of marriage when compared with the Eastern rites, which stress the fact of marriage as an experience of redemption, an extension of baptism, a vocation in the Kingdom within the church.

Third, Western canonists stress the couple as "ministers of the sacrament," whereas the Eastern rites in different ways see marriage as an ecclesial action presided over by the presbyter.

Fourth, whereas the Western church places some dramatic emphasis on the ring blessing and ring giving, particularly in the Anglo-Norman tradition, the Eastern rites tend to keep the ring in betrothal as a preliminary to marriage, a 'sign of a commitment undertaken before the church, and therefore a prelude to the celebration of the marriage to come.

Fifth, the Western rites (all of them eventually, with the exception of parts of Germany) link marriage closely with the eucharist, whereas the link between marriage and eucharist becomes more and more tenuous among the Eastern liturgies.

Sixth, the Western rites reach a climax in the nuptial eucharist when the bride is blessed; the Eastern rites by contrast climax after a liturgy of the Word in the crowning of both the man and the woman.

Seventh, the Western rites tend to opt for readings from 1 Corinthians 6 or 7 and Matthew 19, whereas the Eastern texts (which often include more besides) use Ephesians 5 as the epistle; and although they have Matthew 19 as the gospel (except the Byzantine rite), they draw considerable inspiration from the wedding at Cana (Jn 2:1–11).

Eighth, Western prayers invoke the examples of patriarchal couples and Tobias and Sarah; Eastern prayers do invoke the former, but also abound in invocations of the saints and martyrs, implying that our "elder brethren" cheer on the earthly unions that the church continues to celebrate.

Ninth, Western texts give little for the deacon to do, whereas the deacon takes a full part in the Eastern liturgies.

Tenth, folklore is underplayed in the West. In the East, it is brought into the mainstream of the liturgy and may well account for the Eastern liturgies' enjoyment of different types of symbolism, for example, in the Syrian, Armenian, and Coptic rites' special ceremonies at betrothal.

Eleventh, Western texts step further and further away from an understanding of marriage as "passage" in the primitive sense, and this becomes embodied in the rites. The East, on the other hand, keeps this notion behind various increasingly elaborate liturgies, even when betrothal and marriage are celebrated in close proximity. Special symbolisms at betrothal have been noted. In the Byzantine rite, the fact that betrothal and marriage each begin with the blessing "Blessed is the kingdom . . ." is an eloquent statement of the separate character of the two rites, as being necessary and divinely blessed stages in the lives of ordinary men and women in the Kingdom of God.

Finally, the deep structures of the Western rites are based around the old domestic rites on the one hand and the nuptial mass on the other, which are brought together in the Anglo-Norman synthesis. The Eastern rites, by contrast, consist of a rite of betrothal, centering round the giving of rings, and in most cases some special ceremony; the ensuing marriage liturgy is a synaxis (with or without eucharist) in which the crowning of the couple forms the heart, usually after the readings. These common features in the East point to a common mind on the inner meaning of marriage when brought before God and the Christian community, an inner meaning expanded upon and interpreted by each rite according to its peculiarities and native genius.

NOTES

1. Kenneth W. Stevenson, "Van Gennep and Marriage—Strange Bedfellows?—A Fresh Look at the Rites of Marriage," *Ephemerides Liturgicae* 100 (1986):142ff.

2. Gabriele Winkler, *Das Armenische Initiationsrituale: Entwicklungsqeschichte und liturgievergleichende Untersuchung der Quellen des 3. bis 10. Jahrhunderts* (Orientalia Christiana

Analecta 217) (Rome: Pontificium Insitutum Orientalium Studiorum, 1982), passim.

3. F. C. Conybeare, *Rituale Armenorum* (Oxford: Oxford University Press, 1905), pp. 109–114. See later texts in H. Denzinger, *Ritus Orientalium* II (Würzburg: Stahl, 1864), pp. 451–467, 467–477. See also A. Raes, *Le Mariage dans les Églises d'Orient* (Chevetogne: Editions, 1958), pp. 77–101.

4. Text in Conybeare, op. cit., pp. 110–111.

5. Text in Conybeare, op. cit., p. 112.

6. See Korbinian Ritzer, *Formen, Riten, und religioses Brachtum der Eheschliessung in den christlichen Kirchen des ersten Jahrtausends* (Liturgiewissenschaftliche Quellen und Forschungen 38) (Munster: Aschendorff, 1962), pp. 95–97. Hereafter referred to as *Ritzer*.

7. Texts in Denzinger, op. cit., pp. 386–402, and Raes, op. cit., pp. 139–152.

8. Texts in Denzinger, op. cit., p. 386. My own translation.

9. Texts in Denzinger, op. cit., pp. 402–418, and Raes, op. cit., pp. 139–152.

10. Text in Raes, op. cit., p. 144 (first quotation); Denzinger, op. cit., p. 418 (second quotation); and Raes, op. cit., p. 152 (third quotation). My own translation.

11. See *Ritzer*, pp. 89ff.

12. Texts in Denzinger, op. cit., pp. 419–449, and Raes, op. cit., pp. 157–197. See also G. P. Badger, *The Nestorians and Their Rituals* II (London: Master, 1852), pp. 244–281, and P. Yousif, "La célébration du mariage dans le rite chaldéen," in *La Celebrazione Cristiana Del Matrimonio*, pp. 217–260.

13. Texts in Denzinger, op. cit., pp. 432, 440, and 448. My own translation. See also Jeanne-Ghislane Van Overstraeten, "Les liturgies nuptiales des églises de langue syriaque at le mystère de l'église-épouse," *Parole d'Orient* 8 (1977/78):235–310. And for the Malabar rite, C. Payngot, "The Syro-Malabar Marriage," in *La Celebrazione Cristiana Del Matrimonio*, pp. 261–282.

14. E. Lanne, "Le Grand Eucologue du Monastère Blanc," *Patrologia Orientalis* 28/2 (Paris, 1958), pp. 392–399, and notes. On the practice of anointing, see Jeanne-Ghislane Van Overstraeten, "Le rite de l'onction des époux dans la liturgie copte du mariage," *Parole d'Orient* 5 (1974):49–93. If Van Overstraeten is correct in her suggestion that anointing is connected with baptism, and is an ancient Coptic custom, then my suggestion that it is recent by the time of the White Monastery's Eucologion is wrong; see *Nuptial Blessing*, p. 111.

15. Texts in Denzinger. op. cit., pp. 364–381, and Raes, op. cit., pp. 27–45. See also O. Raineri, "Celebrazione del matrimonio nel rito etiopico," in *La Celebrazione Cristiana Del Matirmonio*, pp. 307–342.

16. Text in Denzinger, op. cit., p. 378. My own translation.

17. Text in Denzinger, op. cit., p. 369. My own translation.

18. See G. I. Passarelli, "La ceremonia dello Stefanoma (Incoronazione) nei riti matrimoniali bizantini secondo il Codice Cryptense G.b. VII (X sec.)," *Ephemerides Liturgicae* 93 (1979):381–391; and G. Baldanza, "Il rito de Matrimonio nel' Euchologio Barberini 336," ibid., pp. 316–351. See also *Ritzer*, pp. 135ff. For a chart with sources, see *Nuptial Blessing*, p. 251, but the procession from the narthex comes during the Psalm, and the "First marriage prayer" occurs immediately before the crowning and not as indicated. For the full text, see J. Goar, *Euchologion sive Rituale Graecorum* (Venice: Javarini, 1730), pp. 310–326, and Raes, op. cit., pp. 49–68. The full English text is in John Meyendorff, *Marriage: An Orthodox Perspective* (St. Vladimir's Press, 1971), pp. 126–144. See also D. Gelsi, "Punti di riflessione sull'ufficio bizantino per la 'incoronazione' degli sposi," in *La Celebrazione Cristiana Del Matrimonio*, pp. 283–306.

19. Text in Goar, op. cit., p. 317. My own translation.

20. See above, n. 18.

21. Text in Goar, op. cit., p. 318. My own translation.

Chapter Four

An Honorable Estate, Instituted of God

INTRODUCTION

There are several ways of looking at what happened in the sixteenth century. The technologist will, perhaps, identify the invention of printing in the previous century as being so advanced by the end of the 1520s that groups and organizations could express their sense of identity by the publication of multiple copies of a single, correct original. The social historian will, perhaps, identify the move toward education and the rise of an articulate middle class as factors that bring to the fore energies and ideas that are to shape the future of Europe. The theologian will add these two insights to the critical one: Europe's ecclesiastical unity, a nervous business throughout the Middle Ages, exploding into various sections that split off from communion with Rome, producing the churches of the Reformation. Marriage rites are one of the many offshoots of their liturgical endeavors. And when the Council of Trent meets to settle *the* Catholic position on everything concerning church life, it has to agree on an irreducible minimum for the marriage liturgy, because the various rites appearing in medieval service books were so different.

Luther appears first on the scene. He produces a short service, based on the noneucharistic marriage rites of the medieval agendas, although it bears clear signs of his own personal style and theology. Calvin works from the liturgical projects of Farel and others; what emerges is a longer rite, to be celebrated on a Sunday in the presence of the whole congregation. Unlike Luther, who keeps both the rings and the joining of hands, Calvin spurns these popish symbols. Later Calvinist rites are compromised by reality (they separate from the main Sunday service) and by the corporate memory of ordinary people (the rings and hand joining reappear).

Thomas Cranmer, who of all the Reformers is faced with the most complex medieval rite, the Sarum Manual, puts together a literary masterpiece that includes all the structural features of the Sarum rite but expresses a Reformed theology of what is enacted. His rite ends (in theory at least) with the celebration of the eucharist. Subsequent revisions reduce his symbolism, and the link with the eucharist becomes increasingly tenuous. And although some of his work is criticized by later Puritans, it is not until the late eighteenth century that his marriage rite is given a new shape, which eventually emerges as the classic North American Methodist form.

Underneath these literary works lie some theological issues. All the Reformers wanted to "reform" the marriage liturgy. Some of them are content to keep traditional symbols, others are not. All of them are united in the need for a vernacular rite, for a stage in the Christian life that is *not* a sacrament; hence Cranmer's description of marriage as "a holy estate, instituted of God himself." He goes on to recall the Ephesians analogy, ". . . signifying unto us the mystical unity betwixt Christ and his Church." For the Reformers, the Ephesians pericope is a foundation text for marriage; it is not a sacrament, but it is important.

Similarly, all the Reformers place the marriage rite under the presidency of the ordained minister, and they try to clothe it with the assembled company of believers, more than just the wedding party. Yet the role of the minister is firmly that of president, so that the two-fold focus of the rites is the consent of the couple and the strong prayer or blessing for the couple, pronounced by the minister.

Four features, however, are noticeable. First, the rites that they produce, for all their corporate focus, eventually become what the jargon calls an "Occasional Office"—a single rite that can be celebrated apart from everything else and performed in a relatively short time. Second, Van Gennep's three stages, which could be discerned in a fossilized form in some of the medieval rites, have disappeared altogether. There is *one* service, and that is all. The Reformers, who might have seen something scriptural in the older division of betrothal and marriage, are products of the Middle Ages. Third, they move out of the home altogether, perhaps for cultural reasons, perhaps because they are suspicious of priests blessing the bridal chamber. Everything has to be done in community. Fourth, just as wives had to promise to obey their husbands in some of the medieval vernacular forms of consent, so was this quality of life enjoined on Reformed women who came to church to be joined to their spouses in the sight of God.

Later developments cause some of these traditions to disappear. Anglicanism sees the reintroduction of the nuptial eucharist (with a proper) in the later nineteenth century. North American Protestants, who do not have laws that require the service to take place in a church building, as in England, can bring the rite back into the home. Twentieth-century Anglican liturgical revision, even as far back as the 1920s, removes the wife's promise to obey. And the American *Book of Common Prayer* of 1928 goes so far as to ask the woman if she wants to marry the man *before* that question is asked of the man, a neat way of introducing equality of the sexes. All this serves to show that when a liturgy is printed, it learns new ways of being flexible; and when a rite is evolving continuously, new features deliberately introduced usually express new perceptions of what is going on.

LUTHER AND CALVIN[1]

Martin Luther's *Order of Marriage for Common Pastors* (1529) is one of the first official marriage rites of the Reformation and it is therefore basic to the development of this liturgy. He is aware of the diverse character of local German services and he expects local pastors to adapt to local circumstances. In practice, Luther's rite seems to have been followed throughout the Lutheran world, perhaps with some additions and survivals here and there. There are examples of some quite outlandishly verbose experiments, but these are exceptional and belong to a later era.

Luther is firm about the need for "the blessing of God and common prayer," and he dislikes too much showy vulgarity on the part of brides in their processions to church. As in the medieval rites, banns are to published beforehand, expressing the public character of marriage. The marriage rite takes the following shape:

Consent (at the church door)

Giving of wedding rings

Joining of hands

Pastor declares the couple married

Pastor recites Matthew 19:6 ("What God has joined together . . .")

Procession to the altar

Solemn reading of Genesis 2:18, 21–24.

Biblical catechesis, including Ephesians 5:25–29, Genesis 3:17–19, Proverbs 18:22

Prayer over couple (with hands stretched over them)

The rite comes in two parts, because Luther uses the church door and the altar. Moreover, its focus is on consent and solemn prayer, clothed with biblical catechesis. The symbolism of ring giving is kept, but the rings are not blessed. (It will be remembered that the *Arrhas* in the Visigothic rite was not actually blessed either, although God's blessing was invoked "on the giving.") Before the pastor declares that the couple are married, Matthew 19:6 is recited. This sequence of ideas and use of the biblical text both recur in later rites.

Then, when the pastor and the couple have walked to the altar, there is an important sequence. First, solemn reading of scripture "over" the couple; next, the catechesis; and third, the solemn prayer. This accords entirely with Luther's understanding of the need to keep the Word read, the Word expounded, and prayer close together. Some of the texts themselves in this rite are worth quoting. First, the short form of consent:

"Hans, dost thou desire Greta to thy wedded wife?" ("Greta, . . . Hans . . . husband?")

Second, the formula declaring their marriage:

"Since Hans (N) and Greta (N) desire each other in marriage and acknowledge the same here publicly before God and the world, in testimony of which they have given each other their hands and wedding rings, I pronounce them joined in marriage, in the name of the Father . . . "

Third, the concluding prayer:

"O God, who hast created man and woman and hast ordained them for the married state, hast blessed them also with fruits of the womb, and hast typified therein the sacramental union of thy dear Son, the Lord Jesus Christ, and the Church, his bride: we beseech thy groundless goodness and mercy that thou wouldst not permit this thy creation, ordinance, and blessing to be disturbed or destroyed, but graciously preserve the same, through Jesus Christ our Lord."[2]

All three texts exemplify the essential simplicity of Luther's rite. The prayer (which recurs in later Lutheran rites, even when other prayers are added) links creation and redemption together, includes allusions to Ephesians 5 as well as to Matthew 19:6. God has instituted marriage for a purpose; *he* keeps the couple together. The whole rite builds up to this prayer as a climax. Survival of earlier tradition is apparent underneath Luther's rite through its use of the shape of the noneucharistic rites of medieval Germany. On the other hand, early Scandinavian rites add a "brudemesse" probably because the nuptial mass was a tradition embedded in previous Catholic practice.

Calvin's rite in the 1542 *Form of Prayers,* by contrast, is lengthier in word but reticent on outward symbolism. It should take place after the sermon and on Sundays when the eucharist is *not* celebrated. The service is in three parts: biblical catechesis (note the reverse position from Luther), the consent, and the prayer:

1. "Our help . . ."/"Who has made . . ."
Biblical catechesis (themes include creation, creation of man and woman, obedience of wife, indissolubility, fidelity, sanctity of the body, and marital virtues)
2. Question to each on basic willingness to marry
Longer question to each on commitment to marry
(wife to obey)

Short prayer for the grace of God
Reading of Matthew 19:3–6
Declaration that couple are married
3. Long prayer for the couple (reproducing themes
and sequence from earlier catechesis)
Short blessing

The symbolism may have gone but the shape is deliberate, and centered around the word of God, as one
may expect. The Bible opens the service, sets the context, and dominates the proceedings. The couple are
then asked preliminary questions to lead up to the solemn consent:

"Do you (N) confess here before God and his holy congregation, that you have taken and do now take for
your wife and spouse (N) here present, whom you
promise to keep, loving and caring for her faithfully,
as should a true and faithful husband his wife; living
piously with her, keeping faith and loyalty with her in
all things, according to the holy word of God, and his
holy Gospel?"[3]

Before they are actually declared man and wife, there
must be a short prayer for grace and a reading (Mt
19:3–6), again placing the word as central to the rite.
Finally, the rite reaches a conclusion with a long
prayer for the couple (similar in structure to the opening catechesis) and a short blessing.

Like Luther's service, the form of consent is passive
(because of medieval antecedents of this genre in both
cases). Calvin's title, moreover, is the form for "con-
firming" marriages, although in later Calvinist books it
is sometimes called the manner of "celebrating," and
even "the liturgy of marriage." But unlike the Lutheran books, which tend to follow the 1529 rite,
Calvin's rite reappears again and again, though there
is a tendency in the nineteenth century to make the
vows active (as in Sarum, and, as we shall see, in

Cranmer), and to have more congregational participation, together with more variety in the prayers. Calvin's rite influences strongly subsequent British rites of the Calvinist traditions. Its peculiarity, above all, is a heavy emphasis on the grace of the Holy Spirit.

THE BOOK OF COMMON PRAYER TRADITIONS

The first *Book of Common Prayer* appears in 1549 and the marriage rite contained in it was altered little in 1552 (the second Prayer Book). Indeed, the rite hardly changed at all in subsequent years until the final version of the whole book in 1662. Because of this marriage rite's influence in later reformed (and, it must be said, modern Roman Catholic) rites, it stands out as a landmark in our whole story, equal in importance to the Gregorian Sacramentary nuptial mass and the twelfth-century Bury rite, with its form of consent immediately prior to the nuptial mass.

When Gregory Dix published his *Shape of the Liturgy* many years ago, he both shocked and delighted many people in the way he treated the liturgical work of Thomas Cranmer. Perhaps his book goes off track when it comes to the Reformation precisely because the author is so obviously out of sympathy with what the Reformers were trying to do. Nonetheless, when he supported the theory (not new) that Cranmer was Zwinglian in his theology, many Anglicans, particularly those of the High Church tradition, found his words difficult to accept. I have discussed Cranmer's marriage rite in some detail and I have concluded that Dix's theory holds true of the marriage rite as well, insofar as Cranmer's theology of marriage liturgy was avowedly Protestant.[4] The emphasis is on the couple giving their consent, and the priest stands as president over the "solemnization of matrimony," the Sarum title. The fascinating character of this rite is that the author manages to use so much medieval Latin material and forge what is, without a doubt, a literary *tour de force*. Here is the order,[5] as it appears in the 1549 Prayer Book, together with the main sources and the most significant alterations made in 1552 and 1662:

Main sources	1549 text	1552 and 1662 main changes
Hermann,* Sarum, et al.	Opening preface	Parts clarified (1662)
York Manual	Request for impediments	
Sarum, Luther	Consent (passive)	
York	Giving away of the bride	
Sarum	Vow (active), hand joining	"Till death us do part" (1662)
Sarum	Ring giving	Delete reference to gold (1552)
Sarum and other medieval sources	Prayer for the couple	Couple must kneel here (1662)
Luther	Matthew 19:6	
Hermann (Luther?)	Declaration of couple's marriage	
Sarum and other medieval sources	Blessing prayer	Not called a blessing (1552)
Sarum and other medieval sources	Psalm 127 (128) or Psalm 66 (67)	
Sarum and other medieval sources	Kyrie, Lord's Prayer and *preces*	

*Hermann is Hermann von Wied, whose Encheiridion (1538) and Consultation (1543) Cranmer knew.

Main sources	1549 text	1552 and 1662 main changes
2 *Sarum* and other medieval sources	Prayer 1	Delete reference to Raphael (1552)
Sarum (Gregorian Sacramentary)	Prayer 2	
Sarum (Gregorian Sacramentary)	Prayer 3 (longer)	Delete reference to Old Testament women (1662)
Sarum (Lanalet prayer)	Prayer 4 (blessing)	Not called a blessing (1552)
Hermann, Luther	Biblical catechesis	
Sarum (Gregorian Sacramentary)	Eucharist recommended	Eucharist hoped for (1662)

The sources and subsequent alterations to the text show Cranmer standing midway between the late Middle Ages and developing Protestantism. Surprisingly, Martin Bucer had little to complain about in the 1549 rite, which may have been one reason why the reformed rite, for all its medieval topdressing, remained acceptable to many, despite the fact that Luther and Calvin had each produced rites that were considerably simpler.

Cranmer's rite begins at the front of the nave, not at the church door, with an instruction that explains what marriage is for. This includes both biblical references (the Ephesians analogy and Christ's presence at Cana) as well as the three reasons for marriage that had been traditional in medieval writing, namely, children, sexuality, and mutual support and comfort. We quoted its opening periods at the beginning of this study, made up as it is of words that are recognizable throughout the English-speaking world. After ending this introduction with a chance for the congregation and then the couple to produce an impediment to the marriage, the priest then asks for the consent of the couple. This comes in two forms, as in *Sarum* and the other British Manuals. The first form is derived from the older passive formula, but it has been slightly adapted to describe marriage as an "ordinance" in reformed style:

"(N), Wilt thou have this woman to thy wedded wife,
to live together after God's ordinance
in the holy estate of matrimony?
Wilt thou love her, comfort her, honor and keep her
   in sickness and in health?
And forsaking all other, keep thee only unto her,
so long as ye both shall live?"[6]

After asking a similar question of the bride, but inserting obedience, the priest then asks:

"Who giveth this woman *to be married to this man?*"

Here is another example of Cranmer's cunning use of antecedents. In the *York* service, the priest asks:

"Who gives *me* this wife?"

In other words, Cranmer is determined to place the spotlight on the couple; the man and woman are to be married and so the priest is not the person to "receive" the woman.

Then each partner makes the marriage vow, again in words taken and adapted from *Sarum*, but with a careful touching up of the prose to avoid a sacramental status for marriage:

"I (N) take thee (N) to my wedded wife,
to have and to hold, from this day forward,
for better for worse, for richer for poorer,

94

in sickness and in health, to love and to cherish,
till death do us part (1549 reads 'us depart'):
according to God's holy ordinance (Sarum reads 'if holy
  church it will ordain'):
and thereto I plight thee my troth."[7]

Once again, the woman promises to obey, and, curiously, she *gives* her troth. But the vow stands centrally in the rite, and many couples familiar with the older versions would scarcely have noticed the deliberate introduction of the new formulation.

The next stage, after the consent and vow, is the giving of the ring. Now, instead of blessing the ring, it is merely placed "on the book" (i.e., the priest's book), and the priest gives the ring to the man to give to the woman. In 1549 this was accompanied with the giving of gold and silver pieces (which were popular in medieval England, a version of the Visigothic *Arrhas*). This was suppressed in 1552, although there is evidence of its survival for long thereafter, down to the present day, even though the liturgy does not any longer refer to it:

"With this ring I thee wed;
With my body I thee worship;
And all my worldly goods with thee I share;
in the Name of the Father . . ."

Once the words "This gold and silver I thee give" are inserted after the first clause (1549), the full text reads almost exactly the same as *Sarum.* But the crucial difference is that the ring and silver pieces are not blessed.

The first of several prayers now appears in a subtle interweaving of ideas taken from the medieval blessing of the ring, although the prayer actually prays for the couple (cf., in principle, Calvin). This is the first prayer in the whole service. Only thereafter does the priest pronounce Matthew 19:6 and declare the couple's marriage (cf. Luther). This first part of the service thus concludes on a thoroughly reformed note. A short blessing provides an eloquent liturgical full stop.

The priest then leads the couple to the altar, a movement Luther kept, and one that couples would have expected to perform. The altar service reads similarly to the medieval one, but with some crucial differences. The eucharist is clearly intended. The special material in the eucharist in the old service book (the nuptial blessing) has been rewritten in order to pray for *both* the man and the woman. It has been placed in the course of the third of a series of four prayers, all of which use later medieval sources. Cranmer's adaptation of the Lanalet prayer (the last of the series of marriage prayers) is worth quoting in full:

"Almighty God, who at the beginning did create our first parents, Adam and Eve, and did sanctify and join them together in marriage: pour upon you the riches of his grace, sanctify and bless you, that ye may please him both in body and soul, and live together in holy love unto your lives' end."[8]

The alterations that were made after 1549 clarify some parts of the rite and also gradually eliminate the Old Testament characters. (The 1928 proposed revision in England even omitted Adam and Eve in the prayer just quoted.) In addition, two prayers are no longer described as blessings in 1552. But the most important change is at the end, when in 1662 it was made clear that the eucharist is no more than hoped for. There was controversy surrounding its appropriateness at weddings, although some couples went to the eucharist on the Sunday after their marriage. The main problem then became how to end the rite appropriately, and the so-called "Book of Comprehension," an attempt to pacify Puritans in 1688 and 1689, provides an answer that many priests may have followed, since it still appears in 1928. This solution consists of a general collect, followed by the blessing from the eucharist ("The peace of God, which passeth all understanding . . ."). The link with the eucharist appears to be severed.

Apart from the ring blessing what had disappeared? Many features, including the sacramental position of the nuptial blessing, other blessings, the use of candles, the sprinkling of holy water over the rings and the couple, the placing of the ring on the first, second, and third fingers before finally resting on the fourth, the canopy held over the couple during the nuptial blessing, and the sacramental role of the priest. As we have seen, English rites avoided giving the priest any special formula to say after the consent that would in any way point to the priest as the "performer" of the rite. Cranmer takes this one stage further, using emphasis in texts and drama, and in the ordering of texts and prayers, to show that the priest is there to represent the church. It is this understanding of the priest that underlies nearly all modern revisions, including the 1969 *Ordo*.

Among the points raised by Puritans against Cranmer's rite was the use of the ring, which they deleted in their own liturgical projects. Still, there was pressure to abbreviate Cranmer's service as well as to clarify certain points in it. When John Wesley was compiling his *Sunday Service of the Methodists in North America* (1784), he incorporated both these criticisms in a rite that took the following shape:

Preface

Consent

Vow (for "troth" read "faith")

Prayer after ring giving (but no ring)

Matthew 19:6

Declaration that the couple are married

Blessing

Kyrie, Lord's Prayer, and *preces*

Four prayers[9]

Wesley followed the liturgical project of the Unitarian Theophilus Lindsey (1774) in deleting the psalm, which would perhaps be superfluous in simple chapel architecture or the open air, since there was no chancel area through which the minister and bridal pair had to pass in order to reach the holy table for the second part of the rite. He also followed the Puritans in eliminating the ring giving. And the end of the service is tidied up by omitting the biblical catechesis, as well as any reference to the eucharist.

Further reductions were achieved by American Episcopalians as well as American Methodists.[10] The 1789 *Book of Common Prayer* takes a radical line, although it keeps the ring. In this rite, the opening instruction is reduced considerably, and the service ends with the prayer that in Cranmer's version leads into the psalm, so that the walk to the altar and the marriage prayers disappear altogether. Similarly, the 1792 *Doctrine and Discipline of the Methodist Episcopal Church* reduces the opening instruction, continues to delete the ring and the psalm, but omits only the second of the marriage prayers, which prays for child bearing. These two rites, therefore, stand as abbreviations of the original, probably for pastoral as well as missionary reasons. We have thus turned full circle and have reached back to the old medieval informal domestic rites. The corporate focus is more tenuous, simplicity is the order of the day, and (unlike Cranmer) things mustn't be said more than once or twice.

This is the form of marriage liturgy that became typical of North American Protestantism. This was either a type of reduction of Cranmer; or an even more drastic reduction; or, on the other hand, English rites inspired by Luther's *Traubüchlein* or Calvin's *Forme des prières*. As we shall see, modern revisions by American Episcopalians and Methodists more than make up for this drastic treatment.

ROMAN CATHOLICISM AND THE COUNCIL OF TRENT

The Churches of the Reformation denied marriage its sacramental status, but with few exceptions framed new rites based on the view that marriage is an ordinance, to be celebrated publicly, in a liturgy centering on the consent of the couple to live a Christian marriage, together with the reading and exposition of the word of God, and solemn prayer.

Meanwhile, medieval Catholicism continued for a time with its considerable liturgical variety. In Chapter Two, we drew attention to the importance of the Anglo-Norman synthesis, with its rite of consent at the church door. This rite eventually reached Rome through the Norman invasion of southern Italy. Thus, the thirteenth-century Pontifical of Sora[11] has this new addition to the marriage liturgy. The French rites continued to develop, dividing into various groups, some of which had the consent at the church door, others holding it inside. The 1498 Lyon rite even introduced Matthew 19:6 as a formula to be said by the priest after the consent had been given. Another custom that seems to be of the fifteenth century is for the priest to wrap his stole round the couple's hands during the recitation of the priestly formula, a practice that as we have seen was imposed on the Maronites. The most interesting rite, however, is that of Metz (1543) that incorporates the marriage within the nuptial mass, so that consent and the priestly joining formula occur at the offertory, and the ring giving and short marriage prayers follow the post-communion. This has the advantage of bringing the mass and the marriage into closer union. Also, the consent is separated from the ring giving, which makes for considerable clarity. The Metz tradition provides inspiration for modern revisions for this reason and is therefore worth noting now.

When the Council of Trent discussed marriage liturgy in its penultimate session of November 1563, however, it decided to make the consent of the partners essential. It also required a priestly formula to be recited immediately after the consent. It was clear that marriage is a sacrament and that the consent of the partners effected the sacrament. The Tridentine decree on marriage, *Tametsi*, is in some respects the liturgical exception, for it overtly encourages local marriage customs to be observed:

"If certain locales traditionally use other praiseworthy customs and ceremonies when celebrating the sacrament of matrimony, this Sacred Synod earnestly desires that these by all means be retained."[12]

This passage is quoted in the Constitution on the Sacred Liturgy of the Second Vatican Council, in the discussion of the liturgy of marriage. The Fathers of the Council of Trent clearly saw no need to impose a rigid uniformity on the Catholic Church regarding this sacrament, and subsequent service books demonstrate that the older customs did, in fact, continue, with the noticeable difference that a priestly formula was usually introduced where it was absent.

The liturgical books of the Council of Trent reflected this in the reforms. It adopted a two-stage revision in the form of the nuptial mass (in the 1570 Missal of Pius V) and the rite of marriage (in the 1614 *Rituale Romanum* of Paul V).[13] If the marriage rite is to vary from one country to another, then it must clearly belong to a special kind of liturgical book, the Ritual locally adapted. On the other hand, the nuptial mass is part of the missal and it had to be standard.

The nuptial mass consists of the chants, prayers, and readings for the eucharistic celebration. Much of it appears in the later medieval Pontificals. The Gregorian mass prayers are prescribed throughout; no Trinity votive, as in some parts of Northern Europe. The epistle is Ephesians 5:22–33; this was rare in the medieval West, except in the twelfth-century Roman Pontifical. The gospel, on the other hand, is the old favorite, Matthew 19:3–6.

The Tridentine nuptial blessing has been shifted so that it no longer comes just before the Peace. It now immediately follows the Lord's Prayer and precedes the *Libera nos*. It is conceivable that those who made this decision wanted to avoid the husband kissing his wife at the Peace, which was common in the Middle Ages, and was usually the only time when provision was made for a husband to kiss his wife inside a church building. This would be changed back to the older sequence in the 1969 *Ordo*. After the dismissal, a short prayer for the couple follows. The priest then exhorts them to hold to their vows.

Austere by comparison with many local service books, the Tridentine nuptial mass does not contain such customs as the canopy, the singing of the nuptial blessing as a preface with introductory dialogue, and other enrichments we have already seen. It was, indeed, a harbinger of the marriage rite contained in the 1614 *Rituale*. Here is the order as it appears in the *Rituale:*

Banns

Three witnesses to be present

Consent (in the vernacular)

Priestly formula: "I join you in matrimony, in the name of the Father . . ."

Holy water sprinkled: couple

Blessing of the ring (medieval, adapted)

Holy water sprinkled: ring

Ring giving, with the invocation of the Trinity

A sequence of *preces*

Short prayer for the couple (medieval, adapted):

". . . if the marriage is to be blessed, the parish priest celebrates the Mass for bride and groom, as found in the Roman Missal, observing everything prescribed there."

This rite was intended to be a minimum, as indeed it was. There is no reference to gold and silver pieces, no psalm, no sequence of prayers for the couple. On the other hand, the priestly formula, so recent in history, is given, and an attitude is perceived that is redolent of what Klauser described as "the epoch of rubricism."[14] Another late medieval addition to the rite is the use of holy water as a symbol of purification.

Local service books,[15] especially in France, Spain, and Germany, continued to prescribe their own customs, and the only sign of what might be called a determination to go its own way can be found in the later phases of Gallicanism, where, for example, the priestly formula is not included in as emphatic a form as the Trent decree clearly envisages.

But other features not contained in the *Rituale* of 1614 persist at the local level. For example, the 1596 Bordeaux rite contains *two* rings. Rites of betrothal are common in French books, particularly in the South. Many of the local Rituals quote from Trent's Decree, stressing the importance of marriage, but there are not a few examples of liberties taken at the pastoral level that the Fathers of Trent would not have liked—for example, the Paris 1839 rite's provision for a form of marriage to be used when one of the partners is not a Roman Catholic.

Apart from frequent rites of betrothal, Neo-Gallican texts also abound in domestic rites after the mass (another absence in the 1614 *Rituale*). The canopy frequently occurs at the nuptial blessing, as do the precious pieces, which are blessed separately from the ring. Moreover, children born before the marriage are legitimized, in several local rites, by being placed under the canopy, with or without a special prayer. Some rites even provided prayers against impotence. Whereas the official texts of 1570 and 1614 provide a minimum text to use at one service, and a somewhat stark one at that, Neo-Gallican rites provide rich texts that see marriage as a passage, as we saw in the Eastern rites. Thus, the French books frequently have the following sequence:

Betrothal

Marriage rite:

    consent and priestly formula

    ring giving

    precious pieces

    Psalm 127 (128)

    marriage prayers

Nuptial mass:

    with nuptial blessing (canopy, preface form)

    concluding prayers

Domestic rite:

blessing of home

blessing of chamber

Further rite:

prayers against impotence

The order of ceremonies varies from one tradition to another, but what we have here demonstrates the strength of conservatism and imaginative innovation, both of which were features of Neo-Gallicanism.[16]

Of all the post-Tridentine liturgical books, the *Rituale Romanum* was the only one to be "commended" rather than "imposed." Some other countries took liberties—for example, English-speaking Roman Catholics in the United States and Britain abbreviated and adapted the *Sarum* (and the 1662 Prayer Book) vows and ring giving.[17] But on the whole, there was a lost opportunity, not least in missionary countries in Africa, Asia, and Latin America.[18]

EPILOGUE

The sixteenth century sees Protestantism and Catholicism locked in various kinds of pastoral and theological quarrels. These affect the marriage liturgy, although it is interesting to see the way in which, in reaction to Protestantism, the Council of Trent produces a simple marriage rite rather than one of the elaborate schemes that France or Spain could easily have produced. The sacramentality of marriage is fought over, although both sides agree that marriage is important and that it must take place in church if it is to be recognized as authentically Christian. This underlying attitude is not antisecular; it is a way for separated churches to clarify their minds and assert their positions over their own. The present pastoral and social fruits of these attitudes consist of ordinary men and women who are often hurt by being required to bring their children up in a church whose authority they resent. We shall be looking at these issues in the next and final chapters of this study.

Meanwhile, it is important to provide a link between the age of confrontation and polemic (the sixteenth century) and the age of liturgical renewal and ecumenism (the twentieth). Various movements in Christianity in the last century can be identified as indications of Western Christianity's search for its own roots. For example, Guéranger's perhaps misplaced enthusiasm for things medieval was part of that development in Catholicism. Similarly, Wilhelm Löhe[19] awakened many Lutherans to the really authentic features of their own tradition, which had been obscured by the "relevance" of the Enlightenment and the hectoring of Pietism, as these affected classical Lutheran liturgy. Anglicans knew a similar *retour aux sources* in the Tractarian Movement. All these affect the marriage liturgy. But one little-known church, which has all but disappeared, the Catholic Apostolic Church, pioneered the way in which much Western liturgy took its path, in its use of tradition—patristic, medieval, as well as reformed—in order to be truly ecumenical.

In their *Liturgy and Other Divine Offices of the Church*,[20] beneath Cranmerian English, we can see a marriage rite that seeks to integrate the Reformation with Catholicism. Here is the scheme:

Structure	Source
Preface	Cranmer, abbreviated
Prayer for the couple	New, referring to vows to be undertaken
Genesis 2:18–24	Cf. Eastern rites
Consent (passive)	Cranmer
Giving away	Cranmer

Structure	Source
Vow (active)	Cranmer: but with insertion on life in the Church
Ring giving	Cranmer, adapted
Prayer for the couple	Cranmer
Declaration	(a) *Ego vos congjungo* (Roman)
	(b) "I pronounce" (Cranmer)
	(c) Matthew 19:6 (Luther, Cranmer, and Neo-Gallican)
Short blessing	Medieval Western
The peace	New
Psalm 44 (45)	Eastern
Kyrie, Lord's Prayer, and *preces*	Cranmer
Prayer 1	Gregorian Sacramentary nuptial blessing adapted, praying for both throughout and with the "crown" allusion at the end
Prayer 2	Cranmer
Prayer 3	Cranmer's "long" prayer
Blessing	Cranmer

A nuptial eucharist follows, clearly recommended, though not always celebrated immediately. This includes Ephesians 5:22–33 and John 2:1–11 as the lections (cf. Byzantine rite), propers in the eucharist itself, and a special Trinitarian blessing of the couple before Communion.

The Catholic Apostolic rite is really the first rite of Western Christianity to set out to use the full riches of tradition in the production of an entirely new liturgy. Cranmerian roots are apparent, but underneath, there is a stronger ecclesiology, which has an Eastern character to it. There is also a desire to integrate the marriage liturgy within a liturgy of the word and eucharist, hence straight bible readings, instead of biblically inspired catchesis, such as we saw in Luther, Calvin, and Cranmer. Moreover, the imagery of the prayers forges out of tradition something new and original. The style may not be that of the contemporary Western churches, but the method certainly is.

NOTES

1. Text of Luther in P. Z. Strodach (Trans.), *Luther's Works*, 53 (Philadelphia: Fortress, 1965), pp. 111–115. Text of Calvin in Peter Barth and Wilhelm Niesel (Eds.), *Joannis Calvini: Opera Selecta*, II (Munich: Kaiser, 1952), pp. 50–56. See the studies by B. D. Spinks, "Luther's Other Major Liturgical Reforms: 3. The Traubüchlein," *Liturgical Review* 10 (1980):33–38, and "The Liturgical Origins and Theology of Calvin's Genevan Marriage Rite," *Ecclesia Orans*, 3 (1986):195–210. See also Kenneth W. Stevenson, *Nuptial Blessing: A Study of Christian Marriage Rites* (Alcuin Club Collections 64) (London: SPCK, 1982, and New York: Oxford University Press, 1983), pp. 124–125.

2. Text in *Luther's Works*, p. 115.

3. Texts in Barth and Niesel, op. cit., n. 1.

4. For texts of 1549/1552/1662 and principal sources, see F. E. Brightman, *The English Rite*, II (London: Rivingtons, 1915), pp. 800–817.

5. See our discussion of Cranmer, *Nuptial Blessing*, pp. 134ff.; see also nn., pp. 233ff. The sources indicated in the order given are from Brightman and my own research. On Hermann's work, see *Nuptial Blessing*, pp. 129ff.

6. Text (with comparisons to sources) in Brightman, op. cit., pp. 802–803.

7. Text (with comparisons to sources) in Brightman, op. cit., pp. 804–805.

8. Text (with comparisons to sources) in Brightman, op. cit., pp. 812–813.

9. *The Sunday Service of the Methodists in North America* (London, 1784), pp. 149–153. Theophilus Lindsey's rite is contained in *The Book of Common Prayer Reformed According to the Plan of the Late Dr. Samuel Clarke* (London, 1774), pp. 72–78 (N.B.: *Second* edition of that year).

10. For the Episcopalian rites, see W. McGarvey, *Liturgiae Americanae* (Philadelphia: Church Publishing Company, 1897), pp. 312–323. See also Marion Hatchett, *The Making of the First American Book of Common Prayer* (New York: Seabury, 1982), p. 49 (1785 proposals at the Boston Convention); p. 56 (Philadelphia Convention); p. 82 (1786 proposals for radical abbreviation); and pp. 125f. (1789 text). For the Methodist rites, see *The Doctrines and Discipline of the Methodist Episcopal Church in America* (Philadelphia: Parry Hall, 1792), pp. 240–243.

11. For text, see M. Andrieu, *Le Pontifical romain au Moyen Age*, I (Studi e Testi 86) (Vatican City: Apostolic Press, 1938), pp. 300–301. For a discussion, see Jean-Baptiste Molin and Protais Mutembe, *Le rituel du mariage en France du XIIè au XVIè siècle* (Théologie Historique 26) (Paris: Beauchesne, 1973), pp. 67, 73, 74, 78, passim.

12. *Concilium Tridentinum*, Sessio XXIV, Caput I (Mechlen: Van Elsen and Van der Elst, 1847), p. 238. See also G. Baldanza, "La grazia sacramentale matrimoniale al Concilio di Trento. Contributo per uno studio storico critico," *Ephemerides Liturgicae* 97 (1983):89–140.

13. *Missale Romanum ex decreto Sacrosancto Concilii Tridentini restitutum* (Antwerp: Balthasar Moret, 1682), pp. xcvi–xcviii, and *Rituale Romanum* (Antwerp: Plantiniana, 1826), pp. 232–235.

14. Theodor Klauser, *A Short History of the Western Liturgy* (London: Oxford University Press, 1969), p. 119.

15. See Stevenson, *Nuptial Blessing*, pp. 168–178.

16. See John Brooks-Leonard, "Another Look at Neo-Gallican Reform: A Comparison of Marriage Rites in Coutances," *Ephemerides Liturgicae* 98 (1984):458–485.

17. See, for example, *Addenda ad Rituale Romanum ad usum Unitatum Statum Foed. Americae et Angliae* (Mechlen: Dessain, 1916), pp. 35–41.

18. Spanish liturgical use of the *jugale* (see p. 47) was taken to areas of the Spanish Empire, including Mexico and the Philippines. See Jakob Baumgartner, *Mission und Liturgie in Mexiko*, 2 vols. (Switzerland: Schöneck and Beckenreid, 1971), for which see Vol. I, pp. 293ff. and Vol. II, p. 382 (the latter lists a *Manual Mexicano de la administracion de los santos sacramentos, conforme al Manual Toledano, 1634*). I am indebted to Father Geoffrey Steel for drawing my attention to this.

19. Löhe produced a neomedieval marriage rite, complete with bridal nuptial blessing, in an interesting series of nuptial offices. See Wilhelm Löhe, *Agende für christliche Gemeinden des lutherischen Bekenntnisses*, in Klaus Ganzert (Ed.), *Wilhelm Löhe: Gesammette Werke* (Neuendettelsen: Freimund-Verlag, 1953, 7/1), pp. 425–437. I am indebted to Thomas H. Schattauer for drawing my attention to this study.

20. Text in *Liturgy and Other Divine Offices of the Church* (London: Chiswick, 1880), pp. 253–261. See also Stevenson, *Nuptial Blessing*, pp. 148–149. This Church started life in England in the 1830's under charismatic influence and emerged as a full-blown church, with twelve "apostles," a rich liturgy culled from many sources and congregations all over Europe and in parts of North America. Only "apostles" could ordain, and the last one died in 1901. But the importance of this church upon the liturgical, ecumenical, and charismatic movements of this century is slowly being realized. See Kenneth W. Stevenson, "The Catholic Apostolic Church—Its History and Its Eucharist," *Studia Liturgica* 13 (1979):21–45.

The Reforms

Chapter Five

Preparations

INTRODUCTION

The marriage rites of the sixteenth-century Reformation and Counter-Reformation set out to solve theological and liturgical problems within the strict confines of those problems as the churches perceived them. Thus, the Reformation liturgies insist that marriage is an ordinance, a public rite presided over by the minister, and that the consent of the couple, together with the reading and exposition of the Word, should be the essentials, along with solemn prayer. The Roman Catholic Church, however, lays down a mandatory form of nuptial mass, which is to be used by those churches that do not qualify under the two-hundred-year rule, and (later) produces a rite in 1614 that admirably expresses the principles enunciated by the Trent Decree, *Tametsi* (1563). Marriage is a sacrament consecrated by the couple, but the priest must still be there for the validity of the sacrament in the eyes of the Church. We have seen how these opposing views produced the rites in question. We have also noted how similar *all* those rites are, in that they opt for a one-stage marriage liturgy, a celebration of the last of Van Gennep's three phases of rites of passage. Those three phases, which we might dare to call "The Shape of Marriage," continue to be the ground on which Neo-Gallican rites introduce the necessary Tridentine features. But, for all their beauty and exuberance, these local diocesan variations fade away in the nineteenth century under the influence of Ultramontanism. It is worth noting that many of the features need not have disappeared. They only went because they appeared in the same books as other services contained in local rituals that could not qualify as legitimate. Guéranger's writings, and subsequent Ultramontanism, chose to ignore Trent's specific encouragement of local *marriage* rites and customs to continue to grow and develop and be used in the liturgy.

Marriage, for all that it appeared last in the 1614 *Rituale*, was still praised and emphasized in conciliar documents. Thus at Vatican I and in the decree *Ne Temere* of Pius X (1907),[1] it is stressed as a vocation of Christians in the world. But one issue raised itself that proved to be of considerable difficulty in the years ahead. What of a Roman Catholic partner wishing to marry someone who was a Christian but who belonged to another Church? One solution was provided in 1914[2] in the form of a papal indult that allowed such marriages to be celebrated, but without the nuptial mass, i.e., the premass rite of consent, with its short prayers over the couple after the consent and ring giving. Such a rite was inherently second class for two reasons.

The first derived from the fact that such marriages were set on the same level as those celebrated during the so-called "closed season," i.e., Lent and Passiontide. We have not traced the origin of this restriction, which goes back far in Christian history, but it has to do with marriage, celebrated with feasting and dancing, as being inappropriate during penitential seasons and because consummation of the marriage was not proper during such times.

The second reason derived from the fact that the devout held the nuptial mass in great esteem. Although the Tridentine books divide the premass consent rite from the eucharist (and the 1614 *Rituale* ends, "if the marriage is to be blessed . . ."), most Catholic families regarded the nuptial mass as something very special, whose absence would be taken as the denial of the rights of every Catholic couple. The special character of the nuptial blessing thus remains an issue that the revisers who compiled the 1969 *Ordo* had to face.

The Roman Catholic Church was beginning to face other Churches. It also had experience of dealing with other cultures. Trent encouraged local customs to be taken into account, and some took these liberties at their face value. Thus, when the earliest known mission *Rituale* was put together for Nagasaki in 1605, both the joining of hands and the ring were omitted, since these customs were not significant in Japanese culture.[3] In the twentieth century, adaptations and transmutations became common, so that the *mangala-sutra* was allowed as a substitute for the ring in the 1960 Anglican Prayer Book for India, Burma, Pakistan, and Ceylon.

NEW PATHS
The first part of the twentieth century saw several interesting attempts to recover things lost as well as to innovate in the interests of imaginative development. Thus, the Anglican Prayer Books of various provinces in the late 1920s (including England, the United States, and Scotland) abbreviate Cranmer's lengthy instruction, delete the bride's promise to "obey" (or else make it optional), and provide a collect and lections for a nuptial eucharist, if required. But text and context interact more subtly, and many Anglican (and other) clergy began to follow post-Tridentine Roman Catholic practice in wrapping their stoles around the joined hands of couples when they recited the words, "Those whom God hath joined together . . ." Cranmer

would have turned in his grave when these practices began, since the priestly symbolism eloquently denies completely the nonpriestly and nonsacramental intention of the original liturgical reviser. Similarly, North American Protestants of various traditions are familiar with the custom of the pastor reciting those words with his right hand raised in blessing. What was originally intended as a scriptural comment on something that had already taken place (the consent of the partners), soon becomes a special formula, said by the minister as an authoritative and performative part of the rite.[4]

In the previous century, British Methodism was innovative in more radical ways. Thus, although Wesley deleted it, the ring returned in the nineteenth century. We find it in the "Primitive" Methodist rite of 1860. The liturgy therein handles the symbolism carefully. The ring is not placed "on the book," nor is it blessed as Tractarian Anglicans began to do, but it is placed directly on the third finger of the bride's left hand, and the groom then says:

"I give thee this ring *as a memorial of our union*, and as a pledge of my love and fidelity."[5]

Cranmer's medievalism is thus drastically changed. But the bride then has her say:

"As such I now receive it."

Such formulas recur in subsequent Methodist rites, and they reappear in the next century as significant expressions of a dominant theme in marriage today—mutuality and equality. It is interesting that the formula for the bride to "receive" the ring also appears in the eighteenth century in the 1720 *Rituale* of Blois.

Another innovative rite was the 1902 Book of Common Order, of the Church of Scotland (Presbyterian), which begins the rite with biblical readings and prays for the couple *before* their consent is given, an interesting branching off from the Calvinist rites of previous Scots-Presbyterian tradition. All this serves to show that Protestantism was becoming much less suspicious of traditional symbolism and more ready to enrich the somewhat bald rites inherited from the Reformation.

FOUR ISSUES
Four issues began to raise themselves for Roman Catholics and others as the twentieth century progressed.

The first concerned the *theology* of marriage. Trent was dominated by post-scholastic theology and therefore produced a scholastic type of marriage rite that insisted on the consent of the partners, but the priest had still to be there. Marriage theology entered a stark phase that was dominated by the contractual side of marriage. Just as bread and wine are consecrated by the recitation of the words of Christ in the context of certain definite ritual actions, so marriage as a sacrament is consecrated by the consent of the partners, who are seen to be the "ministers of the sacrament." Such an understanding has the real advantage of pointing the finger at the laity, and of making them sit up and think. But this understanding has its disadvantages, not least in that it leans rather too heavily on the legal tradition of the Roman Empire, which also taught that consent sufficed for a valid marriage, and leans considerably less on the riches of liturgical tradition in the East and West before scholasticism took over.

There came a shift in Catholic theology from the *contractual* emphasis on marriage to an understanding of marriage as a *covenant*, a theme already present in the old Sacramentaries. An important contribution to this debate came with the publication (in 1963) of Eduard Schillebeeckx's[6] historico-doctrinal study of marriage, which sets the contractual-based debate in a wider historical perspective and also highlights the "problem" of the interchurch marriage. For Schillebeeckx and others, the contractual understanding has two disadvantages. One is that it emphasizes precisely what the Trent Fathers wanted to emphasize: the service celebrated as a sacrament in Church. The other is that it lacks a strong ecclesiological dimension. Both these disadvantages concur with our own analysis. Emphasis on the one, single Church service fails to see marriage as a "passage," as a union in which the partners grow together under God both before and after the Church service, rather than as something that transpires automatically in heaven because the right legal formulas have been uttered according to the correct rubrics. Similarly, the absence of a full ecclesiology of marriage in the liturgy itself inevitably would make partners coming to marriage wonder if their new state of relationship has, indeed, got anything to do with the Church any longer. One thinks, at this point, of the deliberate insertion by the Catholic Apostolics of the words, "in the faith of Christ's Church, and in the ways of God's commandments," in Cranmer's marriage vow. Marriage is also about the rest of the Church. So how can covenant help?

Covenant can help because it places the right balance of emphasis on God, the couple, and the rest of the Church. Covenant emphasizes both the "objective" side of marriage as an act of God in the Christian assembly by two people, as well as the "subjective" side of marriage as a mystery of life in which the partners, their friends, and relatives have to grow in a life-long union. Covenant is a theme that stands up better to biblical scrutiny than contract, because, as we have seen, contract is only one aspect of marriage, whereas covenant can be applied to the whole relationship as something that is changing, dynamic, and full of what Michael Ramsey once described as "an adventure."

The second issue concerns the development of liturgiology as a science. How did the Roman Catholic Church in particular, and the remaining Western churches in general, inform themselves of the roots of liturgical tradition in recent centuries? Various smaller studies were undertaken by commentators, for example, on the *Book of Common Prayer*. But what of the whole medieval tradition? And what of the East?

Dom Edmond Martène is largely responsible for keeping alive and available several important marriage rites of the Middle Ages, through the various editions of his *De Antiquis Ecclesiae Ritibus*.[7] In the first book, Martène provides full texts of rites that include the early Sacramentaries, traveling marriage rites, as well as the more elaborate medieval texts, most of them of French origin. A comparison of these texts gives an excellent bird's-eye view of how the Western rites of marriage developed, and he is even kind enough to provide the Greek Byzantine rite as well.

Then, in 1875, W. G. Henderson[8] published his edition of *The York Manual*, and in an appendix provided no fewer than ten medieval English rites that, when compared, tell the English tale eloquently enough. Shortly before this, in 1863 and 1864, Heinrich Denzinger[9] published his *Ritus Orientalium*, which brought together in Latin translation various definitive texts (most of recent date) of the services (apart from the eucharist and hours) of the Eastern churches. It says something about the quality of all these texts and studies that they are still necessary tools for the scholar today.

Four books, however, have to be added to this list because they all influenced the writing of history and the compilation of new texts, as well as the general appreciation of the collective memory of Christians, both Eastern and Western.

The first came in 1938, when Basilius Binder[10] published his study. Martène, for obvious reasons, placed the spotlight on French rites, both Anglo-Norman and Visigothic. Binder filled in the story regarding Germany and the neighboring countries, in particular with the noneucharistic rites of the late medieval period.

The second, also by a German, was the study by Korbinian Ritzer.[11] This first appeared in German in 1962, although a shorter version was duplicated and available in 1951. Ritzer's documentation is vast, and, although his starting point is Canon Law and social custom, his liturgical account is full. Once more, his book is invaluable for the scholar in that it traces the story from Christian origins right up to the tenth century and beyond. His collection of texts is likewise exhaustive, covering as it does not only the Roman Sacramentaries, but also the Visigothic rites and the noneucharistic rites as well.

A third study appeared in 1958.[12] Unlike the others, it is no more than a series of translations, with notes, of the Eastern marriage rites, carried out by Alphonse Raes, *Le mariage dans les églises d'orient*. It made available in ready form the complex rites of the East at a time when ecumenism was well under way and the Vatican Council round the corner.

Another study appeared after the Council, but it is still important for our survey because one of the authors, Jean-Baptiste Molin, was involved in drawing up the 1969 *Ordo*. The book takes on the story of the French marriage rites from where Ritzer left off, and is entitled *Le rituel du mariage en France du XIè au XVIè siècle*, and it was published in 1974 as a joint work by

Molin and Protais Mutembe. Once again, the study has a complete set of texts that includes two significant landmarks to which we have already drawn attention. These are the twelfth-century English Bury rite, the first known to prefix the nuptial mass with a proper rite of consent, and the fourteenth-century Barbeau rite, the first in France known to have a full "active" vow.[13]

History is thus in a strong position to inform all the Western churches of the evolution of the marriage liturgy from the time of the Roman Sacramentaries right through the many strands of the Middle Ages, down to the present day. This information has been carefully used in different ways throughout this study.

The third issue is one which we have touched upon already and concerns the social development of the countries that have made up the Roman Catholic world. We have seen how the sixteenth century forced the Catholic Church to insist on marriage in church, by couples who would carry out the essential ingredients to make their wedding day lawful in the eyes of the Church.[14] But three factors that are relatively new to the Catholic Church began to be pressing. One is the rise of secularism in the Western world and the increasing laxity of many people to observe "Christian" marriage. This was highlighted in countries like France that required a separate civil marriage before a state official to have the marriage registered lawful in the eyes of the government. In response to this requirement, the Catholic Church insisted that the couple should come to church *as well* to have the marriage legitimated in the eyes of Mother Church. Such a situation, though historically understandable, was bound to set State and Church in a potential confrontation, particularly in view of the Catholic Church's emphasis on consent, which is about all that the secular liturgy before the state official contained. It need hardly be added that an increasing number of couples who no longer attended church with any degree of frequency ceased to bother with the church service; many of a later generation did not even bother to get married.

Another social feature arose in the mission fields of the Third World, in those areas where polygamy was (and is) a long-standing practice of many tribes. Should the Church set itself against polygamy, or should it tolerate it temporarily until such time as the area in question was wholly converted to Christianity? Different views were expressed on this difficult question.[15] It is undeniable that polygamy was practiced in the patriarchal era of the Old Testament. On the other hand, polygamy does not regard the wife as equal in status to the man; and yet wifely subservience lies behind many of the popular marriage customs and vows of the earlier days of the Western medieval church, as well as Catholic and Protestant rites after the Reformation. The official line of the Catholic Church has always been against polygamy; still, the practice lies behind many of the societies at present existing in countries being evangelized by the Church.

Yet another social question concerns divorce, a problem that the Catholic Church has traditionally dealt with through annulment, which in legal terms declares that the original marriage never existed, for example, because the marriage was not consummated or else because the consent of the partners was not maturely or adequately undertaken. Divorce is also a problem that Protestant churches face. Some have their own procedures. Others accept civil law and marry any couples who come to church for another marriage. Still others adopt the perhaps dubious practice of refusing to ratify the consent of these couples, but still offer them a service of blessing, a popular practice in the Church of England. Such a procedure is wonderfully pragmatic, but in the theology it drives a dangerous wedge between consent and blessing, which the marriage liturgy is supposed to hold together. Although the Byzantine understanding of the "death of the marriage" is gaining popularity in the West as a way around the ecclesiological problems posed by divorce, the Roman Catholic Church is still committed to the indissolubility of the (sacramental) marriage bond. Given this, the only way to terminate a marriage canonically is to determine whether or not the bond exists, hence the system of annulments.

The fourth and final issue facing the Roman Catholic Church is about the marriage of Catholic and non-Catholic. Formerly shunned by the devout, it is now common throughout the Catholic world. Indeed, it has since been overtaken by another issue, the marriage of a Catholic with someone who is not baptized, which often means someone who does not believe in God. Traditionally, the Catholic Church has either tried by one way or another to get the non-Catholic to become a Catholic, or else it has required a promise from both partners that children born of their union will be brought up in the Catholic Church. As we have seen, the old liturgical arrangements for the "mixed" marriage consisted of a liturgy of a very second-class kind.

Non-Catholics have frequently resented this sort of intrusion into their religious life, particularly when they have been loyal and faithful to the church of their upbringing. Moreover, there are parts of the Western world where semiforced conversions have left behind them a legacy of bitterness that will take a long time to heal. But such is the way in that the divisions of the sixteenth century have hardened and been brought down from the seminar room into the marriage chamber. This issue was grasped by Schillebeeckx and others. Secularism has its own jokes. Nowadays many pastors rejoice when the couple coming before them for marriage are practicing Christians (even if one of them happens not to be Catholic), in contrast to the couples who are both "good" Catholics on paper, but who are unlikely to reappear in church until the christening, if then. We live in an age in which Christians are, perforce, sharing their faith with each other, in a world that, in outward attitudes at least, is by instinct and commitment definitely a post-Christian one.

THE SECOND VATICAN COUNCIL
The Second Vatican Council has a lot to say about marriage. Indeed, one senses from its decrees on liturgy and the married state within society that the Fathers of the Council took marriage far more seriously than Vatican I, or, for that matter, the Council of Trent. Because the Constitution on the Sacred Liturgy appeared first, what it has to say about the reform of the marriage rite is eloquent testimony to the fresh winds blowing through the thinking of the Church.

"77. The marriage rite now found in the Roman Ritual is to be revised and enriched in a way which more clearly expresses the grace of the sacrament and the duties of the spouses. [Here follows a brief quotation from the Council of Trent.] 'If certain locales traditionally use other praiseworthy customs and ceremonies when celebrating the sacrament of matrimony, this Sacred Synod earnestly desires that these by all be retained.'

"Moreover, the competent territorial ecclesiastical authority mentioned in article 22, para. 2, of this Constitution is free to draw up its own rite suited to the usages of places and people according to the provision of article 63. But the rite is always to honor the requirement that the priest assisting at the marriage must ask for and obtain the consent of the contracting parties.

"78. Matrimony is normally to be celebrated in the mass, after the reading of the gospel and the homily, and before the 'prayer of the faithful.' The prayer for the bride, duly amended to remind both spouses of their equal obligation to remain faithful to each other, may be said in another tongue. But if the sacrament of matrimony is celebrated apart from mass, the epistle and gospel from the nuptial mass are to be read at the beginning of the rite, and a blessing should always be given to the spouses."[16]

Some of this is familiar territory, some of it is not. The Tridentine principle of local variation in the marriage liturgy is upheld, as is the requirement that the partners give their consent. But the rest is both new and deeply traditional. The marriage rite is ecclesiological in that it is about what the Church is doing. It must, therefore, be part of a full liturgy, whether or not the eucharist is celebrated. Moreover, in line with the other reforms of the Council, the special rite of marriage is incorporated into the eucharist by being placed after the gospel and homily. In terms of history, this is exactly what the 1543 Metz tradition does. Furthermore, when the eucharist is not celebrated for pastoral reasons, including when one of the partners is either not a Catholic or not baptized, the readings must still be read and the homily given. More radical is the insistence that the nuptial blessing should refer to *both* partners and that it should be part of the noneucharistic form of the marriage liturgy, thus putting an end to the anomalous character of the "closed season" rite as well as the "mixed marriage" rite.

Before we go further, however, it is worth drawing attention to the fact that marriage figures strongly in one other document of the Second Vatican Council, that of *The Church in the Modern World* (1966), which devotes the first chapter of its second part to "the dignity of marriage and the family." It is careful and perceptive. Its final paragraph is a moving testimony to the Catholic Church's newly apprehended attention to the married state as an essential vocation in the Kingdom of God:

"Let married people themselves, who are created in the image of the living God and constituted in an authentic personal dignity, be united together in equal affection, agreement of mind, and mutual holiness. Thus, in the footsteps of Christ, the principle of life, they will bear witness by their faithful love in the joys and sacrifices of their calling, to that mystery of love which the Lord revealed to the world by his death and resurrection."[17]

Such a wholesome and pastoral atmosphere helped to bring relaxation to the rules about marriages between Catholics and non-Catholics, even to the extent that the old phrase "mixed marriage" is coming to be replaced by the more kindly "inter-Church marriage." Rules subsequently issued by Paul VI reaffirmed the need for children to be brought up in the Roman Catholic Church, but showed much more sensitivity to the real religious commitments of those involved in such marriages who were members of other churches. Clergy from those other churches were permitted, at long last, to take part in the marriage liturgy, in reading, preaching, and praying for the couple. While intercommunion was officially forbidden, the Vatican nonetheless revealed the thin end of what has become a long wedge.

Before we go on to take up the story of the evolution of the new liturgy, a quotation from the Decree on the Apostolate of Lay People (1965) perhaps expresses something of the urgency felt by many of the Council Fathers:

"Christian couples are, for each other, for their children, and for their relatives, cooperators of grace and witnesses of the faith. They are the first to pass on the faith to their children and to dedicate them in it. By word and example, they form them to a Christian and apostolic life; they offer them wise guidance in the choice of vocation, and if they discover in them a sacred vocation they encourage it with all care."[18]

THE 1969 *ORDO:* ITS EVOLUTION[19]

The Constitution on the Sacred Liturgy was passed on December 4, 1963, the fourth centenary, to the day, of the Council of Trent's liturgical decree, which placed all authority in matters liturgical in the hands of the pope. It was thus important for any real continuity with Trent to be made as explicit as possible. Therefore, the quotation from *Tametsi* on the need for local customs to continue was both political and timely. After the Constitution was passed, the *Consilium Liturgicum* set up various study groups that were to be charged with drawing up new rites in accord with the Constitution. It was left to Groups 22 and 23 to deal with the new *Rituale;* Group 23 in particular was given the task of compiling the new *Ordo Celebrandi Matrimonium* in consultation with the other group. These were set up in March 1964. The new *Ordo* was promulgated on March 17, 1969. What happened in the intervening five years?

The chairman of Group 23 was Pierre-Marie Gy, O.P., from the Institut Supérieur de Liturgie in Paris, a well-known liturgical scholar whose own personality and knowledge of history and theology were to prove needful attributes for the years ahead. The secretary of the group was Secundus Mazzarello. The group consisted of the following:

J. Mejia (Columbia), pastoral liturgy

J. Rabau (Belgium), parish priest

127

J. Hofinger (Austria), East Asian Pastoral Institute, Manila

F. Vandenbroucke (Belgium), liturgist

D. Sicard (France), pastoral liturgy

Three liturgical scholars were added: A. Chavasse, B. Löwenberg, and K. Ritzer, the author of the seminal work on the marriage liturgy mentioned earlier. The Chairman of Group 22 was Balthasar Fischer, of the Liturgical Institute, Trier, and among its members were E. Lengeling, F. McManus, B. Luykx, J. Lécuyer, and J.-B. Molin (co-author of the book on French medieval rites cited before). It also co-opted L. Ligier.

The Constitution provided the group with its basic orders. But these needed to be put into practice, which the group began doing at three residential meetings: Strasbourg in 1965, Le Saulchoir in 1966, and Verona in 1966. Within the first two years of its existence, the basic shape of the marriage service had been formulated. Among the questions to be faced were the relationship between the rite when celebrated during the mass and when not, the nuptial blessing itself, the shape of the rite of marriage, and the use of vernacular languages. This latter point becomes far more important after the 1969 *Ordo* was promulgated, because of the liberties that local countries did and did not take.

The group began by looking at the history of the rite, which recent publications were able to clarify. Thus, the priestly formula in the 1614 *Rituale* was known to be a fourteenth-century Norman development, rather than something belonging to deepest antiquity. The meeting at Le Saulchoir produced a document that compared three different structures to the rite of marriage:

Form A (German Ritual, 1950)	Form B (Bury rite, twelfth century)	Form C (Roman)
Blessing of the ring	Blessing of the ring	Consent
Giving of the ring	Consent	Blessing of the ring
Consent	Giving of the ring	Giving of the ring

Such a variety of shape must have appeared baffling, indeed tantalizing to the uninitiated. Yet each reproduces its own tradition, which future local books might or might not follow. In the end, the Roman order is followed, but it is significant that the German 1950[20] rite is the one that was consulted as representing pre-Vatican II innovation. In fact, the 1950 rite is the most important of all these rites, because it provides a collect-type prayer at the start of the service and it also appends in German a Visigothic blessing of the couple, directing the priest to stretch his hands over them during its recitation. The group, therefore, had *one* rite to use as an example of history enriching present practice.

In April 1966, McManus wrote to Gy expressing the need for the new rite to differentiate between the marriage of a Catholic and with a non-Catholic and the marriage of a Catholic with a non-Christian. The action bore fruit in the three types of service provided by the 1969 *Ordo*. However, three points were raised in the preliminary stage in 1966. First, there was the possible use of the Metz order, which placed consent within the mass before the offertory, but the ring giving *after* the mass. Johannes Wagner liked this custom, whereas Martimort did not. Second, there was some discussion on the *ego vos conjungo* formula, which several liturgists took to imply that the priest performed the sacrament. (Later that year, Molin wrote a memorandum that made the distinction that the couples "admit" the sacrament in their consent, whereas the priest "joins them together.") The formula was dropped. Third, the nuptial blessing, which was to cause problems later, was already the subject of controversy. Wagner championed the Roman tradition of blessing the bride alone, as a way of emphasizing her role in a chauvinist world; moreover, an article by De Jong was used in evidence to support such a view. Martimort, on the other hand, thought otherwise, that the blessing should be changed, as indicated by the Constitution itself. (Incidentally, among the many memoranda written to Gy was one by Ritzer on the use of medieval sources.)

In October 1966, the structure of the rite was formulated, as well as the important distinction made by McManus, which has crucial pastoral implications. A draft was written containing two new nuptial blessings: one blessed the bride alone (by Jungmann) and the other blessed both partners (by Ligier). And a Visigothic blessing (with intercalated "Amens") appeared at the end of mass (suggested by Lécuyer).

In April 1967, the draft was discussed with the *Consilium Liturgicum*. It was agreed that McManus' three categories should be incorporated for pastoral reasons in the new rite. It was also agreed that the nuptial blessing should be moved to its former position, before the Peace. Furthermore, an active form of consent was to form the basis of the new rite, as Gy requested earlier in the discussion. He did this as a result of his knowledge of the popularity of the English vow from the Prayer Book, derived from the *Sarum Manual*, throughout the English-speaking world. But the biggest problem concerned the text of the nuptial blessing, about which there was considerable disagreement. Eventually, a compromise was reached, largely through the principle of alternative forms. The old nuptial blessing was to be edited so as to pray for the woman and then the man. Ligier's proposed text, which had a similar structure, was to be shortened. And a third and simpler prayer was to be written probably with a view to being suggested for use at marriages where one partner was not a Christian. There was also a discussion about the preliminary questions before the consent: the authorities insisted that the third of these questions, about bringing up children in the Catholic Church, should appear in the new rite.

Accordingly, Mazzarello edited Ligier's draft of the nuptial blessing. After comments of the *Consilium* were attended to, the final draft was sent to Rome in November 1967, and scrutinized and approved by the *Consilium* in March 1968, subject to further comments by a theological consultant, P. Ciappi, whose particular concern it was to get the descriptions of the third form of the rite (between a Catholic and an unbaptized person) theologically correct. Pope Paul then used the final draft form when he attended the eucharistic congress in Bogota on August 23, 1968. This was particularly appropriate in view of the enriched character of the new rite, quite apart from the fact that one of the members of the Study Group (Mejia) came from Colombia.

The final text was duly issued on March 17, 1969. The main difference in the final text was that consent could be given *either* passively (in the form of a question) *or* actively (in the form of the vow), whereas the earlier version directed a vow only. Thus came to an end several years of hard work that has greatly enriched the sacramental life of the Catholic Church. What stands out as particularly noteworthy are the following features:

Creative use of tradition

Incorporation within the mass

Centrality of consent

Pastoral distinctions into three types of marriage liturgy all of them full liturgies, in their own right

The result is a considerable advance on the "irreducible minimum" model of 1614, for the new *Ordo* has now no fewer than six ingredients:

Reception of the couple

Liturgy of the word

Preliminary questions

Consent

Blessing and giving of the rings

Nuptial blessing

It is to these that we must now look in some detail.

NOTES

1. *Acta Apostolicae Sedis*, 49 (Vatican City: Apostolic Press, 1907), p. 528.

2. *Rituale Romanum* (Ratisbon: Pustet, 1925), pp. 478–479 (" . . . when mass is not said"), and pp. 479–480 (" . . . when the nuptial blessing is not permitted").

3. See P.-M. Gy, "Le nouveau rituel romain du mariage," *La Maison-Dieu* 98 (1969):142 and n. 40.

4. On the "priestly formula," see Stevenson, *Nuptial Blessing: A Study of Christian Marriage Rites* (Alcuin Club Collections 64) (London: SPCK, 1982, and New York: Oxford University Press, 1983), pp. 75, 90, 149, 169ff., and 186ff. See also Joanne Pierce, "A Note on the 'Ego Vos Conjungo' in Medi-

eval French Marriage Liturgy," *Ephemerides Liturgicae* 99 (1985):290–299.

5. See the full text in *Forms for the Administration of Baptism . . . for the use of such Primitive Methodist Ministers as may require them* (London, 1860), pp. 15–23. See also Stevenson, *Nuptial Blessing*, pp. 158ff.

6. E. Schillebeeckx, *Marriage, Secular Reality and Saving Mystery* (New York: Sheed and Ward, 1963), passim. For a more recent discussion of these and related issues, see Theodore Mackin, *What is Marriage* (Ramsey, NJ: Paulist Press, 1982), pp. 239ff. I am also indebted to Susan J. White for her paper, "Beyond the Contract/Covenant Debate: New Images for a Theology of Christian Marriage," presented as a seminar paper, University of Notre Dame, Indiana, April, 1983. "Covenant" becomes a popular theme in non-Catholic rites, for which, see pp. 154ff. (American Episcopalian) and Ch. 7, n. 9 (Ecumenical CCT rite).

7. E. Martène, *De Antiquis Ecclesiae Ritibus*, I–III (Rouen: Behourt, 1700–1702). See also A.-G. Martimort, *La Documentation Liturgique de Dom Edmond Martène* (Studi e Testi 279) (Vatican City: Apostolic Press, 1978). This work is indispensable for identifying the many manuscripts used by Martène.

8. W. G. Henderson, *The York Manual* (Surtees Society 63) (Edinburgh, 1875), Appendix IV, pp. 157*–168*.

9. H. Denzinger, *Ritus Orientalium*, I–II (Würzburg: Stahl, 1863–1864).

10. B. Binder, *Geschicte des feierlichen Ehesegens von der Entstehung der Ritualien bis zur Gegenwart* (Metten: Abtei, 1938).

11. See above, Chapter 1, n. 11; see also our review of the 1982 reprint, *Theologische Revue* 80 (1984), coll. 156–158.

12. See above, Chapter 3, n. 3.

13. See above, Chapter 2, n. 11. On Barbeau and Bury rites, see pp. 39–43.

14. For a discussion of the development of this issue and the Church's varied response to it in Europe, see Bruno Klein-

heyer, "Riten um Ehe und Familie," in H. B. Meyer, H.-J. Auf der Maur, B. Fischer, A. Haüssling, and B. Kleinheyer (Eds.), *Gottesdienst der Kirche: Handbuch der Liturgiewissenschaft*, 8 (Ratisbon: Pustet, 1984), pp. 121ff.

15. See, for example, Adrian Hastings, *Christian Marriage in Africa* (London: SPCK, 1973).

16. Austin Flannery (Ed.), *Vatican Council II: The Conciliar and Post-Conciliar Documents* (Collegeville, MN: Liturgical Press, 1975), p. 23 (Constitution on the Sacred Liturgy, Chapter II, sec. 77, 78). See also text with notes by P.-M. Gy, *La Maison-Dieu* 76 (1963):100–104. See also text with notes on successive drafts by P. Jounel, *La Maison-Dieu* 156 (1983):228–231.

17. See Flannery, op. cit., p. 957 (Constitution on the Church in the Modern World, Chapter I, sec. 52).

18. See Flannery, op. cit., p. 778 (Decree on the Apostolate of Lay People, Chapter I, sec. 11). For a development of this theme, see also Raymond Didier, "Sacrement de mariage, baptême et foi," *La Maison-Dieu* 127 (1976):106–138.

19. I am indebted to P.-M. Gy for allowing me to study his dossier on the work of the Study Group of which he was chairman. In addition, the following should be noted: P.-M. Gy, "Le nouveau rituel romain du mariage," *La Maison-Dieu* 98 (1969):7–31; S. Mazzarello, "De novo ordine celebrandi matrimonium," *Ephemerides Liturgicae* 83 (1969):251–277; C. Braga, "La genesi dell' 'Ordo Matrimonii,' " *Ephemerides Liturgicae* 93 (1979):247–257; G. S. Sloyan, "The New Rite for Celebrating Marriage," *Worship* 44 (1970):258–267; A. Bugnini, *La riforma liturgica (1948–1975)* (Ephemerides Liturgicae "Subsidia" 30) (Rome: Edizione Liturgiche, 1983), pp. 676–686; and A. Nocent, "Le rituel du mariage depuis Vatican II," in *La Celebrazione Christiana Del Matrimonio* (Studia Anselmia 93; Analecta Liturgica 11) (Rome: Pontificio Ateneo S. Anselmo, 1986), pp. 129–144. On the question of the nuptial blessing, see J. P. De Jong, "Brautsegen und Jungfrauenweihe," *Zeitschrift fur Katholische Theologie* 84 (1962):300–322. (I have argued against this view, see *Nuptial Blessing*, passim.) A recent study attempts to show that the prayer over the bride, as it appears in the Leonine and Gela-

sian Sacramentaries, is fifth century, whereas the other mass prayers are earlier; see P. Nautin, "Le rituel de mariage et la formation des Sacramentaires 'Léonien' et 'Gélasien,' " *Ephemerides Liturgicae* 98 (1984):425–457. I would still argue for the custom of praying over the veiled bride as an early Roman practice on the basis of my study of Latin authors, especially Ambrose and Augustine; see *Nuptial Blessing*, pp. 26ff.

20. See *Collectio Rituum ad Instar Appendicis Ritualis Romani Pro Omnibus Germaniae Dioecesibus* (Ratisbon: Pustet, 1950), pp. 80–99; discussed by Kleinheyer, op. cit., pp. 123–125.

Chapter Six

The Rites

INTRODUCTION

One word stands out in the decree promulgating the new *Ordo* that sums up the real message behind the new rite, "this *richer* rite." It can be no coincidence that Chapter 77 of the *Constitution on the Sacred Liturgy* stated that the marriage rite was to be "revised and *enriched* in a way that more clearly expresses the grace of the sacrament and the duties of the spouses."[1] There could be no clearer hint that the 1614 service was found to be poor in comparison.

The "Introduction"[2] comes in four parts. The first, "The Importance and Dignity of the Sacrament of Matrimony," begins with some quotations from the Second Vatican Council, including some that we quoted in Chapter 5. These four opening paragraphs stress the theology of marriage (1) as a way of sharing in the love between Christ and the Church, (2) as a *covenant* of fidelity and procreation that is indissoluble, (3) as a bond in which the partners stick together "in good times as in bad" (see the form of consent in the rite), and (4) as a way of producing children for the continuation of humankind and the enrichment of the Church.

The next three paragraphs relate to the liturgy itself. The priest must be careful both in his preaching and in preparing couples beforehand to make known the

Christian view of marriage (5). The liturgy should stress the Word—a new element in marriages when mass is not celebrated; but it should also stress (6) the consent of the partners, the nuptial blessing *"for the bride and for the marriage covenant,"* and the reception of communion by the whole congregation. The rite should have a certain clarity that highlights these special points. Moreover, Holy Communion is an inseparable part of mass, as the Liturgical Movement has taught us. Finally, matrimony demands and requires faith on the part of the couple (7).

All of this sturdily asserts the emphases in the conciliar documents and sets them within the liturgical framework of the Western tradition. There is, therefore, nothing new. Of particular note are the use of the Ephesians analogy in the opening paragraph and the description of marriage as a *covenant*, not just as a contract.

The second part, "Choice of Rite," explains the three different services provided in the *Ordo*. Never before in the Western tradition have couples been presented with this kind of choice in an official manner. Alternatives are a feature of the recent reforms as a whole. Sometimes they exist for variety, as we shall see later in the service. But at this point, the options exist for definite pastoral reasons. Since the Study Group had to work hard to thrash these principles out, it seemed important to stress them at this point. First of all (8) the second form of service should be used between a Catholic and a non-Catholic; but the first form may also be used, although the non-Catholic should not receive communion "according to general law." We shall return to this point in Chapter 7. If taken at its face value, it means that one of the partners receives communion whereas the other does not, which places a considerable pastoral burden on both.

Folk religion lies behind the next paragraph (9), which alerts priests to be aware that many people only come to church for weddings, and therefore the choice of readings and the homily itself should be carefully prepared. Here is the post-Christendom situation of a Western church openly admitted in an official liturgical document. Then, related to this phenomenon (10) is the fact that secular authorities should not be given special treatment—another Western cultural inheritance. Finally, there are some remarks about the relationship between the marriage mass and the liturgical year (11); Sunday masses take precedence and the old "closed seasons" are opened up.

The third part, "Preparation of Local Rituals," repeats the principles both of Trent and of Vatican II about marriage liturgies. These are indeed (12) to be compiled, but taking into account existing options built into the new rite (13), variety of structure (14), crowning or veiling *of the bride*, and the substitution of local customs for the hand joining and ring giving (15), and encouragement to keep local customs when first encountered in evangelization (16).

This is a particularly telling part, because it opens up many liberties that include structure as well as content. On the other hand, one senses a Western approach to folk custom; just as the nuptial blessing is seen as bridal in the previous section (8), so here the bride may be crowned or veiled (15).

The fourth part, "Right To Prepare a Completely New Rite," only lays down two things, a rule of irreducible minimum and a guideline. The rule is that the consent of the partners and the nuptial blessing must always form part of these rites. This takes us far from the anomalous character of Trent, which on the one hand insisted on consent and on the other said the priest had still to recite the special formula after consent.

The guideline is pregnant with possibilities. In cultures where marriage is normally celebrated over a period of days, new rites should be adapted "to the Christian spirit" and even celebrated at home. Here is a Trojan horse for Van Gennep's rites of passage to return to Catholic unity.

RITE FOR CELEBRATING MARRIAGE WITHIN THE EUCHARIST[3]

Now we come to the first form of service. The *entrance rite* concerns greeting the couple and bringing them into the church. It may be omitted, although Western culture, rather than Eastern, normally makes a special scene out of the arrival of the *bride* in church, so that the official emphasis on *both* partners mixes a little strangely with the lingering Westernisms that are detected in the *Praenotanda*.

The *liturgy of the word* follows, which can have either two or three readings. A homily must be given. The choice of lections is enormous. We shall look at these later on, together with the question of chants and music.

The *rite of marriage* comes now and consists of four elements. The first is the series of *preliminary questions* about free will, lifelong union, and bringing children up in the Church. These three may be omitted (sec "Introduction," No. 14). They serve to build up to the second element, the *consent*, which comes in two forms, each based on old Anglo-Norman models. The first is the active vow, appearing for the very first time in an official Roman formulary of this type, and the second, which may seem preferable for pastoral reasons, is the traditional passive form. The Study Group had wanted the active vow to be the sole formulation at this point. It is interesting to note that "for richer for poorer" has been replaced by the less rhythmical "in good times and in bad" (*inter prospera et adversa*).

The American and British versions keep the old English phrase at this point.

The priest then declares the couple to be married in a formula that is quite different from the *ego vos conjungo* (I join you together) in the 1614 *Rituale*. There had been discussion about this by the Study Group and it was evidently decided to compromise with a short statement, ending in the Matthean pronouncement (Mt 19:6). The result is paralleled closely by no less a tradition than English nonconformity; it is exactly the same in meaning as what Richard Baxter suggested in the abortive Savoy Liturgy of 1661, and also in various English Methodist rites of the nineteenth century.[4] It would have resembled them more closely, and gained in coherence, had the formula been declaratory throughout; the central part meanders into a semi-prayer.

The third element is the *blessing and exchanging of rings*. The blessing is done in a simple prayer. The sample given is the first of three and is based on a twelfth-century rite from Rennes, Normandy. The rings are now exchanged, using a formula based on one of the earliest texts known—the marriage of Judith, daughter of Charles the Bald, to Edilwulf, King of East Anglia in A.D. 856.[5] It is also short and to the point. The prayer of the faithful follows, and, in order to keep the creed from obtruding into the unity of sequence, it is said *after* the bidding prayers. The eucharist follows on from the offertory, and the nuptial blessing is given in its traditional place, between the eucharistic prayer and the Peace. Instead of an introductory prayer, as in the Sacramentaries, the nuptial blessing is introduced by a short bidding and silence, which is a more effective way of building up to it as a special feature of this mass. The eucharistic form of the service gives the text of the *first* nuptial blessing, which is the version that edits the old Gregorian text. The opening paragraphs, which are a little repetitious, may be reduced to one only. Among those portions of the old prayer that have gone are the Old Testament women, what one member of the *Consilium* described at a plenary meeting as "Rebecca and Company." There is something not entirely satisfactory about this prayer, because it compromises between two mutually exclusive views of the solemn prayer, i.e., is it bridal, or is it for both partners? The eucharist ends with a special blessing. The sample given for use in the United States is an expanded version of the first one in the latin text (based on an old Visigothic original).

The form for use with the eucharist brings together the focus on the couple and the ecclesial aspects of the eucharist, so that the spotlight that is placed on them during the marriage rite itself never leaves them. At the offertory, they may bring the bread and wine to the altar, and at the Peace, they kiss each other. The mass is not nuptial in name alone. The couple participate at a profound level, and (unlike so many medieval nuptial masses) they receive communion.

RITE FOR CELEBRATING MARRIAGE OUTSIDE THE EUCHARIST[6]
The second form closely resembles the first, with the obvious difference that the rite does not move into the eucharist at the offertory. Although this form is a considerable advance on its inadequate predecessor (it is a full liturgy in its own right), there is nonetheless something muted about the ending. Everything looks as if the eucharist is going to follow, and yet it doesn't.

The main change comes in the nuptial blessing, which must be given. The general intercessions (prayer of the faithful) may come first, immediately after the exchange of rings. Alternatively, they may be placed between the introductory prayer to the nuptial blessing and the nuptial blessing itself. This has the advantage of bringing together the elements of solemn prayer for the couple. We shall return to this structure later.

No particular nuptial blessing is prescribed with this rite; any of the three texts may be used. Provision is also given for the distribution of communion from the reserved sacrament, which is presumably intended solely for the Catholic partner, in order to ensure that communion is received even in this somewhat inadequate form. A deacon may solemnize this kind of marriage, which, though pastorally needful in some areas, is hardly theologically appropriate and serves to make this form of the rite even more second class. The rite ends with one of the special blessings and (if desired) the Lord's Prayer.

RITE FOR CELEBRATING MARRIAGE BETWEEN A CATHOLIC AND AN UNBAPTIZED PERSON[7]

Two categories of person are envisaged by the title "unbaptized." The first is someone who does not believe in God. The second is a catechumen. Since both categories exist throughout the Catholic world, the rite was drawn up with special care because of the pastoral implications, particularly when the marriage involves an unbeliever. In structure it is the same as the preceding one, with one important exception that concerns the nuptial blessing.

This special feature in the rite may be omitted "if circumstances so require." But if given, the text is the *third* nuptial blessing (No. 121), which is the simplest, stressing the theology of covenant, and praying for the bride and groom together throughout. The Lord's Prayer may be omitted if the nuptial blessing has been omitted, and another prayer may be said by the priest.

This type of marriage clearly needs careful handling. The notes are more definite about the kind of homily to be given in the previous rite than in this one, where it "should speak of the obligations of marriage and other appropriate points."

PRAYER TEXTS: SOURCES AND THEMES[8]
Alternatives abound, and their sources are often as interesting as their themes.

Opening Prayers
There are four of these, whereas there are three Prayers over the Gifts and Prayers after Communion. The first three Opening Prayers match the corresponding other prayers. The fourth (No. 109) is taken from the Fulda Sacramentary, a tenth-century book that contains some Visigothic material. However, in the Fulda book, this prayer, which prays for the couple in a prospective manner, is an alternative Prayer over the Gifts. Perhaps its position in the Fulda Sacramentary looks forward to the nuptial blessing as the performative part of the rite.[9] That could no longer be true of today, when the rite of consent holds such importance.

The other Opening Prayers speak concisely of various images in marriage. The first (No. 106) is a reworking of an older prayer from the 1570 Missal, and uses the Ephesians analogy. The second (No. 107) simply prays for the couple's love. The third (No. 108) prays for the grace of the sacrament and the enrichment of the church.

Blessing of the Rings
The first alternative form (No. 110) is the prayer that appears in the eleventh-century *Benedictional of Robert*[10] and is more lengthy than the others. The second (No. 111) is a new composition, stressing the meaning of the symbolism of the ring.

Prayers Over the Gifts
The first (No. 112), like the first Opening Prayer,
comes from 1570 Missal, and like the second (No.
113), which is a new composition, prays directly for
the couple. It is the third (No. 114), also a new prayer,
which goes over the top in some healthy eucharistic
theology:

"May the mystery of Christ's unselfish love
which we celebrate in this eucharist
increase their love for you and for each other."

Prefaces
Again, there are three. The first (No. 115) comes from
the 1570 Missal with some reediting from the Gelasian
Sacramentary and elsewhere. Predictably, the first
stresses the indissoluble union of man and woman
and the grace of the sacrament. The second (No. 115)
is a new composition, taking in a theme from one of
Leo the Great's sermons. It stresses the covenant theology of marriage:

"Through him you entered into a new covenant with
  your people.
You restored man to grace in the saving mystery of
  redemption.
You gave him a share in the divine life
through his union with Christ.
You made him an heir of Christ's eternal glory.

"This outpouring of love in the new covenant of grace
is symbolized in the marriage covenant
that seals the love of husband and wife
and reflects your divine plan of love."

This is perhaps one of the finest of the new prayers in
the entire 1969 *Ordo*. The third Preface (No. 117) is
also new. Like the preceding one, it waxes eloquent:

"Love is man's origin,
Love is his constant calling,
Love is his fulfilment in heaven.

"The love of man and woman
is made holy in the sacrament of marriage,
and becomes the mirror of your everlasting love."

Hanc Igitur (No. 118)

The early Roman Sacramentaries have always given a
variable insertion to the Canon at this point. The opportunity was taken to adapt the old version into a
conflation of material from the Leonine and Gelasian
prayers with the Gregorian.

Nuptial Blessing

As we have already noted, there are three nuptial
blessings, each now introduced with a short bidding
prayer. The first nuptial blessing (No. 33) is a reediting of the Gregorian original. Among the features of
the old version that have been changed are (1) the
opening reference to the creation of woman from
man, which is now modernized to be egalitarian, (2)
the Old Testament women are now subsumed into a
general category:

"May she always follow the example of the holy
    women
whose praises are sung in the Scriptures;"

(3) some of the allegedly female marital virtues are
omitted and replaced by a section that prays for her
life in the Church.

The second nuptial blessing (No. 120) is the text that
was written by Ligier and abbreviated by Mazzarello.
Its shape and direction are the same as the compromise reached over the old prayer, namely that it prays
for the bride first, then for the bridegroom more

briefly, and then for both at the end. Underneath this compromise, two significantly contemporary themes occur. First, life in the Church and world:

"Holy Father, you created mankind in your own image
and made man and woman to be joined as husband and wife
in union of body and heart
and so fulfil their mission in this world."

Second, marriage as covenant:

"Father, to reveal the plan of your love,
you made the union of husband and wife
an image of the covenant between you and your people."

And this Old Testament image (cf. Hos 4:2, 6:6, and Is 5:1–7) leads into the Ephesians analogy:

"In the fulfilment of this sacrament,
the marriage of Christian man and woman
is a sign of the marriage between Christ and the Church."

The prayer then focuses on both before settling rather more on the bride than the groom. It demonstrates the rule that we have observed earlier that prayers that give special emphasis on one partner begin to differentiate the roles of the husband and wife in ways that may not meet reality. This example, which asks that the bride be "caring for the home," may mix uncomfortably with some modern Western understandings of the reordering of the traditional roles within the family.

The third nuptial blessing (No. 121) is another new composition. It has the simplest style and prays for both partners throughout. It can, therefore, dwell more happily on theological images of marriage rather

than on what duties each is going to try to perform.
The blessing still starts with the bride, but the groom
is included all the time. There is a pastoral aspect here
that is lacking in the others:

"Lord, may they both praise you when they are happy
and turn to you in their sorrows.
May they be glad that you help them in their work
and know that you are with them in their need.
May they pray to you in the community of the Church
and be your witnesses in the world."

It certainly has an affinity with the two new prefaces
looked at earlier.

Prayers after Communion
The first (No. 122) is a reworking of the Post-Communion in the 1570 Missal, with some material from the
1738 Paris Missal (De Vintimille's book). The new second prayer (No. 123) prays openly for the couple. The
third is also new (No. 124), though it, like the corresponding Prayer over the Gifts (No. 114) has a strong
eucharistic slant to it.

Blessing at the End of Mass
Once again, there are three texts. As we have seen,
the inspiration for this Visigothic feature came from
the 1950 German rite. Thus, the first prayer (No. 125)
is based on a longer version that first appears originally in the *Liber Ordinum*, but the Spanish efflores-
cence has been toned down to more sober Roman periods. The prayer is theocentric, pungent, and pastoral.

The second and third (Nos. 126 and 127) are both
new, but based on the Visigothic structure, with the
intercalated "Amens." Whereas the former gives each
person of the Trinity a special job to do, the latter is
based on the Cana theme and is therefore indirectly related to a medieval pontifical blessing contained in the

147

eleventh-century Canterbury Benedictional. It ends on an eschatological note, like so many other nuptial prayers:

"May he grant that, as you believe in his resurrection, so you may wait for him in joy and hope."

These prayers, of course, correspond with the other special blessings at the end of mass that appear in the Missal of Paul VI.

All in all, the provision of prayer in the 1969 *Ordo* is more than lavish when set alongside the austere provisions of the 1614 *Rituale* (for the marriage rite) and the 1570 Missal (for the nuptial mass). Moreover, an attempt has been made to introduce new theological emphases as well as a more pastoral tone to these prayers. It is to be hoped that pastors and couples will take great care in choosing (and, where appropriate, composing) such prayers as they would like for the marriage celebration.

LECTIONS AND CHANTS

The 1570 Missal has one epistle (Eph 5:22–33) and one single gospel (Mt 19:1–6). The new *Ordo* has, by contrast, *eight* Old Testament lections, *ten* New Testament readings, and *ten* gospels. When taken with the need to "enrich" the liturgy with this new *Ordo*, it can hardly be denied that any single one of these lections is inappropriate. Genesis and Tobit obviously figure prominently for the Old Testament (Gn 1:26–28, 31a; Gn 2: 18–24; Gn 24:48–51, 58–67; Tb 7:9–10, 11–15; Tb 8:5–10). But the covenant theme appears in the famous Jeremiah lection, which is a complete newcomer to the marriage liturgy (Jer. 31:31–32a, 33–34a).

Among the second readings are those we have met before (1 Cor 6:13c–15a, 17–20; and Eph 5), but there are choices that are more ecclesiological in their implications for the mission of the Church (Rom 12:1–2, 9–18) as well as for the ordinary life of the Christian community (1 Pt 3:1–9). This latter text is used by the Armenian rite at betrothal.[11]

The gospels include the indissolubility of marriage (Mt 19:3–6; Mk 10:6–9) as well as Cana (Jn 2:1–11). On the other hand, as in the epistles, there is a great deal of teaching about divine love (Mt 22:35–40; Jn 15:9–12; and Jn 12–16). Once more, marriage is increasingly seen as a *particular* relationship within the Church, but also as part of the *wider* life of love and service.

The chants reproduce psalmic material that we have encountered before (Ps 128) as well as hymns of praise and evocation (Ps 33 and 103). Whether or not these chants are used (with the alleluia verses before the gospel), the more popular hymns and songs will weigh more heavily with couples as they prepare for their marriage. Even within the English-speaking world, there exist considerable differences in wedding hymns, which tend to go in and out of popularity. Moreover, pastors will probably divide into those who are ready to indulge in the more overtly sentimental examples of these compositions and those who are more rigid in their views and tastes.

Music plays a more profound role in liturgical celebrations than many liturgically minded clerics will admit. Oftentimes it is the case that music, in all different shapes and sizes, serves powerfully to make the new and somewhat stark liturgies of the Western churches bearable to those who come to church and fail to identify with the rather cold and clinical language that many presiders use in their prayers—less still with the often outlandishly overblown language frequently used in the "welcomes" and "explanations" that seem to butter many public liturgies today.[12]

If a marriage liturgy is to have hymnody as a prominent feature, then it is probably best to divide these hymns according to their *genre*. Thus, an opening hymn should be one of praise and thanksgiving. A hymn between the readings should aid reflection on the meaning of the lections and the spirit of meditation; a hymn of quiet evocation is therefore a good choice to help build up to the gospel and the homily. Thereafter, the rite should not be interrupted until the rite of marriage itself is over. Where the eucharist is not celebrated, a rousing final hymn of dedication fits well with the nuptial blessing.

Other cultures will think quite differently from this Western scheme. Importantly, the hymns and chants serve to *interpret* the liturgical action rather than dominate it. "Flow" is an essential ingredient in any liturgy, and it is just as possible that a bad or inappropriate musical item may wreck the prayerful atmosphere of worship, and a windy celebrant who has insufficient confidence in the liturgy to speak for itself without introductions and explanations can reduce the worship of God to the level of a television interview.

LOCAL ADAPTATION

It is impossible to summarize here how the 1969 *Ordo* has been adapted to local countries' needs. Still, by way of preliminary, the Study Group that drew up the new rite had among its members not only experts in the teaching and practice of liturgy (e.g., Gy and Sicard), but members with strong Third World interests (e.g., Mejia from Colombia and Hofinger from the East Asian Pastoral Institute, Manila). No doubt due to their influence, the *Praenotanda* should encourage adaptations to local cultures, stipulating on the one hand that the consent of the couple and the nuptial blessing should always be given, as well as warning on the other hand that adaptations should be according to "the Christian spirit and to the liturgy" ("Introduction," No. 18).

Among the countries of the Western world, however, considerable adaptation has already taken place. Thus, the German *Feier der Trauung*[13] of 1975 makes two significant alterations in the order. The first follows the German practice of associating the ring giving closely with the consent of the partners. This was written into the 1950 German service, and it was examined by the Study Group as one of three distinct structures to the rite, but rejected for the official Roman version. The second is more radical and concerns the shape of the whole service when celebrated within the eucharist. The nuptial blessing in the 1969 text occupies its traditional position, immediately before the Peace, and it was assumed that this time-honored liturgical climax would remain, because of its associations in the Western liturgies. The only other position that it has occupied in the nuptial mass was after Communion in the Visigothic as well as some later Spanish and French rites. However, the 1975 German rite places the nuptial blessing after the marriage rite and before the prayer of the faithful. This is quite legitimate, since the *Praenotanda* state (No. 14):

"Within the rite of the sacrament of matrimony, the arrangement of its parts may be varied."[14]

It could be argued that to juxtapose the nuptial blessing with the giving of consent interprets the irreducible minimum required of any marriage rite more faithfully than the official text itself, since consent and blessing are brought so closely together. Moreover, the nuptial blessing before communion arose at a time when special blessings (e.g., of oil and other material things) usually occupied this position between the eucharistic prayer and communion. When the blessing is done (on this logic), let it be done at the point of blessing within the eucharist. We no longer live in that kind of liturgical climate, with those expectations, since the only time when a special blessing normally takes place between the eucharistic prayer and communion nowadays is at the Chrism mass on Holy Thursday. Here the option actually written into the new rite to bless the oils instead at the end of the liturgy of the word is normally taken.[15] Furthermore, the nuptial blessing comes before communion in old Western rites because it appeared in this position long before anyone ever thought of having a rite of consent before the mass began.

The French brought out a rite in 1969[16] that made two interesting innovations. First, the formulas for consent are more varied, and they involve at times the bride and groom reciting parts of the vows *together*. This is imaginative and could come across powerfully to congregations as well as to the couple themselves as a new way of symbolizing and expressing the union that they are sealing. Second, the French text also provides a native French form of nuptial blessing in addition to the three official versions. It avoids both of the unsatisfactory features of the official texts: it prays for both partners throughout and does not differentiate roles in a way that would be incongruous with contemporary French society. The new blessing also stresses the ecclesial character of marriage and the common witness of the couple to the values of the Kingdom in the world.

The introductory notes to the 1969 French *rituel pour la célébration du mariage* also make a clear distinction between *three* types of normally noneucharistic marriage: with a catechumen, with a baptized non-Catholic, and with someone not baptized. Moreover, under the last heading, it is envisaged that the person concerned may or may not be an unbeliever, or may have another religion altogether. Official panels of advisors obviously help local pastors with this kind of case. This is yet one manifestation of the modern Western church, living in a multifaith, multicultural world.

In the English-speaking world, the official response to the inherent liberties of the 1969 Roman *Ordo* has been poor by comparison.[17] (A recent investigation conducted by the International Commission for English in the Liturgy [ICEL] has confined this overall view.) Whereas the rites for England and Wales, and those for the United States, have reproduced the Latin text with little adaptation, the 1980 Irish book abounds in alternative forms at the consent and even has an additional nuptial blessing. Most innovative of all is the inclusion of a special prayer, to be recited by the couple, either after the giving of the rings or else after Communion. It is clear that the English-speaking Catholic world is at an early stage in liturgical adaptation. Imagination is not something that people can be taught, but one suspects that the "epoch of rubricism" is still partially with us.[18]

OTHER CHURCHES

Care has been taken throughout this study to set the Catholic rites within a full historical perspective, which (after the Reformation) becomes ecumenical in scope. Chapter 5 introduced some of the ideas that were in circulation among the churches of the Reformation as they set about the task of adjusting their marriage liturgies in the light of changing needs and enrichment through a better knowledge of antiquity.

Alongside the Second Vatican Council came a series of liturgical reforms that changed the outward face of the marriage rites of these churches. Thus, the British Methodist rite was already in the late 1960's working on a model that would place the rite in the context of a synaxis. Moreover, it produced a particularly fine Jewish-inspired thanksgiving, which could be used on its own as a conclusion to a noneucharistic service, or else make up the preface of the eucharistic prayer when the fuller form of the rite was used. Written by David Tripp, it is worth quoting in full:

"Praise God, King of the Universe,
who has created all things,
and man in his own image.
Praise God, who has created courtship and marriage,
joy and gladness, feasting and laughter,
pleasure and delight, love, brotherhood, peace and
   fellowship.

"Praise God, who has sent Jesus Christ,
to save us from sin and redeem our love from
   selfishness,
and has given us the Holy Spirit
to make us one with each other and with him.

"And so with all the company of heaven,
we join in the unending hymn of praise . . ."[19]

By contrast, the United Methodist Church (United States) produced an even more original solution to the question of special blessing amid solemn prayer for the couple. In their 1979 *Service of Christian Marriage*,[20] the long prayer at the end of the noneucharistic form of the service can be adapted for use within the eucharistic prayer when the fuller form of the rite is used. Thus, the "thanksgiving series" becomes the preface and the "supplication for the couple" becomes an extension of the epiclesis. This is an interesting way of expressing particular concern for the couple within the body of the great prayer. It seems inspired by the old Western preface and *hanc igitur*.

The American *Book of Common Prayer* (1979),[21] however, has a number of original features. First, the couple may be "presented" for marriage by family and representatives of the congregation. This clearly recalls the sacrament of baptism. Then, the intercession and nuptial blessing are brought together at the end of the marriage rite itself in a way that reproduces the German Roman Catholic order; both were probably working simultaneously at this shape. Finally, and most original of all, the 1979 Prayer Book makes sense of the lingering Anglican practice of having *both* passive consent *and* active vow. Following the integration of wedding and mass that we observed in the Metz tradition, the compilers of the new Prayer Book went one stage further, so that the liturgy takes the following shape:

Entrance

Preface, explaining the reasons for marriage (Cranmer, adapted)

Consent: passive

Question to the *congregation* for help and support, with response

Liturgy of the word, with the homily

Consent: active (vow)

Ring blessing

Ring giving

Declaration that the couple are married (Mt 19:6)

Solemn intercessions

Nuptial blessing (two forms)

The peace

Eucharist (when celebrated) follows from the offertory

This rite not only stresses the congregational character of the service, but it heightens the drama of the consent of the couple. At the start, they are asked if they will carry out the duties and obligations of Christian marriage. The congregation is asked to support them.

Marriage is therefore a corporate business, not a private agreement. Then the word of God is read and expounded to the assembly. Only after this do the couple make their full and active vows to each other, having come forward to the celebrant from their seats for the second time in the liturgy. This form has been introduced into other Provinces of the Anglican Communion.

The Church of England's *Alternative Service Book* (1980) contains a marriage service that follows the main thrust of modern revision, but is open both to the older Cranmerian shape as well as to the modern synaxis-based rite. It therefore has more flexibility of structure. Whereas other modern rites do not mention the traditional "giving away" of the bride (the custom persists in many countries), English conservatism allows it to happen, but it is optional. Moreover, although two rings are envisaged as the norm, as in other modern rites, there is still provision for one ring, but the bride must verbalize her acceptance of it, using a formula similar to the one noted in Chapter Five in the 1860 Primitive Methodist rite. There is a rich anthology of prayers in a section at the end of the rite. Some of these are old, others new. Particularly fine is a long Jewish-inspired prayer, drafted by Bishop Hugh Montefiore and his wife Elizabeth Montefiore. Its inspiration is both biblical and traditional, and it also betrays signs of being based on the first of the three nuptial blessings in the 1969 Roman *Ordo:*

"We praise you, Father, that you have made all
    things,
and hold all things in being.
In the beginning you created the universe,
and made mankind in your own likeness:
because it was not good for them to be alone,
you created them male and female

and in marriage you join man and woman as one
   flesh,
teaching us that what you have united
may never be divided.
We praise you that you have made this holy mystery
a symbol of the marriage of Christ with his Church,
and an image of your eternal covenant with your
   people.
And we pray for your blessing on this man and this
   woman,
who come before you as partners
and heirs together of your promises.
Grant that this man may love his wife
as Christ loves his bride the Church,
giving himself for it
and cherishing it as his own flesh;
and grant that this woman may love her husband
and follow the example of those holy women
whose praises are sung in the Scriptures.
Strengthen them with your grace
that they may be witnesses of Christ to others.
Let them live to see their children's children,
and bring them at the last
to fullness of life with your saints
in the Kingdom of heaven:
through Jesus Christ our Lord. Amen."[22]

NOTES

1. See Chapter Five, n. 16.

2. See the English text in *The Rites of the Catholic Church as Revised at the Second Vatican Ecumenical Council*, I (New York:
Pueblo, 1976), pp. 534–538 (Latin text of "Praenotanda" in
Ordo Celebrandi Matrimonium (Vatican City: Typis Polyglottis),
pp. 7–10).

3. *The Rites*, pp. 539–546 (*Ordo Celebrandi Matrimonium*, op.
cit., pp. 11–16).

4. See Stevenson, *Nuptial Blessing: A Study of Christian Marriage Rites* (Alcuin Club Collections 64) (London: SPCK, 1982, and New York: Oxford University Press, 1983), p. 156. The text as Baxter proposed it avoids the didactic qualities of the Prayer Book formula at this point, and reads as follows:

"These two persons, A and B, being lawfully married according to God's ordinance, I do pronounce them husband and wife. And those whom God hath joined together, let no man put asunder."

The writer had occasion to ask Père Dalmais what he thought the new Roman Catholic formula was. He looked at the Latin text, and grinned mischievously at me with the words, "Oh! Mais c'est une épiclèse, n'est-ce pas?" ("Oh! But it's an epiclesis, isn't it?) For all the politics behind contemporary revision, modern rites show a remarkable convergence on this type of presidential formula.

5. See Korbinian Ritzer, *Formen, Riten, und religioses Brachtum der Eheschliessung in den christlichen Kirchen des estern Jahrtausends* (Liturgiewissenschaftliche Quellen und Forschungen 38) (Munster: Aschendorff, 1962), pp. 258–260. Hereafter this is referred to as *Ritzer*.

6. *The Rites*, pp. 547–552 (*Ordo Celebrandi Matrimonium*, pp. 17–21).

7. *The Rites*, pp. 553–557 (*Ordo Celebrandi Matrimonium*, pp. 22–26).

8. *The Rites*, pp. 561–570 (*Ordo Celebrandi Matrimonium*, pp. 30–39); see also Gy, "Le nouveau rituel romain du mariage," *La Maison-Dieu* 98 (1969):128–139.

9. Text of prayer in *Ritzer*, p. 371 (No. 2608). This prayer, based on a Gelasian original, was used, in an adapted form, as the Prayer over the Gifts ("secret") in some late medieval rites instead of the corresponding Gregorian text; for a discussion of this point and its possible theological implications, see Stevenson, "The Marriage Rites of Mediaeval Scandinavia: A Fresh Look," pp. 554f. and 557.

10. See H. A. Wilson, *The Benedictional of Archbishop Robert*, p. 157 ("benedic, domine, anulum hunc"); for textual variants in later books using this prayer, see Jean-Baptiste Molin and Protais Mutembe, *Le rituel du mariage en France du XIIè au XVIè siècle* (Théologie Historique 26) (Paris: Beauchesne, 1973), p. 319 (no. 2).

11. *The Rites*, pp. 558–561 (*Ordo Celebrandi Matrimonium*, pp. 27–30).

12. Aidan Kavanagh, *Elements of Rite: A Handbook of Liturgical Style* (New York: Pueblo, 1982), pp. 101f. and passim.

13. *Die Feier der Trauung in den Katholischen Bistumern des Deutschen Sprachgebietes* (Einsiedeln and Köln: Benziger; Freiburg and Basel: Herder; Regensburg; Pustet; Wien: Herder; Salzburg: St. Peter; Linz: Veritas, 1975). See p. 129, on the German structure, in the 1950 *Collectio Rituum*, discussed by the Study Group.

14. See *The Rites*, p. 537 (*Ordo Celebrandi Matrimonium*, p. 9).

15. See *The Rites*, p. 520, para. 12; see also *Ordo Benedicendi Oleum Catechumenorum et Infirmorum et Conficiendi Chrisma* (Vatican City: Typis Polyglottis, 1971), p. 8. Jounel, in writing of the new Chrism Mass, seems to *prefer* the option of blessing the oils after the Liturgy of the Word, on the grounds of being closely connected with the synaxis of the day; see P. Jounel, "La consécration du chrême et la bénédiction des saintes huiles," *La Maison-Dieu* 112 (1972):74f. (whole article, pp. 70–83).

16. *Rituel pour la célébration du mariage* (Paris: Brepols, 1969). See also R. Béraudy, M. Leprêtre, and P. Lionnet (Eds.), *Célébrer le mariage* (Paris: Desclée, 1981), which is an unofficial publication, with several new liturgical texts, and many suggestions for pastoral implementation.

17. *The Roman Ritual* (Dublin: Veritas, 1980). The text of the "Prayer of the Newly Married Couple" (p. 29) is deliberately phrased in a kind of "blank verse," not unlike the medieval Sarum marriage vow. The text is as follows:

"We thank you, Lord,
and we praise you
for bringing us
to this happy day.

"You have given us to each other.
Now, together we give ourselves to you.

"We ask you, Lord:
make us one in our love;
keep us one in your peace.

"Protect our marriage.
Bless our home.
Make us gentle.
Keep us faithful.

"And when our life is over
unite us again
where parting is no more
in the kingdom of your love.

"There we will praise you
in the happiness and peace
of our eternal home. Amen"

On this kind of participation of the couple, see pp. 203ff.
For the rite of England and Wales, see *The Marriage Rite* (Birmingham and Dublin, 1970). For the rite for the United
States, see *Rite of Marriage* (New York: Pueblo, 1969).

18. On acculturation, see Anscar Chupungco, "The Cultural
Adaptation of the Rite of Marriage," in *La Celebrazione
Cristiana Del Matrimonio* (Studia Anselmia 93; Analecta
Liturgica 11) (Rome: Pontificio Ateneo S. Anselmo, 1986),
pp. 145–162.

19. Text in *The Methodist Service Book* (London: Methodist
Publishing House, 1975), p. E13.

20. Text in *A Service of Christian Marriage* (Supplemental Worship Resources 5) (Nashville, TN: Abingdon, 1979), pp. 44f.

21. *Book of Common Prayer* (New York: Seabury, 1979), pp.
422–432. There is also a form for "The Blessing of a Civil

Marriage," pp. 433–434; and a form for "An Order for Marriage," pp. 435–436, following the "agenda" pattern that corresponds to the "Rite 3" orders for the eucharist, pp. 400–405, and burial, pp. 506–507. See also Marion Hatchett, *Commentary on the American Prayer Book* (New York: Seabury, 1980), pp. 427ff. This rite is discussed in Stevenson, *Nuptial Blessing,* pp. 192–195; it has influenced marriage rites in the Anglican Churches of New Zealand, Australia, and Canada, and is generally regarded as the finest in the Anglican Communion today. See below, Chapter 7, n. 9 for the *CCT* rite, strongly influenced by it also.

22. Text of the rite in the *Alternative Service Book* (London: SPCK, 1980), pp. 285–304; quoted prayer, ibid., p. 299.

The Future

Chapter Seven

Unresolved Issues

To suggest that a new liturgy can resolve all issues is a pretentious idea to propound, especially when the rite in question is marriage, which earlier in this study we noted to be, in human terms, a way of coping with disturbance.[1] Indeed, if rite is to be about reality, then there is not only inherent disturbance, there is also another essential ingredient of rite, ambiguity.[2] If the marriage liturgy were to consist of certain predetermined issues, facts, and experiences, then we would reach a hazardous situation in which every single marriage was the same.

Liturgy is, by its very nature, what Price described in another context as "assiduous supposing."[3] Liturgy is about trying to be something that we hope to be but aren't yet. Marriage rites, therefore, have a peculiar way of "supposing assiduously" before God and humankind—the "supposition" being lifelong mutual commitment, and the "assiduousness" being the underlying hope and fear that this might even be the case. There is ambiguity here because liturgy is about evoking, not defining; it is about hidden and subtle forms of meaning, not just about the obvious.

In Chapter Six, we looked at the component parts of the 1969 Roman *Ordo* and noted that in this rite there is a far greater degree of choice of readings than has been known so far in the West. Moreover, some of these readings are old war-horses that are obvious in their immediate meaning because they apply straight away to marriage (Mt 19:3–6), whereas others are less obvious, and more ambiguous, because they are about the whole of Christian life, of which marriage is a part (Jn 15:9–12). Therefore, the new liturgy is more ambiguous than its predecessor. In the choice of word, yes; and certainly in the kind of flexibility of shape and, to some extent, form that may be given to new rites that are composed for other cultures.

Liturgical reform cannot settle all questions, particularly of marriage. This is not to deny that in the history of the liturgy there are some issues that have a habit of recurring precisely because they are about conflicting or shifting views of what is going on in the rite.[4] It is to eight of these issues that we must now turn. Some of them have appeared before. Some of them are not about what the "official" text, drafted by the expert, says, but rather concern how ordinary couples "hear" the rite they celebrate on their wedding day regardless of what the professional liturgist may tell them.

WHO "DOES" THE MARRIAGE?
This question itself is related to the "irreducible minimum" question that arose out of medieval scholasticism, the Council of Trent, and Counter-Reformation Catholicism. Generations of Roman Catholic couples, and others as well, have been taught that even though they have to go through a sometimes lengthy public liturgy, it is they and they alone who "confect the sacrament." Sacrament confectors are beginning to appear as something belonging to a bygone age. Theology does develop. One can see why such a view permeated recent centuries, but it does not mix well with the spirit of the new liturgy, and even the *Praenotanda* of the new rite do isolate the consent of the partners *and*

the nuptial blessing as those ingredients of the marriage liturgy that are essential. Whatever may have been intended by making the couple the sole ministers of the sacrament, it is certainly true that many people today, including theologians, see in the isolation of consent something not only stark but also lacking in the ecclesial dimension. It may be "neat" but it lacks the Church. David Power notes that ". . . to concentrate, for example, only on the moment of marriage when the promises are made" is an action and an attitude that "is to refuse the interplay of images."[5]

Such an analysis of post-medieval Western thinking, shared by many churches of the Reformation, gets right to the heart of the matter. To opt for a one-sided theology of marriage does great disservice to the rest of the liturgy, because it inevitably makes the remainder of the liturgy look second class: rich as it is supposed to be, significant in meaning as it originally was. So the *Praenotanda*'s insistence on the nuptial blessing is an important way of stressing the liturgical and ecclesial character of the sacrament, presided over by an ordained representative of the rest of the Church.

This tension already existed in the 1614 *Rituale*, where the consent of the partners was immediately followed by the priestly joining formula, *ego vos in matrimonium conjungo*. While the experts interpreted this formula in a secondary manner, the *rite itself* could teach otherwise, especially when the priest wrapped his stole round the couple's hands while reciting that formula. Here certainly is an unnecessary ambiguity if ever there was one, particularly as it is now known that members of the Study Group who drew up the 1969 *Ordo* regarded this formula as implying that it was the *priest* and not the *couple* who performed the sacrament.[6]

The real heart of the matter is not about settling who utters the "magic words." It is about the levels of relationship within the liturgical assembly. Once it is insisted upon that the nuptial blessing should be given (which the 1614 *Rituale* did not), then the relationships are better established. The spotlight falls on the couple; the presbyter is there as liturgical president in a properly constituted liturgical assembly. Moreover, the somewhat high-profile nature of the old formula, *"I join you together,"* is now replaced by a richer liturgical language that is full of references to *God* as the one who joins the couple together. The old self-consciousness has gone. Yet, it is true to say that in the churches of the Reformation it will not quite do to downgrade the role of the minister in the assembly itself. Later rites of the Reformation show a gradual shift toward the minister as president, as representative of the rest of the Church, sometimes tying his stole round the hands of the couple while reciting not the 1614 formula but the Matthean pronouncement, "What God has joined together . . ."[7]

To the question, "Who does the marriage?" it must firmly be answered that the spirit of the new liturgy is far more corporate and ecclesial than its predecessor, that *all* marriage rites should nowadays take place within a full liturgy, and that the two elements of the marriage liturgy that focus on its "deep structures" and underlying attitudes (human resolve and divine blessing) are best kept together as a theological unity. Once again, the East can help the West out of what is a theological and pastoral cul-de-sac. Local pastors can do the Church a great service if they help couples understand this essential truth. To carry on talking about confecting the sacrament through consent is to run the risk of rendering the rest of the liturgy, so carefully put together and insisted upon after the Second Vatican Council, null and void.

Although the precise time at which the bridal blessing emerged in the West is not altogether clear, the liturgies of the Roman Sacramentaries opted for a bridal blessing for the simple reason that the marriage rites of pagan Rome stressed the bride's change of state. The bride becomes, in every sense, a "legal person," which is an important change to express in liturgy. Indeed, it may well be that the deliberate introduction of the Ephesians analogy into the nuptial blessing (it appears in the Gregorian text, but not in either the Leonine or the Gelasian) was in some sense a means of justifying this bridal focus: Christ marries the Church, prepared as a bride; therefore, the bride of this marriage is also prepared and presented to her husband.[8]

Admittedly, in much of contemporary Western culture, marriage is still perceived as "the bride's day." And the drama of the liturgy so often interprets it in this way: the bride enters the church on her father's arm and leaves it on her husband's. There cannot be more focus on the bride than that, whatever the text of the liturgy may happen to say by way of mutuality and modern understandings of equality.

Nonetheless, as we saw in Chapter Two, what the Roman Sacramentaries stressed, the rites of the rest of Western Europe (and the whole of the East) implicitly denied. There are precious few bridal blessings that appear in the non-Roman Western rites, and when they appear, they bear the marks of Roman influence. The anomaly is heightened further by the fact that the nuptial blessing came to be restricted to first timers only, so that many marriages involving widows in the later medieval West must have omitted the nuptial blessing itself but have been replete with the other blessings of both bride and groom. The fact remains, however, that deep in the corporate memory of the Roman rite lies an instinct that wants to reserve the blessing to the bride. We find it in Ambrose and Augustine, in the Sacramentaries, in the later medieval rites, and it was obviously represented on the *Consilium Liturgicum*.

The bridal blessing was, indeed, the one issue that caused the most difficulty when the new rite was drawn up. On the one hand, there were those who let historical research affect their attitudes to the future. On the other hand, there were those who saw something special and important in the Roman tradition. The parallel between this duality and the Roman Canon (with its emphasis on offering and its lack of a eucharistic epiclesis) is unavoidable. The parallel can be taken further, however, in the resort to alternatives as a means of enrichment and the lingering Westernism of bridal focus in the second nuptial blessing (and partly in the third). The conflict of interest is further demonstrated when the Constitution on the Sacred Liturgy explicitly states (78) "the prayer for the bride, duly amended to remind both spouses of their equal obligations to remain faithful, may be said in another tongue," while the *Praenotanda* (para. 6) still speak of "the special nuptial blessing of the bride."[9] This sort of contradiction might have been dealt with more decisively; it is similar to the theological problems posed by compiling the Fourth Eucharistic Prayer from good Eastern sources but rewriting them in order to conform to the *ingenium romanum*, with a split epiclesis.[10]

There are two other issues concerning the nuptial blessing that have also been left partially unresolved. The first concerns its position. We have seen how old Roman custom blessed the bride immediately before Communion. This evolved at a time when there was no rite of consent before mass. Tradition lingered, so that this blessing remained in its old position, even after the Vatican Council reforms. It is interesting that the Constitution on the Sacred Liturgy should say nothing at all about its place in the order of things. Also interesting is that the *Praenotanda* (para. 14) should permit variation within the different parts of the rite. And whereas the French, American, and other versions place the nuptial blessing in the old sequence, the German rite (1975) places the nuptial blessing immediately after the rite of marriage, so that solemn blessing becomes closely associated with consent and ring giving.[11]

This, it would seem, is a preferable procedure, because it interprets the meaning of the rite more accurately and avoids separating important foci from each other, which could result in a fragmented liturgy precisely at a time when we want to avoid such a fragmentation. Human resolve and divine blessing are what Christian marriage is all about. Therefore they hold these together, in sequence, so that the one follows on from the other. Such an order would serve to make any "priestly formula" immediately after consent not only meaningless but redundant.

The second issue is about the relationship between the nuptial blessing and other "blessings" within the rite. The new prayers (unlike the British Methodist and Church of England texts quoted in Chapter Six) follow the old Roman literary structure. The British compositions, by contrast, follow the Jewish-Eastern formulation. This issue has been raised by David Power[12] in the following way:

Tradition	*Roman euchology*
Thanksgiving for past and present	Address that includes motivation
Invocation	Invocation over
Intercession	and petition combined

Such a scheme gives us not only the difference between traditional and some modern compositions, it also shows how the old Roman literary shape dominates the new nuptial blessings. But the matter goes even further, because in the marriage liturgy there are three other types of prayer that may be described as related to the notion of blessing.

First, there are the mass prayers. These invariably pray for the couple in an obvious way. Second, there is the blessing of the rings. These prayers, old as well as new, take the literary form of the medieval era, beginning with "bless . . ." (In the Middle Ages, the marriage rite would have been full of other prayers of this kind said over the couple, before mass.) Third, the mass ends with a special blessing, composed in a simplified version of the old Visigothic structure, with the jussive subjunctive in each of the verbs ("May God do this and that"), each paragraph ending with an intercalated "Amen."

There is no incongruity between the nuptial blessing and the mass prayers. But there are different kinds of incongruity between the nuptial blessing and the other two. First, there is a linguistic incoherence between the blessing of the rings and the solemn prayer over the bride (and groom) before Communion. Second, there is a slight theological incongruity between these fine Visigothic prayers and the nuptial blessing itself, precisely because the nuptial blessing is still bridal in its heart, whereas the Visigothic prayers are focused on both partners, and the entire assembly by implication. In other words, the revisers have used their knowledge of history, but perhaps not enough.

DOMESTIC VERSUS ECCLESIAL
The new rite follows in the great tradition of Roman rites that take place within the Church. Part of the collective memory of Western rites from the twelfth century onwards is not just about including consent

within the basic framework of the rite; it is also about making marriage celebrations *public*. On the other hand, we have seen two different types of domestic rite that appear to have been much used in the Middle Ages.

One is represented by such rites as the eleventh-century North Italian formulary, which consists of a simple set of prayers for use at home as a marriage rite said by the priest, without any public mass. (It is conceivable that this rite was used in conjunction with a mass, but the two rites would have been separate.) The other is represented by those domestic rites that are ancillary to later marriage celebrations. Here, the priest goes to the home after the mass and blesses the bridal chamber. These rites are suppressed by the Reformers. They only appear after Trent in those areas that assiduously adhere to their old customs (e.g., France). On the other hand, there are the Eastern and Visigothic rites that still see marriage as a passage, from one form of life to another. Thus we have a series of short services, which are to do with betrothal and preparation and which lead to a longer liturgy, the marriage celebration. Sometimes these rites end with a domestic rite of some sort, e.g., the blessing of the chamber and the removal of the crowns.

The *Praenotanda* (para. 18) end with a nod in the direction of cultures where marriage celebrations normally are spread over a number of days. Clearly, it was envisaged that these cultures should have their customs christianized without being Westernized. Once again, however, the question of the ecclesial character and the liturgical relationships within the assembly is raised. How successful is the new rite of marriage? In Chapter Eight, we shall suggest ways in which it can be considerably enriched further by phasing marriage over the three stages that Van Gennep identified many years ago and that are still inherent to the Eastern rites of today as embodying the "deep structures" of the marriage liturgy.

Meanwhile, the relationship between marriage as "domestic" and marriage as "ecclesial" is worth pondering. It is quite possible for marriage to be authentically "ecclesial" and take place at home, as generations of North American Protestants have known for long. Indeed, these celebrations even express something of the pioneering spirit of early North American settlers. But they mix strangely with certain parts of Europe, particularly in England, where every marriage has to take place either in the Registry Office, in a church building, or in a building set apart for worship by other religions.[13]

But there are immediate practical implications, too, wherever the marriage is celebrated, for the relationship between home and church comes to a head in such matters as where the respective families are seated and whether or not there should be photography, and even videotaping. It is a pity if the popular customs of separating the families persists, especially when one family may be considerably underrepresented. The Church is one, not divided (or at least one hopes so). Photography and videotaping, on the other hand, can obtrude into the liturgy to such an extent that it ceases to be an act of worship. Churches that specialize in this sort of commercialization should either think again, or else invest in even more technical equipment that is hardly visible at all during the liturgy.[14]

However, it must be freely admitted that marriage in the Judaeo-Christian tradition has its roots in the family, and we have seen enough evidence to assume that early Christians celebrated their marriage at home. Although later developments took the church away from the home for such more overtly ecclesial activities as the eucharist, there is still enough evidence to assume that people continued to regard marriage as something appropriate to the home, even if that meant importing a priest to recite a few prayers in a dead tongue over the happy couple. Moreover, the medieval blessing of the chamber makes explicit one aspect of marriage that the new rites regard with some care (as do the Reformers), namely, sexuality. To bless the marriage chamber, or at least to say prayers near the marriage bed, is to ritualize sexuality in a most wholesome manner. Sexuality, which is so fundamental to a biblical understanding of marriage and so natural to the human race, is a theme that does not appear explicit in many marriage texts, although the 1980 Church of England preface to the rite dares to say:

"Marriage is given that husband and wife may comfort and help each other, living faithfully together in deed and in plenty, in sorrow and in joy. It is given, that with delight and tenderness they may know each other in love, and, through the joy of their bodily union, may strengthen the union of their hearts and lives. It is given, that they may have children and be blessed in caring for them and bringing them up in accordance with God's will, to his praise and glory."[15]

But whatever is said in church, prayers at home, whether part of a sequence of church rites ending there or part of a full service celebrated in a domestic context, can have far more force in ritualizing reality, namely, that the couple indeed do make love when they are left alone together and that this lovemaking is part of the natural instincts and affections implanted in us by God.

A domestic rite is clearly a gap. No one is suggesting that, like its medieval counterpart, it should include a warning from a celibate presbyter that the couple should abstain from sexual union for three nights (the so-called "three nights of Tobit").[16] But there ought to be some forms of domestic prayer, with or without the presence of the priest, that pray for the married life of the couple in the home that they are going to inhabit together. Modern secular customs frequently distance the marriage feast from the home. Indeed, there are often times when the couple may live far away from where the celebration takes place. This is one more reason for having such a set of prayers.

In sum, while it is true that "domestic" versus "ecclesial" is not an issue formally raised by the new *Ordo* (except insofar as new rites may be written for cultures in which marriage is normally celebrated at home), history and comparative liturgy raise the issue. And it could be partly resolved by further investigation, followed by liturgical provisions.

THE ROLE OF SCRIPTURE
The new *Ordo* provides every couple with a bevy of lections, perhaps even a baffling assortment. The relationship between readings and the rest of the rite is more subtle, for it concerns also the question of biblical themes in prayers and (indeed) the fundamental question of what biblical themes are appropriate and how they are to be handled.

In the early medieval West, the Gregorian Sacramentary became standard throughout the orbit of Roman influence. Furthermore, the epistle lections that most frequently came to be read with that venerable mass set were either 1 Corinthians 6:15–20 or 1 Corinthians 7:32–35. Yet the central biblical theme for the nuptial blessing is the Ephesians analogy, studiously unread in the mass. It is interesting to note that this pericope takes over in the 1570 Missal.

The first question is whether the traditional biblical lections are adequate.[17] The answer will doubtless reflect the theological attitudes of the person concerned. My overall view is that passages in the Bible that reflect *theologically* on marriage are certainly appropriate for today, even if (as in the Ephesians analogy) they will require careful exposition. Those passages on the other hand that reflect little more than the cultural milieu of the Bible (and there are few of these, e.g., Eccl 26:1–4, 16–21) are not so helpful, nor are they so full of good pastoral and therefore theological images and themes.

The second question concerns the relationship between the lections and the prayers. In Chapter Two, we looked at the Eastern rites and saw how biblical imagery was worked into some quite lengthy prayers (e.g., the Armenian rite). Moreover, there were times when these prayers reflected the pericopes read in the liturgy concerned. Nowadays, knowledge of the Bible is not what it once was in certain spheres of church life. Because of this, and the increased attention to the Bible that is being paid in all the Western churches, it would be an excellent principle if a couple who request the *first* nuptial blessing, which uses the Ephesians analogy strongly, should *also* have the Ephesians passage read as the second reading; indeed, other mass prayers using this theme could also be selected in this way. No one would want to let the liturgy degenerate into one of those didactic "theme services" in which the worship of God lies shredded on the floor like a piece of pulped garlic. Liturgy is supposed to have its own subtlety. At the same time, it should also have its own inner coherence. Looking broadly at the use of scripture in the new rite, therefore, it would seem that the more choice one has in lections, the more the question of inner coherence is raised. It is to this that we must now turn in relation to the prayers.

The 1969 *Ordo* makes much creative use of tradition. The nuptial blessing now appears in three forms, the first two of which lean heavily on older Latin themes. Similarly, the blessings at the end are Visigothic in shape, although only the first is a direct borrowing from a recognized source; the other two are fresh compositions. Other sources have been noted and discussed in Chapter Six.

The question, however, needs to be asked, "Do they cohere?" Kathleen Hughes has recently raised this issue, and there are signs that her work is going to result in a fresh collection of liturgical texts for the English-speaking world. At root, what she is saying is that a collect, a preface, or any other liturgical formulary needs to be not only beautiful, evocative, and rhetorical, it also needs to have a coherence within itself so that, for example, the opening address in a collect relates directly to what is later prayed for. Her researches were based as much upon patristic reading as upon modern linguistic analysis. Prayers should, therefore, consist of the following ingredients:

Opening address: appropriate naming of God; the naming and attributes of God ought to cohere with subsequent petition and have variety.

Petition: the community is both *receiver* and *subject* of God's gracious activity. The petition is therefore integral to the prayer and needs to express both its perceived relationship with God *and* what it wants to do.

Conclusion: this should be in a Trinitarian form.[18]

While the three new prefaces would pass Hughes' test reasonably well, the nuptial blessings clearly do not because their compromised character is so problematical that the inner coherence that they might have gained has been lost. Indeed, Hughes' criteria would be better met by the old Gregorian nuptial blessing than the new form that is based upon it. Similarly, the Opening Prayers result in the old form (No. 106) being more satisfactory than the third (No. 108). Moreover, the third Prayer over the Gifts (No. 114) has some fine ideas, but one senses that if Hughes were to work on it the result would be an even finer rendering of the eucharistic theology of that prayer. The danger of succinct, modern prayers is that they seem to do little more than hand out information. One issue of primal importance in this particular discussion we have already raised from time to time, namely the interaction of a theological or biblical image and its pastoral application to the people concerned. This relates in part to the remarks we have just made about the use of scripture in the liturgy. Images like the Ephesians analogy and the creation of Adam and Eve need careful handling if they are not to be "heard" by ordinary people as propounding a culture-bound message about women.

Clearly, the opening address of prayer ought to have a direct relationship to what is prayed for later on. The new English texts are therefore to be welcomed as not only better translations of the Latin 1969 *Ordo* but improvements in their own right. It is also to be hoped that other new texts will be provided.

ECUMENISM
The 1969 *Ordo* now places the marriage between a Catholic and a non-Catholic in the course of a proper liturgy, and it even allows it to be celebrated during a nuptial mass, although the rules do state that the non-Catholic should not generally receive Communion. There is a great deal to be said for keeping these options and for challenging the assumptions behind them. First of all, the ecumenical movement has pro-

duced a climate all over the Roman Catholic world that is at different phases in development. Within the English-speaking world alone, this differs in Ireland, England, and parts of North America.

Second, the relationship between the Roman Catholic Church and other Churches is itself a variable factor. Rome and the Orthodox Churches have long had a theoretical relationship of accepting the validity of each other's orders and sacraments. Paul VI singled out the Anglican Communion, which he got to know first hand earlier in his life, as having a special place in the ecumenical dialogue between the Holy See and the Churches of the Reformation. Dialogue continues between Roman Catholics and Lutherans, the Reformed Churches, Methodists, and Baptists. To cap it all, the 1982 Lima Statement of Baptism, Eucharist, and Ministry brought together all the major mainstream churches of the world. Nothing will ever be quite the same again.

The tender issues of geography and the churches involved have to be weighed carefully in the planning of the celebration. Indeed, the greatest opportunity for spiritual growth in inter-Church marriages is for each Church represented to learn more about the *ordinary religious consciousness* of the other. Thus, there may be a marriage between a Catholic and a non-Catholic where the non-Catholic partner belongs to a Church whose eucharistic theology is far removed in style and liturgy from that of the Roman Catholic parish concerned. Variety within the Catholic Church is also a growing phenomenon. On the other hand, there will be many couples among whom the non-Catholic partner holds a view of the eucharist that is so embedded in the liturgical and ecumenical movements of this century as to make refusal of Communion not only a disappointment but a gesture perceived as a deliberate hurt. In

180

such circumstances, to give the eucharistic bread and wine to one partner and to deny it to the other runs the risk of undermining the theological connection between marriage and eucharist. Deeper, personal questions are involved here, as well as those of authority within the Church, and pastors should handle them with care and sensitivity. A possible liturgy for these (and other) occasions has been produced by the Consultation on Common Texts,[19] which draws on the modern marriage rites of the member Churches. The two ingredients highlighted as being essential in the 1969 *Ordo* (consent and nuptial blessing) are safeguarded. There are also enrichments, which include involvement of the families at the start of the service, as well as the Episcopalian rite's distinct treatment of the consent of the partners before the Liturgy of the Word and their active vow after it. The entire service is set within a Liturgy of the Word and provision is made to include the eucharist as well. Significantly, this rite relies heavily on the 1979 Episcopalian service. Once again, we encounter a better position for the nuptial blessing—at the end of the marriage, not (as in 1969) just before the Communion. To place the nuptial blessing invariably within the marriage rite serves to make the inner shape of the service identical, whether or not the eucharist is celebrated. It has the double advantage of helping to make the noneucharistic form look less second class.

CHURCH AND SECULAR LAW

In some countries, there are legal requirements that affect the liturgy in different ways. In England, the Roman Catholic rite of marriage is required to begin with the words:

"I call upon these persons here present to witness that I (N) do take thee (N)
to be my lawful wife . . ."[20]

In France, a secular rite must take place regardless of whether or not the marriage is also to be celebrated in church. We have already noted the imaginative ways in which the French rite adapts the form of consent. Clearly, it is the consent within the rite that is most affected by secular law of whatever kind. On the one hand, couples in England will be made to regard the consent as something requiring the utmost attention in order to get it perfect. On the other hand, in France couples will be able to have a slightly different form of consent in their liturgy, having gone through the chore of a secular marriage beforehand.

Each of these affects the liturgy in different ways, not only in outward form (the texts used), but in inner attitude (the feelings and attitudes of the couples concerned). They raise, in different ways, relations between Church and State, which are never entirely satisfactory in Western Europe, unless the French example be regarded as the better since the Church lives a separate existence from the State at the official level. However, both kinds of legal influence (instanced by the English as well as the French) begin to pose the question to which we shall return in Chapter Eight: What is it that makes a marriage "Christian"?

"MOOD"

A text cannot determine a mood. One even hears of laughter at funerals. But a text is required in some sense to carry mood, and the basic unsatisfactory feature of all the new Western rites is that they fail to face the passage character of marriage. In Chapter Eight, we shall suggest ways whereby this could be put right. It is important at this stage, however, to draw attention to one feature that is involved in the marriage-as-passage debate.

Marriage is ambiguous, it is "assiduous supposing." It is thus not only celebration, joy, and making merry, but marriage has its hidden and darker sides. These include the life being left behind, the covering of nudity with special clothes, and fear of the future. Sometimes these realities are expressed most dramatically in movies, where reality can be coped with because it is presented in a stylized form. All three of the darker features just mentioned are the reverse side of a coin. The life being left behind leads into a life together in the future. The covering of nudity leads into the ecstasy of sexual intercourse (although here, again, there is a mystery because sexual life does not always start at marriage, nor is it necessarily "successful" and fulfilling until later). Finally, fear of the future leads into the fact that the couple at least will have each other without social or familial constraints, or at least a reduction of them. The very fact that these contrasts have had to be qualified serves to show that marriage is not meant just to be "happy." It involves pain of all kinds, it brings opportunities for growth, it is not just "honey." The question must be asked: Does the rite express this?

The answer is a qualified "no," because official liturgies find it hard to be cast in the role of a killjoy. An enriched series of rites to be set alongside the one single rite of celebrating the marriage is probably the answer. "Dying-to-living" is probably a betrothal theme. The covering of nudity is perhaps too private for most cultures of the Christian world today, although prayers at home could ritualize this reality. The third and more general theme, fear of the future, is clearly the one that readings, homily, and intercessions could carry most effectively—for example, in the case of the marriage of two disabled or handicapped people, or a marriage involving the husband going off to fight in (or protest against) a war. Once again, these are obvious where they are also at their most dramatic. "Mood," therefore, seeks beneath the surface for hidden fears and expectations that reflect relationships within the family. The official text cannot rubricate that the mother of the bride must cry, but she frequently does, while the father of the bride holds back his tears. Similarly, the couple recite their vows in nervous tones, because ritual is about making disturbance bearable, beautiful, and divinized. What David Power refers to as "the rather jumbled symbols"[21] of marriage liturgy are infinitely more important than getting the words right. They, therefore, have considerable potential for helping to bring life out of death, sexual abandonment out of embarrassment, a future out of a past. And yet, the marriage liturgy cannot carry the whole burden of these important interior and exterior changes of attitude and relationship, which is why it is all the more crucial to see marriage within the whole *economia* of the eucharistic worship and life of the Body of Christ.

NOTES

1. See pp. 7ff.

2. Cf. Aidan Kavanagh, "Learning to live with rich ambiguity is not a fault but a virtue. It is the poverty of precision that is killing us," quoted from *Made Not Born: New Perspectives on Christian Initiation and the Catechumenate* (Murphy Center for Liturgical Research) (South Bend, IN: University of Notre Dame Press, 1976), p. 4.

3. H. H. Price, *Belief* (London: Allen and Unwin, 1969), p. 486.

4. See Kenneth W. Stevenson, *Nuptial Blessing: A Study of Christian Marriage Rites* (Alcuin Club Collections 64) (London: SPCK, 1982, and New York: Oxford University Press, 1983), pp. 63ff., 168ff., and 203ff.

5. David N. Power, *Unsearchable Riches: The Symbolic Nature of Liturgy* (New York: Pueblo, 1984), p. 66.

6. See pp. 126f. This type of thinking lives on in the delegation to deacons of the right to preside at marriage liturgies, which we regard as a retrograde step, which diminishes the ecclesial character of the sacrament, among other things.

7. For stole wrapping, see Stevenson, *Nuptial Blessing*, pp. 152, 169, 173, and p. 237, n. 43. The Hispanic "lasso" would seem more vigorously symbolic.

8. See our discussion on the Sacramentaries, pp. 30ff.

9. See *The Rites of the Catholic Church as Revised at the Second Vatican Ecumenical Council*, I (New York: Pueblo, 1976), p. 535, para. 6 (*Ordo Celebrandi Matrimonium* (Vatican City: Typis Polyglottis), p. 8, para. 6).

10. On this question, see R. Albertine, "Problem of the (Double) Epiclesis in the New Roman Eucharistic Prayers," *Ephemerides Liturgicae* 91 (1977):193–202. See also H.-C. Schmidt-Lauber, "The Eucharistic Prayers in the Roman Catholic Church Today," *Studia Liturgica* 11 (1976):159ff. The seminal work on this issue is John H. McKenna, *Eucharist and Holy Spirit: The Eucharistic Epiclesis in 20th Century Theology* (Alcuin Club Collections 57) (Great Wakering: Mayhew-McCrimmon, 1975).

11. See p. 151.

12. See David N. Power, *Gifts That Differ: Lay Ministries Established and Unestablished* (Studies in the Reformed Rites of the Catholic Church, Vol. VIII) (New York: Pueblo, 1980), p. 143.

13. On the place where marriage is celebrated, cf. "into the Body of the Church, or shall be ready in some suitable house" in the 1789 American *Book of Common Prayer*, see W. McGarvey, *Liturgiae Americanae* (Philadelphia: Church Publishing Company, 1897), p. 312.

14. On the notes for planning the marriage liturgy, see *The Celebration of Marriage*, pp. 5ff. (see p. 7 for "arranging the church").

15. Text in the *Alternative Service Book* (London: SPCK, 1980), p. 288.

16. For a discussion of the origin of this curious tradition, see Korbinian Ritzer, *Formen, Riten, und religioses Brachtum der Eheschliessung in den christlichen Kirchen des estern Jahrtausends* (Liturgiewissenschaftliche Quellen und Forschungen 38) (Munster: Aschendorff, 1962), pp. 176ff., 193ff., and 212–214.

17. Reginald H. Fuller, "Lectionary for Weddings," *Worship* 55 (1981):244–59.

18. See Kathleen Hughes, *The Language of the Liturgy: Some Theoretical and Practical Guidelines* (Washington, DC: International Commission on English in the Liturgy, 1984). I am also indebted to Patrick Malloy, PhD candidate, University of Notre Dame, Indiana, for his unpublished seminar paper, "A Structural Analysis and Comparison of the Nuptial Blessings, 'Deus, Qui Potestate' from the Gregorian Sacramentary and the *Ordo Celebrandi Matrimonium*," May, 1983.

19. See *A Christian Celebration of Marriage: An Ecumenical Liturgy* (1985), and also J. F. Henderson, "A Christian Celebration of Marriage: An Ecumenical liturgy," in *La Celebrazione Cristiana Del Matrimonio* (Studia Anselmia 93; Analecta Liturgica 11) (Rome: Pontificio Ateneo S. Anselmo, 1986), pp. 375–385. The rite in question has a "copresidency," by two pastors representing the two families. Surprisingly, baptism, which could have been a strong theme in this liturgy, is underplayed. On the issue of shared Communion at "rites of passage," see Richard Rutherford, *The Death of a Christian: The Rite of Funerals* (Studies in the Reformed Rites of the Catholic Church, Vol. VI) (New York: Pueblo, 1980), pp. 188–190.

20. Text in *The Marriage Rite* (Birmingham and Dublin, 1970), pp. 15f.

21. See Power, *Unsearchable Riches*, p. 104.

Chapter Eight

Hopes and Fantasies

One of the most important lessons that evaluation of liturgies teaches those with a special interest in worship is that liturgy is not "words, mere words," it is not just prayer. These are only part of the whole picture. In the words of Aidan Kavanagh:

"It is *rite*, a ritual act which embraces more than prayer (things such as credal assertions, proclamations, acclamations, gestures, sights, nonverbal sounds, and smells) and is not reducible to any one of these forms of communication alone. Furthermore, traditional liturgy's deep structures know only two forms of prayer: one is that of thanksgiving and praise, the other is that of petition."[1]

Liturgy, on this estimate, includes a whole range of meaning, expressed by verbal and nonverbal media. When it *is* verbal, the words must be seen in their entire liturgical context. If they consist of praise/thanksgiving and/or petition, then we are near to the roots of the Christian's most primitive ways of calling upon God.

All this is abundantly true of the marriage liturgy. It is not just words, though the texts are vital, even if they are made to mean very different things, either by rubric (the nuptial blessing), church law (the priestly joining formula), or popular piety (the canopy held over the couple). If the words have to carry a certain ambiguity the nonverbal aspects certainly do. This does not mean that liturgy can hide away into obscurantism because the new liturgies are too threatening. This would mean that liturgy has become marginalized from its true task. Such a fate would have disastrous consequences for all the rites, marriage included.

Kavanagh has recently suggested something that is both outrageous and obvious. In a book entitled *On Liturgical Theology*, he distinguishes between "primary theology" and "secondary theology."[2] What he is saying is that whereas the latter has dominated the scene, because it has been taken to mean "primary," in reality this usually academic exercise ought to be subservient to the truly "primary theology," which is the community of faith's act of worship. For the "theologians" of the Church are those millions of people for whom worship is central. Their piety results not from reading a long list of books (not that that is wrong in itself), but from the one activity that distinguishes them from those who are not Christians: *worship*. The fact is that for the vast majority of Christian people who would never call themselves "theologians" in the usual sense of the word, their theology is derived from their gradual, lifelong engagement in the Church's liturgy. It is this phenomenon that no new official text can suddenly correct if popular piety and official liturgy have got out of touch with each other, when the specialists at the supposed center of the Church's existence meet and agree on a new form of service for all and sundry to use.

In Chapter Seven, we noted some features of the marriage liturgy that have been left unresolved or untouched. In reality, these issues will recur because they are part of the many interactions of meaning that go on at marriage celebrations. The most notable reform of the Roman rite, in our view, was the insistence on the importance of consent and nuptial blessing; this is what many couples have actually taken to be the high points of their marriage service, regardless of what they have been told about confecting sacraments by reciting magic formulas. In this sense, the Second Vatican Council has caught up with the rest of its own Church as well as the emerging consensus among the Churches of the Reformation and the Churches of the Orient. We do not need the medieval preoccupation with intentionality in quite such a strong way nowadays because modern Christians on the whole do marry by choice, not by arrangement.

This is one important example of the way in which "primary theology" needs to assert itself over "secondary theology." But such influence is not always good. It can go the other way, so that the "primary theology" of popular expectation that sees marriage in terms of the bride's change of state persists not just in the minds of curial bachelors but also among English peasants. No amount of didactic teaching or self-conscious rubrics (or for that matter Church law) is going to dislodge the old Western understanding of marriage, however pagan its roots, however inappropriate for what we believe to be a truly biblical and contemporary view of the sacrament of matrimony. Here, one looks wryly at the Christian East, where the liturgies are aggressively egalitarian, but where popular customs are often chauvinistic. The 1969 *Ordo* may lack Cranmer's "who giveth this woman to be married to this man," but we know that many brides are walking into church on the arm of their fathers, and they are going to perceive the marriage either in the way that this implies, or quite differently, but they will still adhere to the old custom because they like it. Here, if ever, is incongruity not easily dislodged in a *rite de passage*, that extraordinarily conservative phenomenon in the world of religious activity.

Rite, then, is not only word, but action. Rite is the basis of ordinary Christian believing. Rite is, perhaps, *its own language,* impenetrable to those who come to it asking the wrong sorts of questions. Rite is capable of storing in its collective memory things that are good and true that the official texts of a Church might attempt to deny; and rite is equally capable of absorbing and keeping ways of understanding things that the Church itself might want to affirm. The important thing, however, is that what goes on in rite is critically but sensitively observed, so that the liturgy can change, not just every four hundred years when the Fathers of the Church (Roman, Anglican, Lutheran, or other) say that it should.

With an eye on these observations on how liturgies grow and what they mean, we suggest that there are eight areas where the 1969 *Ordo* could be improved not only when the next official text comes from Rome but also in local adaptations within the foreseeable future. This is not to take an overnegative view of the *Ordo.* We have already seen to what a considerable extent it is an enrichment on its bald and minimalistic 1614 predecessor. But looking at the new rite from the wider context of history and the meaning of marriage rites in general, these points of growth are easily identifiable.

MARRIAGE SHOULD BE PHASED

Van Gennep's three stages are not only accurate renditions of what goes on in primitive societies,[3] but they also point to new ways in which rites of passage can be understood and celebrated by Christians. In fact, however, these ways are hardly new, because they have been known by previous Christians and they are the backbone of the classical liturgies of Christian Initiation both as it emerged in the fourth century as well as in the late ante-nicene period.

But it is also true of marriage. In all the Eastern rites, and in some of the Western rites (notably the Visigothic), marriage is celebrated as a passage from one form of life to another. The rite of separation is betrothal, in which the partners acknowledge their own and their families' undertaking to prepare for marriage. We find this stage throughout the biblical tradition, even in the infancy narratives of the New Testament. Such a rite may be full and public in character (Armenian), or it may be short and "domestic" in its ambience (Visigothic). But importantly it is *ritualized*, and the Church takes an interest in a real-life phase through which ordinary couples pass on their way to married life. It is even possible that when betrothal was used as an option in later medieval and Counter-Reformation France, it inaugurated (imperceptibly) what we would nowadays call "trial marriages." What the Church does when faced with such a phenomenon could result in a revival of a kind of betrothal rite. But this is secondary to our basic contention that couples planning to marry need to express their separation in some public or semipublic *liturgical* manner, rather than in the attenuated and privatized milieu that makes up modern engagement.

Van Gennep next speaks of the period of liminality. Here again, the Eastern and Visigothic rites provide us with material for this phase. The period of liminality can consciously *prepare for* the marriage celebration; therefore, it blesses robes or prepares the bedchamber. Or else it simply prays for the couple as they themselves prepare inwardly for their union. Both these kinds of liminality express aspects of this period of being neither one thing nor another, which is the whole atmosphere of preparation, and it is appropriate that these old rites should take the opportunity of ritualizing them as a way of coping with the disturbance to relationships that liminality causes among people.

Finally, there is the rite of incorporation, which is what the marriage celebration itself is. And it is this alone of the three stages that the modern Western rites embody, no more. Incorporation means being brought together, in the assembly, and numbered among the ranks of those who are married. This is why this liturgy, of all the various rites, expresses joy and wonder as well as moving forward into a new kind of social life together. Moreover, when the phases are celebrated in the way our predecessors did, the rite of incorporation comes as a real climax; it emerges out of a common intent and breaks into the daylight with far greater impact than when the Church solemnly carries out a twenty-minute marriage liturgy as a Saturday afternoon routine. It is interesting that domestic betrothal, with the priest, persists among many Hispanics today.[4]

These stages are felt needs, and the Church ought to ritualize them. Moreover, if the Church were to ritualize them, the result could be a considerable enrichment of its liturgical life and, therefore, of its sacramental theology. (The whole scheme would be even richer if the marriage liturgy also included prayers at home, even around the bedchamber.) Clearly, it would have been a tall order to have expected the Study Group to have provided such a drastic change in the Roman rite. The corresponding Study Group for Christian Initiation was able to suggest the renewed catechumenate partly because it had been restored before the Council and the pastoral and liturgical groundwork had therefore been done.[5] This could not be said of the recent past in relation to the marriage liturgy. But we suggest that a three-stage marriage liturgy be inaugurated not as an optional extra but *as the norm*, from which shorter versions of the scheme could derive their existence. We have got the whole thing the wrong way round. It is symptomatic of a Church that leaves marriage as a special interest in the hands of catechists as an educational exercise (Pre-Cana weekends) or in the hands of marriage encounter experts as therapy (marriage renewal). Both Pre-Cana weekends and marriage encounter are significant developments in the Western churches. But, like liturgy as a whole, marriage gets out of hand when it is relegated to the experts. We must get across to people that marriage is not a private business; it is the concern and interest of the whole Church. It would be a wonderful thing if a simple rite of betrothal were available for use during the liturgy of the word (at eucharist), or the liturgy of the hours, or for use at home. Similarly, local parishes ought to ritualize the period of liminality at least by regularly praying for couples preparing for marriage. Local folk customs associated with marriage could express this stage in a homely way, when the couple's house is prepared, the robes are made ready, and other preparations are going ahead. Were this to become really popular again, we would be able to enrich the Church's life in a way that far overtakes the gains, considerable though they are, of the rite of incorporation supplied by the 1969 *Ordo Celebrandi Matrimonium* and its sister rites contained in the modern service books of the Churches of the Reformation.

What is suggested here corresponds with what is officially laid down for baptism in the Rite of Christian Initiation of Adults. It would be a pity if it were taken over as the latest idea by a small group of Christians fanatical about marriage. It would, however, benefit the Church at large in a much deeper way were it to be a norm available for couples who want something more than even the best that the new marriage rite can offer, or even for couples who could have this fuller scheme explained to them as a possibility, and who might reply, "We like that; let's have it for ourselves." We keep talking about liturgical renewal as a *retour aux sources*. Here, surely, is a way for modern cultures (secular-urban, post-Christian-rural, as well as the near-pagan) to respond to the roots of our primal state before God that is not only deeply traditional but also deeply biblical. Moreover, such ritualization should not end with the wedding itself, especially since the 1970 Missal revives an old provision in mass prayers for anniversaries.[6] All this can serve to celebrate marriage not as something done, but as a stage in a lifelong passage; and it could result in strengthening marriage as an institution at a time when it needs it most.

WE NEED MORE SYMBOLISM

The new *Ordo* provides a minimum of symbolism taken from traditional Western culture. Thus, the couple are solemnly led into church; they join hands at consent; they give each other rings; and the bride may be veiled or crowned during the nuptial blessing. In the eucharist, the couple may offer the bread and wine, and the Peace that follows the nuptial blessing is obviously a special moment for the new husband and wife. The *Praenotanda* also allow for other customs, as long as they are properly liturgical and fully Christianized. Moreover, in the new texts symbolism is much richer, through themes such as love, covenant, fidelity, and through using biblical themes (e.g., the Ephesians analogy) in a more direct way. All this could be even more enriched, particularly as one senses a somewhat tired liturgical climate of what might be termed "theoretical flexibility," in which everyone is talking about the benefits of having liturgies that are flexible but few people are actually producing them. Obviously, there are certain attitudes that move against enriched symbolism. Some people look askance because they want things as straight as possible and do not like change; it is all right for ethnic religion, but not for my environment. There are those who will say that symbols are not "relevant" since we live in an urban and secular culture that has outgrown the need for these childish things. Experience suggests that those who want "relevance" in liturgy are frequently antipathetic to symbolism, but they show remarkable aptitude in one very Western virtue—they talk a lot.[7]

But liturgy is more than words, and this is supremely true of marriage liturgies. Apart from enriching symbolism through the very notion of phasing marriage in the way we have just suggested, we could also make considerable advances in the effectiveness of liturgical celebrations in two ways. The first would be to include within the betrothal liturgy the symbolism of "death to life." The Copts veil the bridal pair completely at the end of this liturgy. The Armenian rite exchanges crosses. The Maronites anoint, but work into the liturgy at this point a symbolism of Bethany rather than kingship. The East-Syrian rite mixes the *henana* whose liquified ash bespeaks the death of the couple to the earlier level of relationships.[8]

It would be a difficult task to suggest a central symbolic act for a rite such as betrothal that is not already a popular liturgy in the orbit of the Roman rite. Veiling would confuse, since the Western tradition associates this with marriage. Anointing we tend to associate with baptism and ordination; perhaps it belongs also with marriage. *Henana* as a drink would mix strangely with the tight-lipped world of modern hygiene. Perhaps the most appropriate and direct kind of symbol would be another old Eastern custom, also known in the West: exchanging gifts, together with the engagement ring(s). Since this actually happens frequently in real life, it would seem appropriate to bring this practice into the public liturgy. If betrothal ever became popular again, it would no doubt bring with it symbolisms both new and old to interpret the passage through which the community is moving.

When it comes to marriage, however, there are three new symbolisms that could easily be adapted, that would make the nuptial blessing (especially if it is moved from its traditional position to a place immediately after the consent rite) a really powerful climax to the liturgy as a whole. One symbol that is thoroughly Western (and still practiced in Lutheran Sweden) is for a large canopy to be held over the couple during the recitation of the solemn prayer.[9] The fact that the marriage canopy is still used by Jews is certainly a point in its favor, and one that is entirely in accord with the continuity of liturgy between Talmudic Judaism and early Christianity that we have suggested at the start of this study.

The other two symbolisms are Eastern. One is an ancient custom that lies at the heart of all the Eastern rites: crowning. Clearly, the *Praenotanda* of the 1969 *Ordo,* in allowing a crowning of the bride, reproduce a Western mentality when it could so easily have suggested the Eastern one in which *both* the bridal pair are crowned. (The *Praenotanda* reflect here the confusion and debate concerning the function of the nuptial blessing, whether it is exclusively bridal or a blessing of both.) Crowning is an image used rarely in Western texts. For example, the Catholic Apostolic rite has a long prayer immediately after the Lord's Prayer and *preces,* introducing the second part of the service. Based on Cranmer's adaptation of the nuptial blessing, it clearly evokes Eastern sentiment as well as symbolism in a fine concluding section:

"Unite their hearts to fear and love Thee;
and may they abide in mutual love one toward the
    other,
and in Thy peace, so long as they both shall live
    upon the earth.
Do thou crown their life with Thy goodness, and

vouchsafe unto them the abundance of such things as they shall need."[10]

The third symbolism comes from the Coptic rite of anointing the couple immediately before the crowning. As we have seen, the symbolism of this kind of anointing is baptismal,[11] and we suggest that, were this custom to be introduced, even as an option only, chrism should appropriately be used. This would connect easily with baptism, confirmation, and ordination, so that marriage is seen as a truly Christian vocation, brought right into the mainstream of the Church's sacramental life. (One remembers the position of the marriage rite in the 1614 *Rituale*, tucked away at the end after burial.) If future years see a revival of interest in baptism, then the liturgical use of chrism in the other three contexts (confirmation, ordination, and marriage) can be acknowledged as real and living extensions of baptism, as ways of living out the Christian faith in the world. Here the anointing could be performed either before crowning, or under the canopy, immediately before the nuptial blessing. Or else the couple could be anointed without either crowning or canopy. In an age that is seeing a renewed interest in liturgical symbolism, it would be a mark of imagination and maturity if the Christian West were to adorn marriage with symbolisms that are new to its tradition.

This prayer reaches the heart of the crowning symbolism, which is about God's bounty and goodness as well as a way of focusing attention on the bride and groom as the object of the congregation's earnest prayer to God.

There are two customs not as telling as crowning, anointing, or veiling the couple, but which are nonetheless nearer to our culture. One is the old Spanish practice of binding the couple together, which many Hispanics do using a lasso. Older Spanish custom placed this ceremony within the nuptial mass. Usually it takes place nowadays at the reception afterwards. North Americans who are not part of this tradition may be forgiven if they prefer such a "binding" during the liturgy itself, when the formality of the occasion would make it easy to cope with this many-leveled symbolism.[12] Historically it belongs with the nuptial blessing. Another custom is to present the couple with a Bible or prayer book; or else they exchange these during the liturgy. Once again, the custom is optional, and it can be done informally at home or formally during the liturgy. This sort of symbolism could help to relieve the heavy burden already carried by the wedding rings.[13] Native American customs, such as the exchange of feathers, enhance the rite within that culture.

If these and other symbolisms are adequate for using at home, they could also be incorporated into the liturgy in church. Still, binding the couple and presenting them with books could be performed at home, so that the other customs (crowning, anointing, veiling) take place in church. Whatever we do, it is not enough to let symbolism in liturgy be purely verbal. This is what is wrong with so many liturgical celebrations today. There is, arguably, good reason to introduce the crowning as an alternative to the canopy. Preferable to the canopy, the crowns not only symbolize the presence of the deity, but they also speak of victory and peace. Whether the crowns are made of flowers, or metal, or some other material matters little. They could be held by the closest relative, as is the custom in the East. The possibilities are enormous. Above all, they could interpret the best, most deeply traditional, and most wholesome understanding of the nuptial blessing as a solemn prayer of praise and supplication for the bride and the groom.

If these symbols are considered appropriate, or if others are introduced, then two words of caution are in order. First, they are interpretative and should remain secondary to the essential ingredients, which are the consent and the nuptial blessing. Second, they must be allowed to remain symbols and not degenerate into an exercise in education or aesthetics. To put it bluntly, they must not be introduced by a long and specious explanation by a celebrant who trusts neither the liturgy to do its job nor the congregation to relate to a welcome piece of nonverbal liturgy in a wordy world. Nor must they become the object of over-scrupulous artistic folk who may rigidly maintain that everything must be of the very finest. We Westerners have to learn what it is to *relate to* symbolism, instead of wanting to understand it all the time. We also need to learn what place vulgarity has in the worship of ordinary men and women. If we introduce new symbolisms only to make them the object of yet one more example of minimalism of performance and predetermined meaning, then we might as well not bother at all.

WE NEED NEW TEXTS

In Chapter Seven, we looked at the way in which linguistic analysis could produce criteria for improving the present prayers, so that they have an inner coherence. This exercise may also provide entirely new prayers suited to local languages, which is entirely in accord with the spirit of the *Praenotanda*. There is, however, one area that could benefit from closer study of ancient models. The new prayers, as we have seen, are very Western and Latin in their formulation; even the Visigothic blessings at the end of the mass have been changed to conform, and thus are not too exuberant. Eastern texts provide us with examples of two significant kinds of liturgical prayer. One is the prayer of thanksgiving (Coptic) and the other is the psalmic chant (Syrian).[14] In Chapter Six, two British prayers, Methodist and Anglican, were quoted in full as examples of how an ancient thanksgiving prayer pattern can produce a euchology that is both traditional and contemporary. When new texts are written, it would be both enriching liturgically and beneficial theologically if there were some additional nuptial blessings that were constructed along similar lines, perhaps even opening with a eucharistic dialogue. The nuptial blessing would thereby gain a great deal, as a prayer for the couple that emerges out of praise and thanksgiving for creation and redemption rather than simply out of a small and local private context.[15]

Hymnody, of course, is a shifting area of liturgical development. The Syrian tradition, noticeably in the East-Syrian rite, has a peculiar religious psychology that sometimes produces an atmosphere akin to the chorus of a Greek tragedy, so that the congregation becomes an onlooker and commentator, gazing at a drama in which it is already involved. Perhaps some of the hymns frequently sung at weddings bear the marks of earnest supplication in a somewhat sentimental manner. The hymns quoted in Chapter Three use biblical and pastoral images that refer not only to the particular context (the celebration), but to the sacrificial love of God, of which marriage is a partaker. In that sense, the congregation is both onlooker and fervent suppliant. What we need are good marriage hymns, not just general hymns that have a marriage focus simply because they are sung at a wedding. The Danish Lutheran Church is fortunate in having a fine selection composed by one of its greatest hymn writers, Nikolai Grundtvig.[16] There is a pressing need for much more of this kind of hymnody elsewhere in the Christian world, perhaps modeled on the Eastern mixture of biblical imagery and pastoral comment.

The 1969 *Ordo* upgrades the noneucharistic form of marriage from something of a necessary nuisance to a proper liturgy in its own right, and it realistically recognizes that there is a difference between the marriage of a Catholic with a non-Catholic, and of a Catholic with someone who is not baptized. But even these important concessions result, particularly in the case of marriage between a Catholic and a non-Catholic, in a rite that is considerably less full than when the eucharist is not celebrated. There may be good reasons for this since we live in a divided Christian world, and it is beneficial for ordinary men and women to feel the pain of division.

Still, there is something to be said for enriching this noneucharistic liturgy, so that it seems like more than a mass that stops short before the offertory. Recent developments of word liturgies followed by distribution of the reserved sacrament in areas short of priests only serve to show this impression as one that many will take to be true. One way is to make more of the symbolism of the marriage liturgy. Another way that would help considerably would be to move the nuptial blessing so that it invariably comes straight after the rite of consent, whether or not the eucharist is celebrated.

Two other possibilities exist. One is to use incense at solemn services when the eucharist is celebrated, and also when it is not celebrated, as in the Eastern rites. The couple could be censed at the nuptial blessing, as well as at the start of the rite, although one offering of incense may well suffice.[17] Another possibility would be to conclude the noneucharistic liturgy with a solemn thanksgiving, ending in *Sanctus*, or some other chant. The weak point in the noneucharistic liturgy of marriage is similar to Cranmer's; it does not end well.

One of the assumptions that has recurred in this study is that liturgy should ritualize reality. Traditional Catholic teaching about divorce and marriage, however, makes this difficult, because it is based on the principle of annulment, which says that the marriage did not really exist.

It is not our intention to enter in the complex question of divorce, which has exercised many people (including theologians) in all the Churches for a considerable time.[18] But when a couple come to church for the celebration of their marriage after a divorce or annulment, the book assumes that the rite will be the same as if there had not been a divorce. This is a fundamental weakness because most people who go through a divorce carry with them a sense of failure that the Church ignores at its peril. There are various ways of ritualizing this, including the simple, old-fashioned method of private confession. But there is enough uncertainty about how to move forward in the reconciliation of penitents throughout the Roman Catholic world for this particular issue to remain problematical for some time to come.

Conceivably, some couples may want to express their penitence in a public liturgy, for example, at betrothal, or at one or other of the suggested rites of liminality outlined earlier. It could even be that a simple rite of penitence should appropriately be part of the wedding liturgy itself, as has been the practice in the Byzantine rite.[19] The function of this element is not to impose guilt, but to help to lift it by ritualization. Obviously, good pastoral relationships and mutual understanding between couples and pastors and counselors are critical in this context. For the whole reality of failure to be swept under the carpet is, in our opinion, misleading. Some Churches go so far as to suggest a service for the termination of a marriage. This solution, though founded on good intentions, is open to more misunderstanding and heartbreak than it is intended to alleviate.

WE NEED MORE ACTIVE PARTICIPATION BY THE COUPLE AND THE CONGREGATION

For most couples, nerves are very tense on the day of the wedding. One way the nervous disposition can be helped through the passage of marriage is for the couple to do certain things in public, including shaking hands with everyone at the reception, making speeches, and dancing. The new *Ordo* introduces an active vow as the preferable form of liturgical consent. It is good that an increasing number of couples recite these words from a card, or by heart, instead of following the priest clause by clause, phrase by phrase.

Even granted this significant innovation, the note struck in most celebrations of marriage is that of *passivity*. One option that could be built into local rites is for the consent to include a portion said by the bridal pair *together*, as in the French rite. It would also be appropriate for the bridal couple to recite prayers, either individually or together. Some couples would run a mile to avoid this sort of practice. Others, however, would enjoy it and find it helpful. Participation is not just about everyone making as much noise as possible; it is about something much deeper and more profound in the human spirit.

This could be extended so that wider participation is carried out by the congregation, resulting in their doing more than just singing the hymns and reciting the responses to prayers and psalms. The 1979 American *Book of Common Prayer* inserts a new feature after the couple's initial expression of consent, when the celebrant addresses the congregation:

"Will all of you witnessing these promises do all in your power to uphold these two persons in their marriage?"[20]

The strength of this intervention is that it stresses the whole concern today with marriage as corporate and communitarian, in contrast to the earlier concern with the intentionality of the individual partner in marriage. The weakness, however, is that it takes the form of question and answer that reflects the contemporary Church's general concern for *orthopraxis* (right action) rather than with *orthodoxy* (right worship). The liturgical genre is familiar to us, as the faithful renew their baptismal vows on Easter Eve and priests renew their priestly vows at the Holy Thursday Chrism mass. If a less self-conscious way could be found of expressing these many-leveled relationships in the marriage liturgy, we might discover a real breakthrough in making that vital connection between the world of worship and the world as we know it to be.

THERE NEEDS TO BE MORE EMPHASIS ON THE PRESENCE AND ROLE OF THE SPIRIT

In the medieval West, some Northern rites introduced the Votive Mass of the Trinity as part of the marriage liturgy, so that the Trinity mass prayers each preceded the (older) Gregorian Sacramentary nuptial mass prayers. Some other rites introduced another votive form, the Mass of the Holy Spirit. These included some French and Spanish dioceses. Among the French was Metz (always a bilingual area); it has a rite that already has a special place in liturgical history because it pioneered the way of bringing the marriage rite into the mass instead of having it beforehand. Metz did not, however, leave things there. At the end of mass, when the ring ceremonies have been performed (they come at this point in the Metz rite), the 1543 marriage liturgy ends with the *Veni Creator* and a short series of blessing prayers. Some French dioceses in this century adopted the *Veni Creator* and inserted it between the ring giving and the ensuing marriage prayers before the nuptial mass.[21]

These developments show a desire to bring the Holy Spirit into the heart of the marriage liturgy, and the use of the *Veni Creator*, a hymn to the Holy Spirit of love, is an eloquent statement of the Church standing in need of the gifts of the Spirit at marriage as well as at ordination and other times. And yet, in spite of all the interest in Spirit theology in the twentieth century, which has resulted in an enriched eucharistic theology and liturgy, there is no mention of the work of the Holy Spirit in marriage in any of the new mass prayers. They stress such themes as mutual love, but they do so in a Christocentric manner, which might be taken to exclude the Spirit, although such Christocentricity is understandable because of the biblical themes of Christ and marriage (Cana and the Ephesians analogy). It is only at the end of the second blessing concluding mass that the Spirit is directly mentioned (No. 126), but here the idea is plain rather than specific:

"May the Holy Spirit of God
always fill your hearts with his love."[22]

When faced with yet one more lingering Westernism, one longs for something of the richness of the Coptic prayer over the oil, beseeching God for the gift of the Spirit in all kinds of virtues. Perhaps new texts could redress this balance.

THE PRAENOTANDA NEED THEOLOGICAL ENRICHMENT

Each of the new Roman Catholic services is introduced with an official statement that outlines the meaning of the rite concerned, its continuity with previous services, the importance of new features, and those areas of flexibility within the new service. The 1969 *Ordo* is no exception. But even though it alludes to important statements of the Second Vatican Council about marriage, the *Praenotanda* still live in the older world of legal images of marriage that mix somewhat strangely with the new (and primitive) images that appear in the liturgical texts.

Thus, love abounds in the new prayers, a salient example being the third preface (No. 117).[23] But love as a theme only seems to occur incidentally in the *Praenotanda*. On the other hand, although covenant appears consistently in the prayers, there are only two references in the *Praenotanda*; these are significant enough. Faithfulness also is a theme taken up by several of the prayers and is focused particularly on the marriage vow. But the *Praenotanda*, while stressing faithfulness from time to time, tend to do so as a means toward emphasizing indissoluble union rather than as part of the freedom God gives his children. Family life and children also appear in the prayers as fruits of marriage; yet the *Praenotanda* read somewhat coldly about this theme, and also briefly. Finally, while growth in faith is a subject taken up by a few of the prayers, it does not occur in the *Praenotanda* at all.

Local versions of the *Ordo* clearly have an opportunity to expand on all this, so that introductory material can allude not only to the official prayer texts, but also to such new compositions in local languages as are deemed admissible. There is a great deal to be gained by responding positively to these new (and traditional) prayer themes, and the more that introductory material expresses (and even quotes) these texts, the more effective will local versions prove to be in catechesis and in liturgical celebration.

The *Praenotanda* are under official scrutiny,[24] and likely will be rewritten, a process that will probably result in an enriched theology of the whole rite. Meanwhile, local Episcopal conferences have the opportunity to supplement this official statement with notes of a more practical nature about how the celebration is to be planned and presented. Buildings and cultures vary; what is of paramount concern to one couple may be of little interest to another. Nonetheless, these notes, whether produced centrally at the national level or locally at the diocesan level, should set out to clarify the *meaning* of the rite and keep a close watch on local customs as well as secularizing practices that may obscure or hinder the impact of the liturgical experience. Perhaps one of the reasons for so many folk customs lingering on at marriage in society today is because of the poverty of marriage liturgies of the recent West. This issue, a dominant theme in our study, is too important to set aside. It needs to be worked at. Perhaps some of the suggestions made in this chapter will encourage local pastors and couples to take an approach to marriage celebrations that is both traditional and innovative.

NOTES

1. Aidan Kavanagh, "Liturgy and Ecclesial Consciousness," *Studia Liturgica* 15(1982/1983):6.

2. Aidan Kavanagh, *On Liturgical Theology* (New York: Pueblo, 1984), passim.

3. See pp. 7ff. See also J. M. Schmeiser, "Marriage: New Developments in the Diocese of Autun, France," *Église et théologie* 10 (1979):369–386, for a description of an important partial revival of this approach to marriage.

4. I am indebted to Salvador Aguilera for his paper, "Mexican-American Nuptial Tradition," presented as a seminar paper, University of Notre Dame, Indiana, April, 1983. In this tradition, betrothal is ritualized, using family and close friends.

5. Aidan Kavanagh, *The Shape of Baptism: The Rite of Christian Initiation* (Studies in the Reformed Rites of the Catholic Church, Vol. I) (New York; Pueblo, 1978), pp. 95ff. and passim.

6. Texts in *The Sacramentary* (New York: Catholic Book Publishing Company, 1974), pp. 851 (Anniversary), 852 (Twenty-Fifth Anniversary), 853 (Fiftieth Anniversary). See Latin texts in *Missale Romanum* (Vatican City: Typis Polyglottis, 1970), pp. 754–756. No such provisions can be found in the 1570 Missal. Anniversary masses are, however, to be found in the old Sacramentaries. The new texts should not be overlooked.

7. See David Power, *Unsearchable Riches: The Symbolic Nature of Liturgy* (New York: Pueblo, 1984), passim.

8. See above, pp. 67ff.

9. See Kenneth W. Stevenson, *Nuptial Blessing: A Study of Christian Marriage Rites* (Alcuin Club Collections 64) (London: SPCK, 1982, and New York: Oxford University Press, 1983), p. 129 and p. 233, n. 10; for the earlier history of this practice, see ibid., passim. A contemporary illustration of this practice during a Swedish Lutheran nuptial eucharist in Uppsala Cathedral in 1980 is to be found in Åke Andren, *Svenska Kyrkans Gudstjänst: Bilaga 4—Aktenskap och vigsel i dag—Liturgiska utvecklingslinjer* (Stockholm: Gotab, 1981), p. 269.

10. Text in *Liturgy and Other Divine Offices of the Church* (London: Chiswick, 1880), p. 419.

11. See pp. 71ff.

12. See above, n. 4. I am indebted to Father Robert Hoffner for clarifications of current practice; once, when performing the binding together with the lasso, Hoffner had the uncomfortable experience of the bride fainting! If the binding is carried out in the liturgy, it could be performed by the family or close friends.

13. Giving a Bible at marriage became popular in nineteenth-century French and Swiss Reformed rites. See J.-J. Von

Allmen, "Bénédiction nuptiale et mariage d'apres quelques liturgies de l'église Réformée," in *Mélanges Liturgiques offerts au R. P. Bernard Botte* (Louvain: Abbaye du Mont César, 1972), pp. 15f. and nn.

14. See pp. 62ff.

15. For this reason, "ad hoc" compositions, especially for the nuptial blessing, should not just pray for private concerns that the couple happen to feel at the time, but they should be set within the context of the *whole* of God's redemptive plan. Writing new nuptial blessings is an art that is slowly emerging. The "fourth" nuptial blessing in the Irish *Celebration of Marriage* (pp. 25ff.) is a good example of the "interim" character of much modern prayer writing; it combines some old biblical images with some understandable sentimentality. An alternative form of consent that included the old Visigothic "do you love N." would compensate, and add beauty and a human touch to the rite altogether.

16. See *Den Danske Salmebog* (København: Haase, 1953), nos. 734–741 (Grundtvig composed nos. 735, 736, 738, 741, and translated 737 from the German original by Paul Gerhardt).

17. Compare Coptic practice in this regard, pp. 71ff.

18. See our discussion, *Nuptial Blessing*, p. 211, of making a liturgy for divorce itself. See John H. Westerhoff and William H. Willimon, *Liturgy and Learning Through the Life Cycle* (New York: Seabury, 1980), pp. 121–131. This practice goes beyond the bounds of our view.

19. See A Nelidow, "Caractere penitentiel du rite des deuxiemes noces," in *Liturgie et Rémission des Péchés* (Ephemerides Liturgicae "Subsidia" 3) (Rome: Edizione Liturgiche, 1975), pp. 163–177.

20. Text in *Book of Common Prayer*, p. 425. The 1985 *CCT* text includes this question, but prefixes it with a question to the families:

"Do you, the families of N. and N.,
give your love and blessing to this new family?"

Ritualized betrothal would obviate the need for this kind of formula. For the text of an Irish prayer by a couple, see above, Chapter 6, n. 17.

21. For the text of the Metz rite, see Molin and Mutembe, *Le rituel du mariage en France du XIIè au XVIè siècle* (Théologie Historique 26) (Paris: Beauchesne, 1973), pp. 316–318. It is not known what practice was followed at Metz before 1543, the earliest marriage text so far discovered. On the *Veni Creator* and its use at Metz and this century, see ibid., p. 58.

22. Text in *The Rites of the Catholic Church as Revised at the Second Vatican Ecumenical Council*, I (New York: Pueblo, 1976), p. 570 (*Ordo Celebrandi Matrimonium* (Vatican City: Typis Polyglottis), p. 39).

23. Covenant is a dominant theme in the American *Book of Common Prayer* (1979), United Methodist (1979), and the CCT (1985) rites, among many others.

24. I am indebted to Father Vernon P. Decoteau for his paper, "Reflection on the Theology of the Roman Rite of Marriage," presented to a seminar at the University of Notre Dame, Indiana, April, 1983.

Chapter Nine

Application

No liturgy is perfect, nor is it unchanging. As we have seen already in many different examples, the liturgy of Christian marriage is a supreme example of word and symbolic action, in context. There is an intermeshing of these features throughout. In the West, one of the weaknesses of much of the tradition has concerned the *ecclesiological* dimension, which has been frequently lacking. If the 1969 *Ordo* is to be imaginatively adapted, it has many different ways in which it can be further enriched.

Ecclesiology is as much part of what the official Church teaches as it is what goes on in the average Catholic marriage liturgy. And it is now time to pull together some of the thoughts expressed earlier about the 1969 *Ordo* in order to apply them to what goes on in local Churches. Much of the groundwork for this has been done already; we have looked at the new rite not only in its historical context but also in its various options and in its sequence of drama as these fit into what has happened before in history. We have also noticed how these fit together in themselves. Now we must suggest ways in which the phasing of the marriage liturgy through preliminary rites can be achieved, since we regard this as vital for pastoral as well as theological reasons. Some of these suggestions may not fit many cultures and contexts that are within the orbit of this book, but it is to be hoped that they will receive sympathetic consideration.

The couple normally go to see the pastor concerned at some stage in their preparation for marriage. Such preparation will vary from one place to another. It is likely to involve two things. One is some sort of course about marriage itself, which may be undertaken with other couples at Pre-Cana weekends. The other is a discussion about what will go into their marriage liturgy. Already, clergy are under pressure to emphasize more of the various new rites than their predecessors. Marriage is certainly in such company.

We suggest that, if at all possible, the couple (or couples) ritualize their intention to marry within a public betrothal liturgy, perhaps during Sunday mass, in the same way that the catechumenate is inaugurated according to the revised Rite of Christian Initiation of Adults.[1] This could take place after the homily or Creed, and consist of simple questions and answers between the celebrant and the couple. Alternatively, the couple themselves could address the assembly, with the news that they plan to marry and wish to bring this commitment before God and his Church in order to ask for the fervent prayers of the Christian community. Betrothal could then be brought to a suitable climax in a prayer by the celebrant, with the laying on of hands. The engagement ring could be given to the woman just before this prayer; and the man could receive some suitable symbol. Some congregations may even wish to experiment with the bold symbolism of the Coptic rite, where both partners are veiled in a large cloth, completely covering them, in the latter part of the betrothal rite; the veil is removed at the end.

The next stage is that couples preparing for marriage are prayed for by the assembly regularly, both at home and in church, in private and in public. Only in this way will ordinary Christians understand that mar-

riage is not just a big special occasion, but an important stage in the whole of the life of the community,
however fragmented that community might be.

The next stage for the couple is now the two parts of
normal preparation mentioned earlier. Pre-Cana weekends are popular, though they are not universally satisfactory, and one hears of priests and couples complain-
ing that they degenerate into another formality and
lose their depth. Perhaps this is because they have
been set up with the very best of intentions as an educational and therapeutic exercise, but with no attempt
to *ritualize* them. As we have seen in so many local
rites down through history, rite is the primal means
for the Christian to cope with reality. The disturbance
and confusion that is so much a part of this liminal period of engagement needs to be brought into public
worship. Pre-Cana weekends perhaps need to be
rethought. But we certainly suggest that couples attend worship between engagement and marriage and
that there be occasions when they are prayed for in a
special way. Possibly, the Liturgy of the Hours could
meet this need; a vespers could be celebrated during
these weekends, or else the couple could attend a Saturday or Sunday evening Vespers at which there are
special readings and hymns and prayers. One thing is
of vital importance. If, as is often the case, the couple
have already begun to "live with each other," in whatever degree of formality, these rites are still gone
through as basic steps along the road to marriage.

The other feature of preparation concerns planning the
marriage liturgy. Here, the Church has a golden opportunity for catechesis, not only for the couple but for
the whole community as well. (How many average
Catholics ever attend a marriage liturgy, except one
for people with whom they have a strong connection,
either through being related to them or being close

friends?) There is widespread ignorance about the meaning of the marriage liturgy among most Christians today, largely because the rite has become marginalized from regular liturgical diets. If one only attends these services on occasion and by invitation, there is even greater chance that the more sentimental aspects of the liturgy will obscure what is actually happening.

This catechesis of the couple when they plan their liturgy may well be the best means of helping them to grasp the inner meaning of Christian marriage, insofar as this is possible *before* they are finally man and wife and involved in all the daily activities of married couples, from making love to cooking for each other and having friends in for a meal. When they look at the marriage rite together with the priest and anyone else (musicians, lectors, and others), it is hoped that they will *not* be looking at it for the first time. One of the marvellous features of Rite of Christian Initiation of Adults is that it has begun to bring baptism into the ordinary consciousness of Christians, so that they begin to feel that baptism belongs to all of them. A similar such exercise with marriage could well result in many couples becoming familiar and enthusiastic about what may go into their own marriage liturgy.

Among the points for discussion should include the following:

Readings

Prayers, including the nuptial blessing

Music

Other participants (lectors, deacons, ushers)

Each of these points to many other aspects of the liturgy, thus a fruitful discussion is bound to emerge. It is important that too much not be expected of the couple. Middle-class, educated, articulate Catholics could revel in this sort of exercise. Some of them may have alternative nuptial blessings in mind. Other couples may be put off by the formality and intensity of this kind of planning. They should not be dismissed by naive clerics for being apathetic, because they may be the kind of people who think deeply but talk little.

The *readings* provided are many and varied, as are the *prayers*, which include the three official nuptial blessings. It is likely that *music* will play a larger part in discussion because there is considerable enthusiasm for music in special liturgies at present; people are, in general, more knowledgeable about music than about those other aspects that make up the liturgy. It is vital, however, that the music not take over the rest of the liturgy. It is there to interpret and comment. We have already suggested a few guidelines here.[2] Enthusiasm sometimes needs to be curbed a little. A suitably "phased" marriage could do precisely this.

Participation by other people normally means family and close friends, from those who read the lections and the bidding prayers to those who help give out service sheets at the back of church. Many couples will want to have special printing for their liturgy. These booklets should contain a minimum—not a maximum—so that the congregation can engage in what is going on, rather than be buried in typescript during the liturgy itself.

Readings and prayers may often be specially chosen and it is part of the preparation toward marriage that an attempt is made for couples to look carefully at the selection available. They may even want other readings and prayers not provided. Throughout this process of consultation, the priest has a good chance to get to know the couple, which means that when he comes to preach his homily, he will be addressing a context that is familiar to him.

There are other features that make up the preparation for marriage: the home, presents, the reception, arrangements for photography. All this is part of the disturbance of liminality, even if the disturbance is also symptomatic of modern secular living. Frequently, these activities bring to the fore tensions between people who are adjusting to one another (e.g., in-laws). But that is part of what the marriage rite is about, and it need hardly cause surprise.

MARRIAGE

As we have seen, the marriage liturgy is made up of two essential ingredients: the consent of the partners and the nuptial blessing. These two are clothed with various other elements to make up no less than six stages:

Reception of the couple

Liturgy of the word

Preliminary questions

Consent

Blessing and giving of the rings

Nuptial blessing (before Communion, at a nuptial eucharist)

We have suggested earlier that the nuptial blessing ought to come immediately after the blessing and the giving of the rings, even when a nuptial eucharist is celebrated. Similarly, the preliminary questions make much better sense if they come at the beginning of the rite, before the liturgy of the word, as happens in several other modern rites, including the 1979 Episcopalian *Book of Common Prayer*.[3] This means that they are preliminary in character and that the consent is built up to as an important climax in the liturgy. Hopefully, each of these structural alterations will be made the next time a new text is issued, whether in English or any other language.

Now we look at each of these stages in turn.

Reception of the Couple
The most common way in which this part of the rite is normally performed shows the traditional Western emphasis on marriage as the bride's change of state. The scenario is well known, popular, and embedded in the expectations of many local cultures. The groom comes to church some time before the liturgy starts and checks what the ushers are doing, whether out of necessity or as a means of controlling his nerves. He then goes to the head of the nave and sits with the best man until the entrance of the bride in her solemn procession. Similarly, the priest emerges from the sacristy and walks straight to the head of the nave and waits upon the bride's appearance on the arm of her father or a close friend. The drama of her arrival is further enhanced by special music and by the fact that the congregation turns to look at her as she walks up the central aisle.

The new rite in fact suggests that the priest meet *both* partners at the church door, unless he is going directly to the altar. This is a tiny statement against prevailing convention. We suggest that the bridal focus, however popular, is unsound from a theological point of view, since we are at last emerging out of the old Roman thinking about marriage, now that the nuptial blessing is beginning to be seen as a blessing of *both* partners. Therefore, the actions of the liturgy should interpret clearly that new and deeply traditional understanding of what is happening. The bride and groom should either arrive at church together, or else in two separate processions. (In the East, the custom is for the bride to be escorted by two *men* and for the groom to be escorted by two *women*.)

When they arrive at church, they may then walk up the nave, led by the priest and the other ministers, so that the congregation sees a mélange of each of the partners with their supporters, together with the priest and other ministers. In some places, a robed choir often lends dignity to this procession. Such a new direction for the reception of the couple would better serve the Church by making a stronger theological statement about what marriage is. And it also provides for folk customs (albeit changed) to continue.

Music for the entrance of bride and groom may vary between an organ voluntary or a hymn. If there is a voluntary first, then there should be a hymn sung when the couple have arrived at the head of the nave. A hymn is an ample expression of joy and thanksgiving, and it can also serve the double purpose of compensating for any trivializing of the procession that might have taken place (e.g., photography).[4]

At the head of the nave, or wherever is the most suitable place, there should be special seating for the couple. The chairs may be decorated with flowers or by other means. In some countries, there is even a large floral arrangement on the floor around these chairs. On these chairs, the couple are to rest for the first two readings and the homily. Provided that the chairs do not eliminate important vistas (from nave to lectern and nave to altar), they may be placed appropriately in the middle of the space between the nave and the sanctuary area. But if they do obtrude, then the chairs should be placed to the side, preferably opposite the lectern. How the family and close friends are to be seated will depend on where the couple are seated.

Liturgy of the Word

The entrance rite concluded, preferably with an ecclesial rather than bridal procession, the marriage liturgy moves straight into the Liturgy of the Word. At a eucharist, the penitential rite comes first, but there are good reasons for regarding this preparatory rite as superfluous at a nuptial mass. After an introduction by the celebrant, the *Gloria in excelsis* is a suitable doxology for the occasion. Care will have been given to the selection not only of the prayers but also the readings.

When there is a mass, encouragement is given for *three* readings, although many people may want to hasten this stage of the liturgy by having only two. In view of the fine Old Testament and Apostle pericopes that are in the Lectionary for this occasion, it is hoped that this temptation will be resisted. If family or friends are involved in reading the first two lections, then they will need to rehearse carefully, especially in an unfamiliar church. It is vital that such readings be performed well. There may well be people attending the marriage service who hear the Word read from the Bible rarely. It is also possible that the bride and groom will want to read these lections, which would be a noble statement about their commitment and participation.[5]

A deacon, if one is available, should read the gospel. At the homily, the preacher should apply one or other of the main biblical themes to the congregation at the service.[6] Often, close friends are asked to preach, which provides opportunities both for personal allusions (that need to be carefully handled by any preacher) and for some reflection on marriage in that particular assembly. It is important that the preacher realize that the liturgy in question is an opportunity for all married couples (and the unmarried, too) to reflect on the meaning of marriage. If the wider view of marriage that underlines this study is to be taken seri-

ously, then we may one day arrive at a stage when local congregations will see marriage as not just "the
marriage of A and B," but rather as a celebration that
affects all the dimensions of that community.

Preliminary Questions

The homily ended, the marriage rite moves into its
first special stage. The celebrant should stand in a central position. The couple come forward, preferably
with their escorts. (If they are escorted, then reposi-
tioning these preliminary questions at the start of the
service would have even more impact on the rite as a
whole.) The designation of space should be such that
the priest and the couple are clearly visible and central; and the support groups should be clearly standing in a supporting capacity. The deacon (or assistant
minister, if there is no deacon) could well make this arrangement. (We have already seen how the main
Latin tradition has neglected the role of the deacon in
marriage liturgies, in contrast to the East.[7])

The questions should be asked *as* questions, with a certain formality. Unless the bride and/or the groom took
part in the lections, this will be the first time that their
voices are heard in the assembly. One issue that
should be resolved well beforehand (it may be a matter of parish policy) is whether the answers to these
questions will be made over a microphone. The current fad for this device is not entirely to be welcomed.
Two obvious rules of thumb should be noted. Only
use a microphone if the acoustics demand it; and if
one spoken part of the liturgy is delivered through a
microphone, then all others should be as well (unless
there are good reasons, e.g., a "stage direction" for
one part of the congregation). In other words, if the
priest uses the microphone when he asks the couple
these questions, then the answers should be given in
that way.

Consent

The liturgy now reaches a high point with the consent of the partners. This should be performed in a different way from the preliminary questions (another reason for moving them to the start of the liturgy). The partners join hands. They should face each other so as to be clearly visible to all the congregation, with the priest between them and the altar. Nothing and no one should intrude into this solemn part of the rite.

In a literate society, there is no need for the priest to prompt them. They can read the vows from cards, or, better still, memorize them and speak them directly to each other. When this part of the liturgy is performed well, it carries an overwhelming impact. When it is performed badly, it can be embarrassing. It does not matter if they make a mistake. And if microphones have been used for the questions, they should also be used for the vows. By preparing for this part of the liturgy and by performing it, the couple are already engaged in a special relationship with each other before and under God. The rhyming quality of these vows provides opportunity for learning them, whether by memorization or just in order to become familiar with them. The vows are not minispeeches.[8] They are a special, unique type of liturgical speech unparalleled elsewhere, and rightly so.

Immediately after the vows, the priest recites a short formula that declares that the couple are now married. The couple should not kneel for this secondary (and perhaps unnecessary) section. In times past, the priest has either joined their hands or wrapped a stole around them. This was convenient and easy when they were standing directly in front of him, facing the altar. But three reasons suggest that he should refrain from carrying out these symbolic actions. First, it places a high-profile role on what the priest is doing.

Second, it is more important for the couple to be facing each other for the vows (and for that part of the rite to make its own powerful impact in this way) than it is for the priest to seem to exercise his power by joining the couple together. Third, however, if he joins their hands and/or wraps his stole around them, he implicitly detracts from the great importance that should be attached to the nuptial blessing, which (according to the 1969 *Ordo*, but not according to the 1614 *Rituale*) is the other essential ingredient in the rite. In view of what we are about to suggest as accompanying symbolic actions for the nuptial blessing, it is much better if the priest recites this formula without any movement of his hands. The primal and basic hand joining at marriage is done by the partners when they make their vows to each other.

Blessing and Giving of the Rings
The couple now perform the symbolic action of exchanging rings. Most couples opt for two rings nowadays. In the new rite it is a simple ceremony, consisting of the blessing, the giving, and the interpreting words said by each partner. The deacon or other minister can once more assist the priest by bringing the rings to him. The same arrangement should persist as for the vows, with the partners standing in such a way that they are facing each other, but turned slightly toward the priest while he is receiving and blessing the rings. When the rings are given, the partners should once more face each other.

There is scope for other blessings and presentations at this point: either coins or jewelry, or a Bible or a prayer book. It is to be regretted that many couples exchange these gifts during the liturgy without proper recognition being given to them, and the priest should take care to inquire what (if anything) they wish to give each other as extra symbols.

Nuptial Blessing

After the giving of the rings and other gifts, the official text moves into the *bidding prayers*. But if there is no eucharist, the *nuptial blessing* is given before the bidding prayers. All that has been said so far suggests that the nuptial blessing belongs as soon after the consent and ring giving as possible. Assuming that the nuptial blessing comes at this stage, the meaning of the rite now indicates another important climax, so that the ring giving is seen as linking the consent and the blessing. This is a needful part of the inner meaning of marriage, which is essentially about the offering to God of a resolve in order to ask for his blessing and strength.

The couple stand together, facing the priest, who introduces the nuptial blessing with one of the formulas, or else in his own words. (A deacon, if available, should say this part.) The silence between this introduction and the blessing is a significant step in the liturgy, because it points forward to the nuptial blessing as a central feature. Stretching his arms towards the couple, the priest then recites the blessing. In times past, it was sometimes chanted, and in churches where the eucharistic prayer is chanted, the nuptial blessing might also be sung in this way. Careful thought should be given to the use of the voice (not rattled off as if it were a mere formality). Priests who study carefully its sequence of ideas have a better chance of reciting or chanting it effectively. It is a special point in the rite. It deserves a special atmosphere.

For this reason, it would add to the attitude of people to marriage if there were some accompanying symbolisms.[9] One of the weaknesses of marriage in the Catholic tradition in recent years has been that all the fun is excluded from the liturgy. During the nuptial blessing, the support groups could hold a large canopy over the couple, as used to be the case in

223

many parts of Northern Europe in the Middle Ages, and is still an option in the Swedish Lutheran rite. The nuptial canopy could be the property of the church, or else be specially made for the occasion. All that is required is four poles and a strip of cloth. More elaboration is possible, in the carving of the wood-work and in the richness and decoration of the cloth. Such a canopy symbolizes many things, but above all the presence of God and the concern of the congre-gation.

During the nuptial blessing, the priest could anoint each partner with chrism, symbolizing marriage as a vocation of Christian people, and therefore as an ex-tension of baptism. Each of the nuptial blessing texts provides opportunity for this action in the second part, after the opening address has led into the suppli-cation. If new blessings are written and authorized for use that pray for both spouses throughout, there can still be a suitable stage at the start of the supplicatory section of the prayer for each to be anointed. If this custom is introduced, it is hoped that chrism will be used in abundance, as a lavish perfume with which to fill the church. We also suggest that incense be offered during the nuptial blessing. The deacon could walk around the couple, censing them, and thereby symbol-izing the prayer that the Church is offering to God for their future life together.

Still another symbol is appropriate for the nuptial blessing, perhaps as an alternative to the canopy. In all the Eastern rites, crowning is the climax of the rite, and in the Coptic Church it is associated with anoint-ing. The crowns could be held over the couple during the nuptial blessing, whether or not a canopy is to be used; or the crowns could be an adequate substitute for the canopy, although both together would speak volumes about the importance of marriage in general and the nuptial blessing in particular. Such crowns can be made from flowers, or from various forms of metal, richly decorated. Family and friends could place them over the couples' heads at the start of the blessing and remove them at the end. They can also be exchanged from one head to the other, as a symbol of the unity of love of which marriage proclaims and symbolizes.

One more symbol is the Hispanic lasso, the binding of the couple together. It is a pity if this old custom is relegated among many Hispanics to the reception, and it would be appropriate for it to be carried out either during the nuptial blessing, or immediately after it, perhaps during the singing of a hymn or the chosen music. As an interpretative formula following the blessing, it could lead the liturgy to a suitable point of climax and quiet. Above all, these various symbolic actions, together, could celebrate all the aspects of the deity that marriage needs to ritualize so badly in our impoverished liturgies today: the divine presence (canopy), marriage as a vocation (anointing), special graces in marriage (crowning), solemn intercession (incense), and the joining of two into one flesh (binding). It would be far better if our liturgies went in for richer symbolism and risk going all out than for the current liturgies to remain so dull and cerebral in their texts, to be relieved only by excessive musical items.

Many couples enjoy two other special items, which might also be included at the interlude occurring between the nuptial blessing and the bidding prayers.[10] One is a special hymn or song, that the couple choose. There are inherent dangers in this custom, because the special hymn or song could ruin the atmosphere of the liturgy at this vital point. Far better that considerable thought be given to a really fine chant or a song. The other is the "marriage candle." This could be offered either now or else at the offertory; or (if there is no eucharist), during a hymn preceding the final blessing. The growing popularity of this candle is doubtless a symptom of the dearth of symbolism in marriage liturgy. And it could well be that if some of the symbolism that we have suggested earlier are introduced and were to capture peoples' imaginations, then the special hymn and marriage candle might fade out of the picture altogether.

Rest of the Liturgy

After the nuptial blessing at a noneucharistic service (and, in our view, when the eucharist is celebrated), the bidding prayers follow. These are different in character and shape from the nuptial blessing. Whereas the nuptial blessing sets out to place a particular marriage within the context of God's redemption of the world, and to pray for that marriage, the bidding prayers set out to universalize the particular marriage in question with the concerns of the whole Church. They should, therefore, not pray exlusively for the partners in the marriage; they should include petitions for wider concerns, because the Christian assembly never focuses on one concern lest it run the risk of losing connections between various intentions and aspirations in its life of prayer and service. Some texts that are used at this point gush with sentimentality, introvertedness, and an unhealthy obsession with two people. They should, rather, pray for the world to which the assembly has to return, however long the wedding reception is to be. They might even pray realistically about the need for all couples, not just the couple in question, to grow in the sacrament of matrimony, to change and develop, and forgive and renew each other as each partner grows older in the sight of God. Some of these cautionary remarks could also be directed towards couples who want to write their own nuptial blessing. With the bidding prayers, the first part of the eucharist ends.

At a eucharist, the couple may be involved at the offertory. The Peace should first of all be exchanged between the partners and then among the congregation. Their special marriage kiss should be clearly visible to the whole congregation. Whether or not the eucharist is celebrated, the whole liturgy reaches its conclusion with the special blessing.

If we have suggested ways of "solemnizing" the entrance of the couple along egalitarian lines at the start of the liturgy, then we can allow for the recession of the couple at the end of their marriage liturgy to take on an atmosphere of benevolent fun, without any priestly intervention as some sort of sacerdotal killjoy. The liturgy should end with the couple and support group moving down the central aisle. Now photography can have free rein, and liturgy and life merge into a different level of relationship as the marriage celebration moves from the Table of God's Word to the table of the wedding breakfast.[11]

A word concerning robes and colors. White is the normal color for the bride's dress and the priest's vestments in many countries today, but this is a comparatively recent tradition. In the Middle Ages, the bride simply wore the most sumptuous attire she could manage, and the priest frequently wore red; the nuptial canopy was often of this color, too. With the current revival of interest in national costumes, it would be better if white became but one color among various options, depending on tastes, traditions, and local customs.[12]

AFTERWARDS
Marriage does not stop with the liturgy. Occasionally newly married couples gather for enrichment sessions. Once again, these run the risk of allowing the educated and articulate to "take over," with education and

therapy dominant. There are many married people who could not cope with the level of vocal participation that these activities demand. This period of time needs responsible handling. But there are three ways in that marriage as an extension of baptism can be applied in local Churches.

One of the ways is for couples who have been recently married to be prayed for in eucharistic bidding prayers. We pray for the hungry and the unemployed, the local bishop, and the civil authorities; yet we seldom pray for marriage as an institution in the lives of millions of people today. The second is for couples to be given the opportunity to renew their marriage vows at special liturgies. The texts for these renewals need to avoid the current tendency towards self-consciousness, and the theological danger of Pelagianism. It is God's free gift of grace, after all, that makes it possible to speak of his love being experienced between two people. For this reason, such vow renewals should immediately be followed by solemn prayer, along the lines of the nuptial blessing itself. The third is for couples to come to mass at anniversaries. The 1970 Missal contains prayers for these occasions, and they are a hallmark of just how much more concerned are the new rites with marriage than were their predecessors after the Council of Trent. No special ceremonies are needed on these occasions. The eucharist is the eucharist, and it can look after itself.

NOTES

1. See *The Rites of the Catholic Church as Revised at the Second Vatican Ecumenical Council*, I (New York: Pueblo, 1976), pp. 40ff.

2. See above, pp. 149f.

3. See above, p. 155.

4. See above, p. 174.

5. See above, p. 203f.

6. See Reginald H. Fuller, "Lectionary for Weddings," *Worship* 55 (1981):244–59.

7. See above, pp. 56ff.

8. See Kenneth W. Stevenson, *Nuptial Blessing: A Study of Christian Marriage Rites* (Alcuin Club Collections 64) (London: SPCK, 1982, and New York: Oxford University Press, 1983), pp. 79f.

9. See above, pp. 194ff.

10. For the prayer by the couple in the Irish rite, see n. 17 in Chapter 7 (for the text).

11. For suggestions about domestic prayer, which does not require the presence of the priest, see above, pp. 7ff., 36ff., and 190ff.

12. See illustrations in H. S. Kingsford, *Illustrations on the Occasional Offices of the Church in the Middle Ages from Contemporary Sources* (Alcuin Club Collections 24) (London: Mowbrays, 1921), pp. 34–45 (with notes). On the color of the vestments and the canopy, see W. St. John Hope and E. G. Cuthbert Atchley, *English Liturgical Colours* (London: SPCK, 1918), pp. 158f. The illustration described in Chapter 8, n. 9, depicts Swedish national costumes worn by the bride and her supporters (who hold two of the poles for the canopy) and military uniforms by the groom and his supporters (who hold the other two poles). Doubtless the male costume should vary much more, too; the secular "black tie" of recent years has become uniformly drab.

Chapter Ten

Postscript

On June 28, 1985, a statue was unveiled in the English
West Country. Such an event might provoke little comment; after all, what difference should a statue make
except to the owner and the sculptor? But the context
provided ample opportunity for the media to descend
on one of England's loveliest Cathedral cities (Wells)
and gaze up at the solemn unveiling of a large statue
of the figure of Christ, reigning from heaven, bestow-
ing his blessing on the world. Another excuse for media coverage was that the Prince of Wales was the distinguished visitor who performed the unveiling.

The Dean and Chapter had been faced with a problem. Their Cathedral has one of the most elaborate
Gothic West fronts in Europe, and most of the other
statues had survived the Reformation except the figure
of Christ. All that remained of him was his legs.
(There is some speculation that the figure might have
been the victim of severe winds blowing in from the
Atlantic, but most people agree that such an idea is
too kind to the manic iconoclasm of the Reformation
era.) In the end they decided to take a considerable
risk by commissioning a distinguished sculptor who
was also a Christian to replace the diminished figure
in his own way. David Wynne spent a long time re-
searching and thinking about this, his most public and
risky project. Conservationists raged because they
wanted the (authentic) legs only, as a matter of principle. Meanwhile, Wynne smoked his pipe, said his

prayers, and worked away with his chisel. When the Risen Christ was hauled into place and unveiled, most people agreed that the result was a masterpiece. It harmonized completely with its surroundings, but at the same time it was original because it expressed something of the twentieth century's religious experience; it did not attempt to copy the medievalists. Once more, a visible figure of Christ stood atop a marvellous vista of what someone described as "the chivalry of heaven."

Wynne's sculpture is a parable of what this book has been trying to say. Tradition is important because it informs us of our roots, nowhere more than when it touches on supposed "real life" in the marriage liturgy. Moreover, this book urges that once proper attention is paid to our own corporate roots as Christians in the one holy catholic and apostolic Church, we are in a position to apply the past to the present in order to make the future.

Liturgy is not something that ever remains static. Thus, the Western debate about whether or not marriage is a sacrament is not of primary importance; most Orthodox have an open mind on how many sacraments there should be, and most Protestants agree that marriage is at least a "sacramental rite," only using such a qualifying expression to keep baptism and the eucharist as two rocks on which the sacramental system is built.[1] Moreover, what we have suggested about marriage as a "passage" is intended to enrich pastoral practice and also give the Church an impetus to relate better its whole range of sacramental theology to real life experiences. For marriage continues long after the celebration is over, and those couples who keep coming to the eucharist to give thanks for "growing old together" witness to an ancient tradition whereby marriage anniversaries are brought into the ambit of a special gathering at the Lord's Table.

Still, the statue remains visible to anyone who comes to Wells to look at it, and the same is true of marriage. Anyone can marry. Unbelievers can live fulfilled married lives without ever embracing the Christian faith, though God is still present in their relationship, whether or not he is perceived and accepted. Contrariwise, Christians who go to mass every Sunday and are deeply involved in every conceivable activity of the local church are capable of failing to respond to the grace that is so readily made available to them through the Body of Christ. In this sense, specifically *Christian* marriage is the same marriage that anyone else can live, but with the essential difference that it is brought into the context of pertinent values and graces opened to us in the Scriptures, and in the life and witness of the Church, nourished through its faith and worship. It is not for Christians to hold up *their* marriages as being intrinsically superior to anyone else's; and worse still for one branch of Christianity to do it to another. Little of substance divides Christians today regarding the theology of marriage; and if there are differences, they are more of emphasis than of principle, many of which are to be found spread diversely among the ranks of various Catholic theologians themselves. The contractual emphasis of medieval and post-medieval times has given way to the covenantal view, and both are now being superseded by the grander ideal of marriage as *ecclesial*, of the couples forming a "mini-Church" that is also part of the "wider Church." What is of great ecumenical significance is that both the drift toward the view of marriage as covenant and the ensuing movement toward marriage as ecclesial have taken place among all the western Churches. So great is the extent of our growth together in the mystery of Christ's love and unity.

Christian marriage cannot ensure a better and more lasting relationship than any other religion or ideology can do with its adherents. But it can provide both the *context* and the *safeguards* for that relationship to be better and more lasting. What goes on in our marriage liturgies is therefore of the utmost importance. The best advertisement for Christian marriage, however, is not an elaborate or efficient ecclesiastical scheme, but rather partnerships of faith, hope, and love that transcend stress and problems and regard the sacrament as a *continuing* means whereby God can be met as much in good times as in bad. Vow and blessing go hand in hand.

The Wells statue is visible for all to see, but it stands there only as a result of a particular decision taken by a group of imaginative and informed people who sought to replace medieval legs with a modern figure that would be complete in itself. The twentieth-century Western rites, Roman Catholic included, have gone as far as replacing the body as well. Let us hope that, next time around, the face will appear.

Meantime, there are countless opportunities to be seized that may result in further integration between the life of the local church and the experiences of couples young and old. Not every liturgy can or should be a grandiose deluxe business. There is every evidence to assume that many medieval rites at the local level, outside the superlative confines of those magnificent cathedrals, were a bit of an amorphous jumble.[2] Nonetheless, with better information about the tradition of which we are a part and with more imagination brought to bear on how local liturgies are planned, prepared, and presented, we may hope that this sacrament that symbolizes the mystical union between Christ and his Church may find a fresher and more stable foundation within the life of the Christian community. A lot is demanded. Priests who will give more time. Other ministers who will fight against the pressures that marginalize this liturgy to the later hours of the back end of the week, where only the invited can attend, who often (even when they profess a strong Christian faith) domesticate marriage into a pet that is cuddled and stroked and fed and then put back firmly into its place. Marriage in Christian reality is, by contrast, a roaring lion with strength and vigor and health and dignity that challenge faithful and faithless alike to reach out for a better way of living together under the shadow of the King of Kings and Lord of Lords.

Marriage is ultimately about our doctrine of God, no less. It is about the way we celebrate God's very heart and existence, his love stretching out to us as we enjoy each other's company and go so far as to procreate successive generations who may become God's people on earth, where he reigns in glory and vulnerability. Edward King, who was Bishop of Lincoln (England) at the turn of the century, had this to say about marriage:

" . . . one of God's greatest gifts, one of the closest symbols of what he is, and of the union between himself and us."[3]

NOTES

1. See Geoffrey Wainright, *Doxology: The Praise of God in Worship, Doctrine, and Life* (New York: Oxford University Press, 1980), pp. 77f. See also Theodore Mackin, *What Is Marriage* (Ramsey, NJ: Paulist Press, 1982), and John Meyendorff, *Marriage: An Orthodox Perspective* (St. Vladimir's Press, 1971), which have proved invaluable for this study.

2. See pp. 36ff. I have recently edited the marriage rite contained in a twelfth-century manuscript; it was used in the environs of Hamburg. It was probably a "missionary" rite, and

it perhaps brings us nearer to "ordinary" local services than the central texts of a pontifical character. Written on rough parchment, it contains many errors, and the prayer immediately before mass breaks off in a lacuna. See Kenneth W. Stevenson, "The Marriage-rite from an early 'Ritual-Votive Missal' (Rome, Bibl. Vallicelliana, Cod. B. 141, 11th century)," *Ecclesia Orans* 3 (1986), pp. 181–193.

3. See B. W. Randolph (Ed.), *The Spiritual Letters of Edward King* (London: Mowbrays, 1910), p. 48, extract from a letter "To a Friend—On His Marriage," dated Sunday, July 30, 1876.

Appendix

Evolution of the Rite

CHART 1: ORIGINS

Talmudic Jewish

Betrothal
Contract

⎫
⎬ ?
⎭

Crowns
Evening feast at the
groom's house
Seven blessings

Early Christian (?)

Betrothal

Crowns (?)
Domestic rite

Blessings

(a) Early Medieval Western (Roman rite and domestic rite)

Betrothal (domestic)

Nuptial Mass (Gregorian Sacramentary):
Mass prayers
Special readings (various)
Nuptial blessing (bride only) before Communion

Domestic rite (Pontifical of Egbert):
Blessing of the couple at home
Blessing of the ring
Blessing of the bedchamber

(b) Byzantine (Eighth century texts onwards)

Betrothal (at the church door):
Special prayers and ring giving

Crowning (= marriage)
Psalm 127
Three marriage prayers
Crowning
Readings: Ephesians 5:20–33 and John 2:1–11
Further prayers
Blessing and sharing of the cup
'Dance of Isaiah' (walk in circle)
Removal of crowns
Conclusion

CHART 1: ORIGINS

1. *Talmudic Jewish* is from documents whereas *Early Christian* is conjectural.

2. *Early Medieval Western* is reconstructed from the Gregorian Sacramentary (sixth century onwards) and the Pontifical of Egbert is taken as a sample (eighth century). But the outline given is the fullest form; many couples would have done without the nuptial mass, had simply a betrothal, and (later) the domestic marriage rite.

3. The Byzantine rite, like all the Eastern texts, has a proper betrothal liturgy.

4. In *all* the above forms, marriage is *phased* by gradual experience and ritualization of those phases.

CHART 2: LATER WESTERN AND REFORMATION

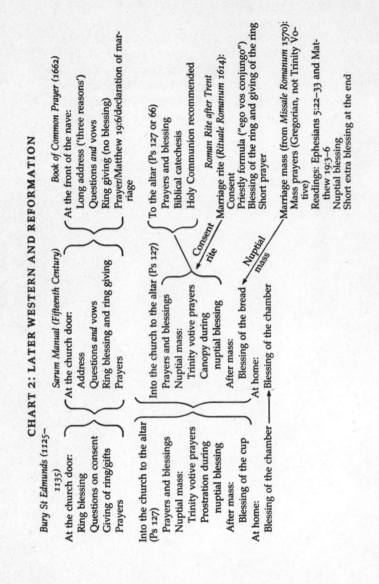

Bury St Edmunds (1125–1135)

At the church door:
Ring blessing
Questions on consent
Giving of ring/gifts
Prayers

Into the church to the altar (Ps 127)
Prayers and blessings
Nuptial mass:
Trinity votive prayers
Prostration during nuptial blessing
After mass:
Blessing of the cup
At home:
Blessing of the chamber

Sarum Manual (Fifteenth Century)

At the church door:
Address
Questions *and* vows
Ring blessing and ring giving
Prayers

Into the church to the altar (Ps 127)
Prayers and blessings
Nuptial mass:
Trinity votive prayers
Canopy during nuptial blessing
After mass:
Blessing of the bread
At home:
Blessing of the chamber

Book of Common Prayer (1662)

At the front of the nave:
Long address ('three reasons')
Questions *and* vows
Ring giving (no blessing)
Prayer/Matthew 19:6/declaration of marriage

To the altar (Ps 127 or 66)
Prayers and blessing
Biblical catechesis
Holy Communion recommended

Roman Rite after Trent

Marriage rite (*Rituale Romanum 1614*):
Consent
Priestly formula ("ego vos conjungo")
Blessing of the ring and giving of the ring
Short prayer

Marriage mass (from *Missale Romanum 1570*):
Mass prayers (Gregorian, not Trinity Votive)
Readings: Ephesians 5:22–33 and Matthew 19:3–6
Nuptial blessing
Short extra blessing at the end

Consent rite

Nuptial mass

1. Bury order prefixes the consent rite to the older nuptial mass. The consent formulas are initially directed by rubric, but then develop their own vernacular style, culminating in the Sarum vow: "I . . . take thee . . . to my wedded wife."

2. Consent replaces betrothal, resulting in *phasing through the building* (at the church door, before the altar, at home afterwards), instead of phasing through separate experiences.

3. The Prayer Book relies heavily on Sarum, whereas the Trent books provide the irreducible minimum. However, Trent officially encourages local rites to continue and develop. N.B.: The "priestly formula" after the consent in the *1614 Rituale*.

4. Other Reformation books provide much simpler versions of marriage liturgies. Wesley (1784) omits the ring (Puritan tendency) and the psalm (no "chancel" in chapel architecture), thus producing considerable reduction.

5. Whereas medieval rites phase, ending up at home, Reformation and Post-Tridentine simplify and opt out of the home altogether (unless local rites maintain this latter custom).

CHART 3: MODERN RITES

Ordo Celebrandi Matrimonium (1969)	Book of Common Prayer (1979)	Consultation on Common Texts (1985)
Set within the eucharist, or else synaxis	Set within the eucharist, or else synaxis	Set within the eucharist, or else synaxis
Collect	Address (modern version of 1662)	Address (cf. 1979 Prayer Book)
Readings (choice)	Preliminary questions, including to the congregation	Preliminary questions, including to the family and congregation (optional)
Homily	Collect	Collect
Preliminary questions	Readings (choice)	Readings (choice)
Consent (question or vow)	Homily	Homily
Ring blessing and ring giving	Vows	Vows
Declaration of marriage	Ring blessing and ring giving	Ring blessing and ring giving
Bidding prayers	Declaration of marriage	Declaration of marriage
Eucharist from offertory onwards	Prayers	Prayers
Nuptial blessing after the eucharistic prayer	Nuptial blessing	Nuptial blessing
Special blessing at the end (choice)	Peace	Peace
Nuptial blessing precedes the bidding prayers when no eucharist is celebrated	Eucharist from offertory onwards, if celebrated	Eucharist from offertory onwards, if celebrated

1. There is no phasing whatever, either as in the early period (phasing through experience), or in the Middle Ages (phasing through the building and ending at home). Everything takes place within the main area of the church building and within the liturgical context of the synaxis, which may be followed by the eucharist.

2. The 1969 *Ordo* juxtaposes preliminary questions to the consent; the two other rites divide them from each other by the Liturgy of the Word, thereby heightening the drama of the consent.

3. The 1969 *Ordo* retains the traditional western position for the nuptial blessing, after the eucharistic prayer; the two other rites place the nuptial blessing after the consent form, within the first part of the liturgy.

4. There are options written into the *CCT* (1985) rite, including the phrase "the giving of" between "bless" and "these rings," so that Reformation sensitivities about blessing inanimate objects are not awakened. The influence of the 1969 *Ordo* on the 1979 Prayer Book rite is obvious, but the improvements made in the internal unity of the rite in 1979 are equally apparent in the 1985 CCT rite.

Bibliography

SOURCES

Addenda ad Rituale Romanum ad usum Unitatum Statum Foed. Americae et Angliae. Mechlen: Dessain, 1916.

The Alternative Service Book. London: SPCK, 1980.

Andrieu, M. *Le Pontifical romain au Moyen Âge*, I (Studi e Testi 86). Vatican City: Apostolic Press, 1938.

Badger, G. P. *The Nestorians and Their Rituals*, II. London: Master, 1852

Barth, P., and W. Niesel (Eds.). *Joannis Calvini: Opera Selecta*, II. Münich: Kaiser, 1952.

Béraudy, R., M. Leprêtre, and P. Lionnet (Eds.). *Célébrer le mariage*. Paris: Desclée, 1981.

The Book of Common Prayer, 1662.

The Book of Common Prayer. New York: Seabury, 1979.

Brightman, F. E. *The English Rite*, II. London: Rivingtons, 1915.

Brooks, E. W. *Joseph and Asenath*. London: SPCK, 1918.

(Catholic Apostolic) *Liturgy and Other Divine Offices of the Church*. London: Chiswick, 1880.

CCT (*Consultation on Common Texts*). *A New Ecumenical Liturgy for the Christian Celebration of Marriage*, 1985.

Charles, R. H. *The Apocrypha and Pseudepigrapha of the Old Testament*, I. Oxford: Oxford University Press, 1913.

245

Collectio Rituum ad Instar Appendicis Ritualis Romani Pro Omnibus Germaniae Dioecesibus. Ratisbon: Pustet, 1950.

Conybeare, F. C. *Rituale Armenorum*. Oxford: Oxford University Press, 1905.

Den Danske Salmebog. København: Haase, 1953.

Denzinger, H. *Ritus Orientalium*, II. Wurzburg: Stahl, 1864.

Deshusses, J. *Le Sacramentaire Grégorien*, I (Spicilegium Friburgense 16). Fribourg: University Press, 1971.

Doble, G. H. *The Lanalet Pontifical* (Henry Bradshaw Society 74). London, 1937.

The Doctrines and Disciplines of the Methodist Episcopal Church in America. Philadelphia: Parry Hall, 1792.

Eizenöfer, L., P. Siffrin, and L. Mohlberg. *Liber Sacramentorum Romanae Ecclesiae* (Rerum ecclesiasticarum documenta; series maior: Fontes; 4). Rome: Herder, 1960.

Die Feier der Trauung in den Katholischen Bistümern des Deutschen Sprachgebietes. Einsiedeln and Köln: Benziger; Freiburg and Basel: Herder; Regensburg: Pustet; Wien: Herder; Salzburg: St. Peter; Linz: Veritas, 1975.

Férotin, M. *Le liber Ordinum en usage dans l'église wisigothique et mozarabe d'Espagne du cinquième au onzième siècle* (Monumenta Ecclesiae Liturgica V). Paris: Firmin-Didot, 1905.

Flannery, Austin (Ed.). *Vatican Council II: The Conciliar and Post-Conciliar Documents*. Collegeville, MN: Liturgical Press, 1975.

Forms for the Administration of Baptism . . . for the use of such Primitive Methodist Ministers as may require them. London, 1860.

Greenwell, W. *The Pontifical of Egbert* (Surtees Society 27). London, 1853.

Goar, J. *Euchologion sive Rituale Graecorum*. Venice: Javarini, 1730.

Henderson, W. G. *The York Manual* (Surtees Society). Edinburgh, 1875.

Hertz, Joseph (Ed.). *The Authorized Daily Prayer Book*. New York: Bloch, 1946.

International Committee on English in the Liturgy, Inc. *Rite of Marriage*. New York: Pueblo, 1969.

Lanne, E. "Le Grand Euchologue du Monastère Blanc," *Patrologia Orientalis* 28/2. Paris: 1958.

(Lindsey, Theophilus.) *The Book of Common Prayer Reformed According to the Plan of the Late Dr. Samuel Clarke*, 2d ed. London, 1774.

Löhe, Wilhelm. "Agende fur christlichen Gemeinden des lutherischen Bekenntnisses," in Klaus Ganzert (Ed.), *Wilhelm Löhe: Gesammelte Werke*. Neuendettelsen: Freimund-Verlag, 1953, 7/1.

Luther's Works, 53. Philadelphia: Fortress, 1965.

The Marriage Rite. Birmingham and Dublin, 1970.

Martène, E. *De Antiquis Ecclesiae Ritibus*, I–III. Rouen: Behourt, 1700–1702.

Martimort, A.-G. *La Documentation Liturgique de Dom Edmond Martène* (Studi e Testi 279). Vatican City: Apostolic Press, 1978.

Martini, Aldo. *Il Cosidetto Pontificale di Poitiers* (Rerum ecclesiasticarum Documenta; series maior: Fontes; 14). Rome: Herder, 1979.

McGarvey, W. *Liturgiae Americanae*. Philadelphia: Church Publishing Company, 1897.

The Methodist Service Book. London: Methodist Publishing House, 1975.

Missale Romanum ex decreto Sacrosancto Concilii Tridentini restitutum. Antwerp: Balthasar Moret, 1682.

Missale Romanum. Vatican City: Typis Polyglottis, 1970.

Ordo Benedicendi Oleum Catechumenorum et Infirmorum et Conficiendi Chrisma. Vatican City: Typis Polyglottis, 1971.

Ordo Celebrandi Matrimonium. Vatican City: Typis Polyglottis, 1969.

Raes, A. *Le Mariage dans les Églises d'Orient.* Chevetogne: Editions, 1958.

The Rites of the Catholic Church as Revised at the Second Vatican Ecumenical Council, I. New York: Pueblo, 1976.

Rituale Romanum. Antwerp: Balthasar Moret, 1826.

Rituale Romanum. Ratisbon: Pustet, 1925.

Rituel pour la célébration du mariage. Paris: Brepols, 1969.

The Roman Ritual. Dublin: Veritas, 1980.

The Sacramentary. New York: Catholic Book Publishing Company, 1974.

Schönfelder, A. *Liturgische Bibliothek,* I. Paderborn: Schöningh, 1906.

A Service of Christian Marriage (Supplemental Worship Resources 5). Nashville, TN: Abingdon, 1979.

The Sunday Service of the Methodists in North America. London, 1784.

Wilson, H. A. *The Benedictional of Archbishop Robert* (Henry Bradshaw Society 24). London, 1903.

Wilson, H. A. *The Pontifical of Magdalen College* (Henry Bradshaw Society 39), London, 1910.

Wilson, H. A. *Liber Evesham* (Henry Bradshaw Society 6). London, 1893.

LITERATURE

Albertine, R. "Problem of the (Double) Epiclesis in the New Roman Eucharistic Prayers," *Ephemerides Liturgicae* 91 (1977):193–202.

Andren, Åke. *Svenska Kyrkans Gudstjänst Bilaga 4—Äktenskap och vigsel i dag—Liturgiska utvecklingslinjer.* Stockholm: Gotab, 1981.

Baldanza, G. "Il rito del Matrimonio nel' Euchologio Barberini 336," *Ephemerides Liturgicae* 93 (1979):316–351.

Baldanza, G. "La grazia sacramentale matrimoniale al Concilio di Trento. Contributo per uno studio storico critico," *Ephemerides Liturgicae* 97 (1983):89–140.

Baumgartner, J. *Mission und Liturgie in Mexiko*, 2 vols. Switzerland: Schoneck and Beckenried, 1971.

Binder, Basilius. *Geschichte des feierlichen Ehesegens von der Entstehung der Ritualien bis zur Gegenwart*. Metten: Abtei, 1938.

Braga, C. "La genesi dell' 'Ordo Matrimonii,' " *Ephemerides Liturgicae* 93 (1979):247–257.

Brooks-Leonard, John. "Another Look at Neo-Gallican Reform: A Comparison of Marriage Rites in Coutances," *Ephemerides Liturgicae* 98 (1984):458–485.

Bugnini, A. *La riforma liturgica (1948–1975)* (Ephemerides Liturgicae "Subsidia" 30), Rome: Edizioni Liturgiche, 1983.

Chupungco, Anscar. "The Cultural Adaptation of the Rite of Marriage," in G. Farnedi (Ed.), *La Celebrazione Cristiana Del Matrimonio* (Studia Anselmiana 93; Analecta Liturgica 11), pp. 145–162. Rome: Pontificio Ateneo S. Anselmo, 1986.

Coyle, John K. "Marriage Among Early Christians: A Consideration for the Future," *Église at Théologie* 8 (1977):73–89.

Crouzel, H. "Deux textes de Tertullien concernant la procédure et les rites du mariage chrétien," *Bulletin de Littérature Ecclésiastique* 4 (1973):3–13.

Dauvillier, J. *Le mariage dans le droit classique de l'église depuis le décret de Gratien (1140) jusqu'à la mort de Clément V*. Paris: Receuil Sirey, 1933.

De Jong, J. P. "Brautsegen und Jungfrauenweihe," *Zeitschrift für Katholische Theologie* 84 (1962):300–322.

Didier, Raymond. "Sacrement de mariage, baptême et foi," *La Maison-Dieu* 127 (1976):106–138.

Duval, A. "La formule 'Ego vos conjungo' au Concile de Trente," *La Maison-Dieu* 99 (1969):144–153.

Fuller, Reginald H. "Lectionary for Weddings," *Worship* 55 (1981):244–259

Gelsi, D. "Punti di riflessione sull'ufficio bizantino per la 'incoronazione' degli sposi," in G. Farnedi (Ed.), *La Celebrazione Cristiana Del Matrimonio* (Studia Anselmiana 93; Analecta Liturgica 11), pp. 283–306. Rome: Pontificio Ateneo S. Anselmo, 1986.

Gy, P.-M. "Le nouveau rituel romain du mariage," *La Maison-Dieu* 98 (1969):7–31.

Hastings, Adrian. *Christian Marriage in Africa.* London: SPCK, 1973.

Hatchett, Marion. *Commentary on the American Prayer Book.* New York: Seabury, 1980.

Hatchett, Marion. *The Making of the First American Book of Common Prayer.* New York; Seabury, 1982.

Henderson, J. F. "A Christian Celebration of Marriage: An Ecumenical Liturgy," in G. Farnedi (Ed.), *La Celebrazione Cristiana Del Matrimonio* (Studia Anselmiana 93; Analecta 11), pp. 375–385. Rome: Pontificio Ateneo S. Anselmo, 1986.

Hope, W. St. John, and E. G. Cuthbert Atchley. *English Liturgical Colours.* London: SPCK: 1918.

Hruby, K. "Symboles et textes de le célébration du mariage judaïque," in G. Farnedi (Ed.), *La Celebrazione Cristiana Del Matrimonio* (Studia Anselmiana 93; Analecta 11), pp. 15–28. Rome: Pontificio Ateneo S. Anselmo, 1986.

Hughes, Kathleen. *The Language of the Liturgy: Some Theoretical and Practical Guidelines.* Washington, DC: International Commission on English in the Liturgy, 1984.

Jounel, P. "La consécration du chrême et la bénédiction des saintes huiles," *La Maison-Dieu* 112 (1972):70–83.

Kasper, Walter. *Theology of Christian Marriage.* New York: Seabury, 1980.

Kavanagh, Aidan. *The Shape of Baptism: The Rite of Christian Inititation* (Studies in the Reformed Rites of the Catholic Church, Volume I). New York: Pueblo, 1978.

Kavanagh, Aidan. *Elements of Rite, A Handbook of Liturgical Style.* New York: Pueblo, 1982.

Kavanagh, Aidan. "Liturgy and Ecclesial Consciousness," *Studia Liturgica* 15(1982/1983):2–17.

Kavanagh, Aidan. *On Liturgical Theology*, New York: Pueblo, 1984.

Kingsford, H. S. *Illustrations of the Occasional Offices of the Church in the Middle Ages from Contemporary Sources* (Alcuin Club Collections 24). London: Mowbrays, 1921.

Klauser, Theodor. *A Short History of the Western Liturgy*, 2d ed. London: Oxford University Press, 1969.

Kleinheyer, Bruno. "Riten um Ehe und Familie," in H. B. Meyer, H.-J. Auf der Maur, B. Fischer, A. Haüssling, and B. Kleinheyer (Eds.), *Gottesdienst der Kirche: Handbuch der Liturgiewissenschaft*, 8. Ratisbon: Pustet, 1984.

Lindars, Barnabas. *The Gospel of John* (New Century Bible), 2d ed. London: Oliphants, Marshall, Morgan and Scott, 1977.

Mackin, Theodore. *What Is Marriage?* Ramsey, NJ: Paulist Press, 1982.

Marriage and the Church's Task. London: Church Information Office, 1978. A report of the General Synod of the Church of England.

Mazzarello, S. "De novo ordine celebrandi matrimonium," *Ephemerides Liturgicae* 83 (1969):251–277.

Melia, E. "Symboles et textes de la célébration du mariage dans la tradition patrisique et liturgique en Orient," in G. Farnedi (Ed.), *La Celebrazione Cristiana Del Matrimonio* (Studia Anselmiana 93; Analecta 11), pp. 29–50. Rome: Pontificio Ateneo S. Anselmo, 1986.

Meyendorff, John. *Marriage: An Orthodox Perspective*. New York: St. Vladimir's Press, 1971.

Molin, Jean-Baptiste. "Symboles, rites et textes du mariage au moyen âge latin," in G. Farnedi (Ed.), *La Celebrazione Cristiana Del Matrimonio* (Studia Anselmiana 93; Analecta 11), pp. 107–128. Rome: Pontificio Ateneo S. Anselmo, 1986.

Molin, Jean-Baptiste, and Protais Mutembe. *Le rituel du mariage en France du XIIè au XVIè siècle* (Théologie Historique 26). Paris: Beauchesne, 1973.

Mpongo, L. La célébration du mariage dans les religions afridcaines," in G. Farnedi (Ed.), *La Celebrazione Cristiana Del Matrimonio* (Studia Anselmiana 93; Analecta 11), pp. 343–360. Rome: Pontificio Ateneo S. Anselmo, 1986.

Nautin, P. "Le rituel de mariage et la formation des Sacramentaires 'Léonien' et 'Gélasien,' " *Ephemerides Liturgicae* 98 (1984):425–457.

Nelidow, A. "Caractère pénitentiel du rite des deuxièmes noces," in *Liturgie et Rémission des Péchés* (Ephemerides Liturgicae "Subsidia" 3), pp. 163–177. Rome: Edizioni Liturgiche.

Nocent, A. "Le rituel du mariage depuis Vatican II," in G. Farnedi (Ed.), *La Celebrazione Cristana Del Matrimonio* (Studia Anselmiana 93; Analecta 11), pp. 129–144. Rome: Pontificio Ateneo S. Anselmo, 1986.

Passarelli, G. I. "La ceremonia dello Stefanoma (Incoronazione) nei riti matrimoniali bizantini secondo il Codice Cryptense G.b. VII (X sec.)," *Ephemerides Liturgicae* 93 (1979):381–391.

Payngot, C. "The Syro-Malabar Marriage," in G. Farnedi (Ed.), *La Celebrazione Cristiana Del Matrimonio* (Studia Anselmiana 93; Analecta 11), pp. 261–282. Rome: Pontificio Ateneo S. Anselmo, 1986.

Pierce, Joanne. "A Note on the 'Ego Vos Conjungo' in Medieval French Marriage Liturgy," *Ephemerides Liturgicae* 99 (1985):290–299.

Pinell i Pons, J. "La liturgia nupcial en el antiguo rito hispanico," in G. Farnedi (Ed.), *La Celebrazione Cristiana Del Matrimonio* (Studia Anselmiana 93; Analecta 11), pp. 87–106. Rome: Pontificio Ateneo S. Anselmo, 1986.

Power, David N. *Unsearchable Riches: The Symbolic Nature of Liturgy.* New York: Pueblo, 1984.

Price, H. H. *Belief.* London: Allen and Unwin, 1969.

Raineri, O. "Celebrazione del matrimonio nel rito etiopico," in G. Farnedi (Ed.), *La Celebrazione Cristiana Del Matrimonio* (Studia Anselmiana 93; Analecta 11), pp. 307–342. Rome: Pontificio Ateneo S. Anselmo, 1986.

Randolph, B. W. (Ed.), *The Spiritual Letters of Edward King*. London: Mowbrays, 1910.

Ritzer, Korbinian. *Formen, Riten, und religiöses Brauchtum der Eheschliessung in den christlichen Kirchen des ersten Jahrtausends* (Liturgiewissenchaftliche Quellen und Forschungen 38). Münster: Aschendorff, 1962, 1982.

Rutherford, Richard. *The Death of a Christian: The Rite of Funerals* (Studies in the Reformed Rites of the Catholic Church, Volume VI). New York: Pueblo, 1980.

Schmeiser, J. M. "Marriage: New Developments in the Diocese of Autun, France," *Eglise et Théologie* 10 (1979):369–386.

Schillebeeckx, E. *Marriage, Secular Reality and Saving Mystery*. New York: Sheed and Ward, 1963.

Schmidt-Lauber, H.-C. "The Eucharistic Prayers in the Roman Catholic Church Today," *Studia Liturgica* 11 (1976):159–176.

Sloyan, G. S. "The New Rite for Celebrating Marriage," *Worship* 44 (1970):258–267.

Spinks, B. D. "Luther's Other Major Liturgical Reforms: 3. The Traubüchlein," *Liturgical Review* 10 (1980):33–38.

Spinks, B. D. "The Liturgical Origins and Theology of Calvin's Genevan Marriage Rite," *Ecclesia Orans* 3 (1986):196–210.

Stevenson, Kenneth W. " 'Benedictio Nuptialis': Reflections on the Blessing of Bride and Groom in Some Western Mediaeval Rites," *Ephemerides Liturgicae* 93 (1979):457–478.

Stevenson, Kenneth W. "The Marriage Rites of Mediaeval Scandinavia: A Fresh Look," *Ephemerides Liturgicae* 97 (1983):550–557.

Stevenson, Kenneth W. *Nuptial Blessing: A Study of Christian Marriage Rites* (Alcuin Club Collections 64). London: SPCK, 1982, and New York: Oxford University Press, 1983.

Stevenson, Kenneth W. "The Origins of Nuptial Blessing," *Heythrop Journal* 21 (1980):412–416.

Stevenson, Kenneth W. "Van Gennep and Marriage— Strange Bedfellows?—A Fresh Look at the Rites of Marriage," *Ephemerides Liturgicae* 100 (1986):138–151.

Stevenson, Kenneth W. "The Marriage-Rite From an Early 'Ritual-Votive Missal' (Rome, Bibl. Vallicelliana, Cod. B. 141, 11th Century)," *Ecclesia Orans* 3 (1986):181–193.

Stevenson, Kenneth W. "Marriage Liturgy: Lessons from History," *Anglican Theological Review* 68 (1986):225–240.

Studer, B. "Zur Hochzeitsfeier der Christen in den westlichen Kirchen der ersten Jahrdunderte," in G. Farnedi (Ed.), *La Celebrazione Cristiana Del Matrimonio* (Studia Anselmiana 93; Analecta 11), pp. 51–86. Rome: Pontificio Ateneo S. Anselmo, 1986.

Taft, Robert F. "The Structural Analysis of Liturgical Units: An Essay in Methodology," in Robert F. Taft, *Beyond East and West: Problems in Liturgical Understanding*, pp. 151–164. Washington, DC: Pastoral Press, 1984.

Turner, Victor. *The Ritual Process*. London: Routledge and Kegan Paul, 1969.

Van Gennep, Arnold. *Les Rites de Passage*. Paris: Librairie Critique, Emile Mourry, 1909.

Van Overstraeten, Jeanne-Ghislane. "Les liturgies nuptiales des églises de langue syriaque et le mystère de l'église épouse," *Parole d'Orient* 8(1977/1978):235–310.

Van Overstraeten, Jeanne-Ghislane. "Le rite de l'onction des époux dans la liturgie copte du mariage," *Parole d'Orient* 5 (1974):49–93.

Von Allmen, J.-J. "Bénédiction nuptiale et mariage d'après quelques liturgies de l'église Réformée," in *Mélanges Liturgiques offerts au R. P. Bernard Botte*. Louvain: Abbaye du Mont César, 1972.

Wainright, Geoffrey. *Doxology: The Praise of God in Worship, Doctrine, and Life*. New York: Oxford University Press, 1980.

Westerhoff, John H., and William H. Willimon. *Liturgy and Learning Through the Life Cycle*. New York: Seabury, 1980.

Winkler, Gabriele. *Das Armenische Initiationsrituale: Entwicklungsgeschichte und liturgievergleichende Untersuchung der Quellen des 3. bis 10. Jahrhunderts* (Orientalia Christiana Analecta 217). Rome: Pontificium Institutum Orientalium Studiorum, 1982.

Yousif, P. "La célébration du mariage dans le rite chaldéen," in G. Farnedi (Ed.), *La Celebrazione Cristiana Del Matrimonio* (Studia Anselmiana 93; Analecta 11), pp. 217–260. Rome: Pontificio Ateneo S. Anselmo, 1986.

Index

Catholic Church, Roman, 8, 19, 113, 115, 119, 121, 122, 123, 126, 180

Catullus, 31

Censing, 65, 72, 74, 201, 224, 225

Ceylon, Anglican Prayer Book (1960) for, 115

Change of state, marriage as bride's, 22, 23, 31, 66, 169

Chants, 148–150, 225; *See also* Hymns; Music in liturgical celebration

Charles the Bald, 140

Chavasse, Antoine, 128

Chrism Mass, 152, 204

Christian Initiation, Study Group for, 192

Chrysostom, John, 21

Church of England, 9, 122, 156, 171, 175
Prayer Book of the, 44

The Church in the Modern World (1966), 125–126

Church of Scotland (Presbyterian), 116

Ciappi, P., 131

Civil marriage, 121

Clement of Alexandria, 19

Cologne rite (1485), 49

Common Order, Book of (1902), 116

Common Prayer, Book of; See: Book of Common Prayer

Communion
Anglican 180
Holy, 137
prayers after, 147

"Conjungo," 45

Consensus facit nuptias, 50

Consent, 8, 40, 50, 51, 52, 65, 66, 67, 77, 87, 88, 89, 90, 91, 94, 97, 99, 100, 101, 103, 105, 113, 114, 117, 121, 123, 129, 130, 131, 132, 137, 138, 139, 155, 166, 168, 172, 182, 188, 201, 203, 216, 221, 223, 240, 242

Methodist Church
American, *98*, *154*
British, *116*, *171*
Methodist rite
British, *140*, *153*
North American, *85*
Metz order, 129
Metz rite (1543), 99, 100, 125, 204
Metz tradition, 155
McManus, 129, 130
Microphone, use of 220, 221
Middle Ages, 17, 28, 44, 47, 52, 84, 86, 93, 101, 119, 121,
    172, 173, 224, 227
"Ministers of the sacrament," couple as, 117
Missal
Bobbio, *45*
Roman, *102*
Missal of Paul VI (1970), 148, 194, 228
Missal of Pius V (1570), 100, 144, 147, 148, 176
Missale Romanum (1570), 34, 240
Moghila, Peter, 77
Molin, Jean-Baptiste, 120, 121, 130
Montefiore, Bishop Hugh, 156
Montefiore, Elizabeth, 156
Moses, 38
Music in liturgical celebrations, 149, 214, 215, 218; *See also*
    Chants; Hymns
Mutembe, Protais, 121
Mythology of ancient Near East, 11

N
Nagasaki, 115
Nazianzus, Gregory, 21, 24, 75
Ne Temere of Pius X (1907), 114